acquiring and developing income-producing real estate

the world trade center, new york city. ten million square feet of office space.

acquiring
and developing
income-producing
real estate

richard h. swesnik

reston publishing company, inc.
a prentice-hall company
reston, virginia

Library of Congress Cataloging in Publication Data

Swesnik, Richard H
  Acquiring and developing income-producing real
estates.

  Includes index.
  1. Real estate development. 2. Real estate
investment. I. Title.
HD1391.S93   332.6'324   78-31472
ISBN 0-8359-0126-2

10 9 8 7 6 5 4 3 2

Printed in the United States of America

contents

chapter eight: your development begins 159

chapter nine: your property is leased...................173

chapter ten: other ways for you and them 185

chapter eleven: will they come back? 193

chapter twelve: you and them and special risks 197

chapter thirteen: sharpening your negotiating skills ..205

preface

If you are a real estate salesman, broker, builder, contractor, developer, lawyer, accountant, property manager, appraiser, mortgage banker or broker, commercial leasing specialist, investor, a real estate oriented thinker with a background in urban planning or economics, or any person within the general framework of the real estate business and are not worth at least one million dollars, you should consider the extraordinary profit opportunities in acquiring or developing real estate investments. If you are worth over one million dollars and would like more, you can probably get it faster as a developer than by any other route.

Practically all of the wealthy real estate entrepreneurs became so through organizing investors into groups that developed or acquired income-producing properties. For almost thirty years, I have observed other developers, syndicators, and the general commercial real estate scene. Hopefully, what I have observed should be helpful. Only fools must learn by constantly making errors. Intelligent people strive to achieve by avoiding the errors made by others.

First of all, you must have absolute integrity. You cannot be even a teeny liar. You can end up losing your real estate license, be subjected to major fines, and possibly be sentenced to a penitentiary by promising something (orally or written) that you cannot fulfill.

You will probably do better if you are a "fits and spurts" type of worker, as that is the nature of the job; there are many starts and stops in real estate development.

You cannot be supersensitive or have thin skin. You are not God. You do not control markets. You cannot make a winner out of a failure. You are mortal and will make mistakes, conceptually or operationally. Sometimes you may be just plain unlucky, but most successful developers seem to make their own luck. In the event of a near failure, or even a total failure of a single project, you will be despised by most investors, probably criticized by all, pressured by bankers, and criticized by lenders. And if you did not follow all the legal and accounting rules, you can be harassed by the Internal Revenue Service, the Securities and Exchange Commission, real estate license law officials, and your state securities administrator.

None of us like criticism, even that which is intended to be constructive. If you need the love and approval of *everyone*, developing real estate is not for you. If your project does well, it was expected to do well and rarely will anyone compliment you or thank you for a job well done. If it does not do well, all hell will break loose. At any rate, if you are successful, you still will not win a popularity contest. Developers seem to have only a few lasting or close personal relationships outside of their immediate families. You will probably make a good deal of money and for this reason, you will be envied, even though your family may adore you. You will make some business enemies because you chose to do business with the ABC Company instead of the XYZ Company.

The rewards in this business are mainly financial although there are some other rewards. You will appreciate the social and economic contributions you are making, even if others may not. Real estate development is the very essence of capitalism—putting money to work, which creates jobs and space for people to live, work, and shop. Every investor is a capitalist at heart. Thus, you will be helping our basic system with each new venture. Since you will control the design and the specifications of the building you develop, much of what you create will outlive you. Singularly, you will have a real chance to get off your aesthetic jollies.

The main reward is money, which among other things can give you status, although much can be said for keeping a low profile. This business is also excruciatingly challenging and exciting. The writer knows of no one in the business who ever died of boredom.

It is difficult *not* to make important money when you consider the many benefits available to the organizer of real estate syndicates. Properly organized successful real estate syndicates should give the organizer

1. A "nontaxable" piece of the action: at least a serious financial interest in the project with all of the characteristics and benefits of an equity ownership but not a capital interest. This is explained in detail later.

2. Leasing and management fees at a slightly higher rate than that usually charged. Since these fees are computed on the gross income, they are truly "off the top."

3. Original loan fees, currently at 1% and if not originally obtained, then certainly refinancing fees of at least 1% of the gross amount obtained.

4. Casualty insurance commissions: fire and extended coverage, partnership liability, and if required, rental insurance. Later on you will discover how easy it is to become an insurance agent.

5. The exclusive right of resale of the property that is being developed or acquired at 5% of the gross selling price.

There are other areas where the developer may also earn money, such as owning the parking rights in an office building, owning the washing and drying machines concessions in an apartment development, and even owning the vending machines such as for cigarettes, candies, and stamps. Later on you will make the decision regarding these other fees, but for reasons that will be explained, you may not want to take them.

A recent private development by the writer developed combined fees and income of $150,000 per year, and assuming an 11-year ownership life, a resale commission of $625,000, if sold at the original cost. If no refinancing of the property occurs, or if there is no increase in the value of the property, the combined benefits over the 11 years total a staggering $2,275,000. It should be also noted that this development was accomplished *without investing any of the developer's personal funds.*

How are these earnings possible from just a single development? They occur because of the combination of financial benefits to the developer. The substantial monies flowing to the organizer are routine in the offices of the nation's larger firms that specialize in the acquisition or development of large income-producing properties.

Since World War II, real estate development has grown and prospered as new demands for every conceivable form of space has increased due to our burgeoning economy. Yet the decade of the 1960s saw real estate developments in the doldrums and out of public favor, especially in the East. Several "big name" developers and some syndicators had gotten themselves, and consequently their investors, in a good deal of financial trouble.

If the guidelines outlined in this book are followed, neither the investor nor the developer can get into financial trouble—unless our total economy suffers a severe financial depression for an extended period of time. Not many people, even the most conservative economists, feel this will happen.

The demise of some of the "swinging syndicators" in the 1960s could be traced to trying to "force" profit opportunities; selecting poorly located or sloppily constructed properties; using too much leverage; paying too high a price for money; or a combination of these factors. Yet others engaged in developing income-producing properties did none of these things and not only survived but escalated modest net worths to very substantial holdings. Two such entrepreneurs, starting with very little, today have individual net worths in excess of $50 million.

Thus, it is not only important to have a positive strategy and know what to do, but also it is probably even more important that your strategy and policies focus on what you will *not* do.

Some books have been written by scholars or serious observers of the syndicated real estate field. I do not claim expertise as either a scholar or a journalist. This is, after all, a relatively new field with no serious written work to guide neophytes.

I have made most of the major mistakes that are inherent in real estate development. I must continually design out errors in the partnership agreements, get rid of common design errors in buildings, research the public's space needs, and continually study the needs of the investors. I must keep abreast of the federal income tax laws affecting investment in income-producing properties and spend a tremendous amount of time studying the building plans and specifications.

This book is, therefore, very untheoretical—it is pragmatic and hardnosed in every way. All of the knowledge contained herein is empirical, gleaned from moments of exquisite suffering. Nothing is borrowed from anyone. However, we would like to express our gratitude to William A. Kelley, Esq., partner in the law firm of Dechert Price & Rhoads of Philadelphia, an eminent real estate tax attorney and contributing editor of The Journal of Real Estate Taxation who reviewed and edited this manuscript to conform with recent tax legislation, most specifically the Revenue Act of 1978.

There are very few quotes in the book, a few footnotes, no junk—just the stuff with which you can make it big. Herein, hopefully, are pointed out most of the pitfalls of developing income-producing properties, while on the other hand, the most positive and rewarding facets of the business are explained in considerable detail.

A scholarly work reveals all the facets, examines them all, attempts to urge the reader into an evaluation and ultimately the right decision. You do not have time for all of this intellectual exercise and neither do I. Do it my way— you will love your future net worth. Undeniably, this is the surest way to achieve an economic orgasm.

to sylvia

"give not, get not"

r.h.s.
8/31/78

the australian embassy, washington, d.c. the facade is pink tennessee marble. normally the cost of marble is not justified, but for an embassy it is appropriate.

you:

the developer or syndicator

chapter 1 outline

Why would you either acquire or attempt to develop income-producing properties? Mainly you would do it either because you have money to invest or your friends and acquaintances have surplus funds. You have examined the alternatives of other forms of investing and found them wanting.

other investment alternatives

the stock market

For years, the securities industry has been urging us to own a piece of America through the purchase of equities (common stocks) in America's "blue chip" companies. It was the "in" thing to do. You had liquidity. Such investments would always rise with the times, thus keeping pace with inflation. And besides, the market was the only organized investment vehicle that was available to almost everyone. Securities dealers had offices in virtually every city of any size in America.

Own a piece of America. Buy blue chips, stay conservative, and watch your assets grow!

Let us examine the advertisements and the subsequent actions that led many people to invest in the market. Let's take a few blue chip stocks selected at random, examine what they sold for in mid-1965 and then again in mid-1975. Most paid dividends, generally in the 3 to 6 percent (at cost) range.

	1965	1975 (Adjusted for stock splits)
GM	97-1/8	43-1/2
G.E.	96-1/4	46-5/8[1]
A.T.&T.	67-3/8	48-7/8
IBM	458-1/4	208-1/4
Xerox	143	68-1/2[2]
ITT	55-7/8	24[3]

You purchased, let's say, 100 shares of each stock. Your total investment was $91,787.50 in mid-1965. In mid-1975, you liquidated and you received $64,637.50, excluding commissions.

True, you were liquid the entire decade of ownership. Inasmuch as liquidity of an asset means the ability to rapidly convert an asset to cash without losing the principal, there were times the investor could have liquidated, but where could he invest the proceeds?

---

[1]GE split 2 for 1 in 1971.
[2]Xerox split 3 for 1 in 1969.
[3]ITT split 2 for 1 in 1968.

How did these stocks do to protect the investor from inflation? In mid-1965, the Consumer Price Index (CPI) of the Bureau of Labor Statistics (BLS) of the Department of Commerce was at 94.7 (1967 = 100). In mid-1975, the CPI was at 160.6, an increase of approximately 70 percent. If nothing else, the securities market proved that these five randomly selected common stocks **did not** move up consistently with inflation during the ten-year period. While inflation **increased** an average of 7 percent per year, the value of the common stocks **decreased** an average of 2.7 percent per year.

You were liquid, but in actual investment practice, hardly anyone knows when to liquidate. Perhaps a few professionals do.

What really happens to investors in the market is as follows: Investor Smith visits securities dealer A and buys, upon recommendation, (let's say) three different stocks. One goes up dramatically, and Smith sells it. He is still left with two stocks, neither of which is selling at the price he paid for them. Smith doesn't sell, because he is not emotionally comfortable taking the loss. He hopes, no, he **knows,** they will eventually go up in value. Psychiatrists call this type of knowing "infantile megalomania." Next, Smith finds securities dealer B and the process repeats itself. After three visits to securities dealers, Smith has sold off three winners and sits with six losers—none of which he will sell. Ask any of your friends, and you will be able to check the validity of the stock market investor's habits. It has been jokingly said that this process could not endure if there were not so many securities dealers.

What is of serious concern is that capital is really needed to preserve our American enterprise system, but the lessons of the last decade still remain. Thus, capital to be raised is not only more costly these days, but the company that seeks to raise it must have an impeccable track record of many years standing.

what about bonds, debentures, or preferred stock?

As long as inflation is with us, and we have learned that inflation can exist during a recession, one must be careful about commiting funds for the long-range period because fixed income securities rarely, if ever, cover the rise in inflation. When you consider the federal and state income taxes that are paid on the interest received from the bonds and debentures as well as preferred stock dividends, an investor surely is a consistent loser in terms of **real** money.

investing in art

There are some alternatives to investing in the market. Art dealers claim (and they may be right) that fine art will indeed go up in value and move with inflation. But how to avoid the pitfalls? Top art and museum officials frequently act as advisers to rich investors. Serious investing in art also requires a serious amount of money. People with net worths in excess of $10 million may find this form of investment intellectually and aesthetically stimulating and indeed financially rewarding if and when they ultimately sell the work of art.

More often than not an emotional attachment develops toward a fine work of art and such emotionally owned works are rarely sold, so there are no known methods to test the theory of their increase in value. Frequently the more expensive pieces of art are given away to charities. There are limitations on charitable deductions tied to the gross income of the donor. If the donor has a tremendous income and donates at appraised value a valuable piece of art he can take the deduction at its full value regardless of how cheaply he acquired it years ago. There are more would-be buyers than would-be sellers for a Rembrandt and this has the effect of increases in value through the operation of the principles of supply and demand. Suffice it to say, this really is not an investment vehicle for the average person.

investing in coins, stamps, and diamonds

The same can be said for the most esoteric alternative forms of investing, such as coins (numismatics) stamps (philately), and diamonds, all of which seem to keep up with inflation, but like art all require knowledge and skills not available to the average investor.

back to real estate

the attractions of real estate

The only real alternative to the stock market seems to be real estate investments. Anybody who bought a home as long as ten years ago and sold it recently realizes the tremendous increase in real estate values.

What has caused these increases in value? Land (meaning buildable lots) has consistently gone up in value due to its increasing scarceness in desirable locations. In addition, the home's reproduction costs, due largely to inflation along with increasing labor costs, have really jumped in value.

The same tremendous rise in value has occurred in well-located shopping centers, office buildings and apartment houses where free-market forces have been allowed to operate.

a major problem: rent control

In many major cities such as New York and Washington, D.C., plus some of the Washington, D.C. suburbs, rent controls have drastically altered what apartment owners can do.

Rent controls are readily put on apartments when operating costs are escalating. This happens because consumer groups lobby for such controls and virtually always succeed in convincing the politicians to pass rent-control legislation. Any person can understand that there are more apartment house renters who can vote than apartment house owners who can vote. Thus, it is politically expedient to pass rent control legislation. However, in the long run, such controls contribute to severe housing shortages because if ownership is not profitable, projects are abandoned. New construction practically grinds to a halt resulting in very few apartment buildings with very few vacancies for the large number of families seeking such rent-controlled units. The long-term result is always predictable. Very little new housing is produced and wholesale abandonment of older properties rapidly occurs. Condominium conversions from rentals are attempted, which the owners hope will allow them to get some of their cash equities back. New York City is a prime example of a rent-controlled city going downward. (The real estate tax base becomes seriously eroded in cities where rent control is left on for more than five years.)

Because politicians of both major parties make short-term decisions (their tenure is short), the long-term seriousness of this issue is known only to the urban planners who work for local governments. Unfortunately they have little voice in "the political decision-making process." The long-range consequences are also known to real estate professionals, but they are badly organized for lobbying purposes. There are too many national groups and associations relating to real estate development, construction, and ownership to form one major lobbying group. As a result, local governments respond, in the main, to citizen groups.

There is no easy solution to the rent control problem. This being so, developers or persons contemplating acquiring income-producing properties would do well to avoid residential acquisitions in cities where consumer groups have political muscle. This situation is unfortunate because garden apartments in cities unfettered by residential rent controls are one of the safest of all real estate investments. They also are the least expensive form of housing in the United States.

risks and rewards of going it alone

your own or borrowed money

A question that must be answered is: Should you develop income-producing property yourself using only your own or borrowed money? If you wish to take the entire financial risk, the answer is yes. As an observer of the income-producing development field, I answer, **no!** Many of the nation's largest developers who have gone it alone are no longer working in the real estate field. Because of the large financial equity requirements in developing real estate, a developer going it alone will find several major problems. At the outset, especially when he is searching for a permanent loan commitment from a major lender, he will necessarily have to demonstrate his financial ability to carry the project from its inception to relatively full occupancy. Even if he starts with enormous personal funds, it is impossible to have every project a winner. Thus, if the project is slow in renting up, which can be terribly expensive, where are the extra funds coming from? The debt must be serviced and usually there is substantial negative cash flow during the rent-up period. Cash flow is defined as all the money left after operating a given property for one year on a cash basis. Stated another way, cash flow is all the cash income less all the cash outlays, including servicing of debt. Negative cash flow is defined in the same manner, the only difference being there is a shortage of cash monies after the full year's operations.

The demise of several large developers can be traced to ill-conceived projects, sloppy construction, poor locations, but most serious of all, **inadequate equity dollars.** Thus, if one really desires to limit financial losses, be he a developer or an investor, he must make certain to see that the property is not burdened with too much debt.

In times when mortgage money is plentiful, the lenders sometimes become too aggressive in their lending policies and frequently lend too much money to a developer. If everything works wonderfully, he may actually "borrow out." "Borrowing out" is a colloquialism used by developers that means borrowing **all** the funds for a project. A "windfall" means borrowing **more** than all the funds necessary to develop a property. "Borrowing out" has tempted many developers into going it alone, without any investors. Frequently, when the rent-up process is slow and demands for funds are necessary because of negative cash flow, the developer, unwelcome at local banks because he is too much of a risk taker, tries to get money elsewhere. This usually means the secondary market. The primary market is limited to institutions funding first mortgages, such as savings banks, insurance companies, savings and loan institutions, and pension funds. There are no such limitations in the secondary market. This market is for the large risk taker and the lenders are large risk lenders. As a result the cost for money is "ungawa." Ungawa is my term for anything in real estate unusually large or highly expensive.

No one, repeat, no one can stay in the secondary market and make enough money out of cash flow to pay back the debt, which usually bears an ungawa rate of interest. The observation here is that all funds borrowed for a real estate mortgage (in some states called deeds of trust) should be borrowed at a long-term rate that usually bears a close relationship to the long-term triple A corporate bond rate. Rates of interest usually charged by secondary lenders are generally four to eight points above this rate and are for the short term. To make matters worse for the borrowers in the secondary market, the rate is usually "floating"; it rises and falls with the prime rate. This means a rate six points above prime can be a disaster if the prime rate moves up quickly. This rapid rise in the prime rate has occurred frequently enough to eliminate the unwary developer who has had to go to the secondary market.

equity partners

The developer who avoids high rates of interest in his long- and short-term borrowings will necessarily have other equity partners. The conclusion is simple: reduce the risk to yourself and you reduce the risk to other partners. You will also definitely reap all the rewards for being a developer, but by reducing your greed you will ensure that there will be other projects to develop in the future. It is not necessary that as a developer you must own it **all.** It is only necessary that you structure your ventures intelligently, and invite others to participate with you in the development or acquisition process by putting up equity monies, then you may all prosper. The benefits to the developer are so great it is not necessary to own the building entirely by one's self. You will be amply financially rewarded by the other benefits to make this business highly desirable for you— just forego owning all the property yourself. Isn't it better to own smaller percentages of a large number of properties safely financed than to own one large property that is over financed and in which you could lose your entire investment?

Besides, when a lender knows that your modus operandi is such that you are always well-capitalized with other investors joining with you, you frequently can borrow money at a cheaper rate and for a longer period of time. This not only makes for a safer investment, it increases the cash flow of the property because the debt service requirements are lower. It might come as a surprise to neophyte developers that there are still many lenders more interested in the safety of their loans than in their profitability. Ideally a mortgage lender would like both safety and a high yield, but he knows he can't have it both ways. He rarely opts for the higher yield. Those lenders that opted for higher rates are in serious financial trouble or are no longer around.

The group ownership approach then is a worthwhile owning vehicle. It allows the developer to go to the traditional marketplace for relatively inexpensive money, which he can afford to repay with ease in normal circumstances.

The burden of raising the monies from investors is no burden at all as the developer will discover if he follows the guidelines outlined in Chapter 7.

The task of managing properties owned by partnerships is just a little more bothersome than managing properties owned by only one person. But it is also easier in some respects because the developer, as general partner, is making the day-to-day decisions for the other owners. He does not need to agonize over a decision made because a single owner is out of town when a major emergency occurs. If the property is owned by a group of partners, the responsibility for decision making is his in the first instance and normally the other partners are rarely consulted.

The timing of refinancing (going back to the original lender for a **new** and **larger** loan) and sale are the ultimate responsibility of the developer and both of these functions are very rewarding. They rarely are as rewarding in the case of a single owner or in selling the property for a single owner. If the business of developing were not so rewarding, then all properties would be owned by individuals alone. This, of course, is no longer true. Most of the major properties built in the last twenty years are owned either by large corporations, major lenders, or partnerships. Because the safest way to own properties is in the joining of capital with others, many techniques of ownership that are safe have been worked out by successful developers.

real estate investment trusts

The period from 1965 to 1975 saw the proliferation of mortgage real estate investment trusts which sought higher yields than that which a developer with a good track record would pay. As a result, trusts with enormous amounts of money to loan lent money to inexperienced developers, who were usually in not the best locations, and occasionally to risky one-purpose buildings such as hotels, motels, and automobile dealerships. They frequently lent money to second-home and resort property developers.

As of this writing, most of the major real estate investment trusts that dealt more or less exclusively in mortgages are either in bankruptcy or will soon be there. The quality developers just did not deal with them (the mortgage trusts) because of the higher costs of money when compared to the traditional sources of mortgages: the savings and loan associations, the savings banks, the insurance companies, and the pension funds, most of whom were not suckered into making loans at high rates of interest but rather took the conservative approach, seeking safety instead of high yield. They are still around today.

the question still remains: acquire or develop

The answer lies with the individual. The temperament of the syndicator or developer, the **need** for certain kinds of developments (such as office buildings, apartments, or shopping, centers), and availability of "future" commitments all influence the choice. In the absence of lender commitments for the future, of course, the development cannot begin. Notwithstanding any of the foregoing market conditions, the techniques needed for syndication of existing properties have been carefully developed. You should not consider merely acquiring and syndicating properties while foresaking the development of these properties. There is much money to be made in syndicating existing properties, but there is much more money to be made in **creating** real estate investments.

The question most frequently asked by the person considering the acquisition or development of income-producing property is how much is a **fair** amount to charge the group as either syndicator or developer. The question is a fair one. Generally speaking, when one seeks answers for problems, the answers can frequently be found in history. Aristotle, who was born in 384 B.C. and died at the age of 62 (322 B.C.), certainly was considered one of the greatest and most influential thinkers in Western culture. Somewhere very early in my commercial real estate life, I heard a story about Aristotle that impressed me. While the story may not be true, it nonetheless could have happened. As the story goes, Aristotle was teaching the sons of many famous people; among those he tutored was Alexander the Great. At any rate, Aristotle lost his lease, yes, lost his lease, in the school where he was teaching. The owner of the building wanted to use it for some other purpose, and there was Aristotle with many of his pupils and no place to teach them.

Because many of Aristotle's pupils were from wealthy homes, he thought it would be proper to approach his pupils' fathers for help in locating a new school. The following deal was struck. The fathers told Aristotle they would put up all the money if he used all the funds to build a school, and, while they would be 100 percent owners at the beginning, they stated that as soon as they received their money back in the form of rents, that Aristotle would own 50 percent of the real estate and they would own 50 percent. During the period of ownership by the students' parents, Aristotle received a small salary from tuition fees. At the time the fathers received all of their monies back, he continued with his same small salary, but proceeded at that point as 50 percent owner to pocket half of the monthly rents that he paid to the owners, among whom he was now the largest. He remained as a tenant, of course, but half the cash flow was now flowing to him.

There is a splendid lesson to be learned from observing Aristotle's procedure in solving his problem of providing space for his students. The real lesson here is if a promoter or developer or syndicator were to offer a participation to several investors in the owning of income-producing properties and everything were done at cost and without commissions or fees of any kind to the promoter, developer, or syndicator, then the venture that Aristotle structured would remain fair even today. If the developer were to receive nothing except management and leasing fees, for example, while he was managing the properties, he would one day own 50 percent when all of his invited investors had their monies returned to them. One can readily observe that the problem with this owning strategy by the promoter, developer, or syndicator is that he must wait until all the monies have been returned to the investors before he enjoys any of the fruits of his labors. One can also observe that it must be a financial success in order for the promoter to reap any benefits from copying Aristotle's method of organizing a group of investors.

The modern syndicator, developer, or promoter is unwilling to wait until all the dollars have been returned to the investors before he participates in any of the benefits that he ordinarily receives. Because he is unwilling to wait, he must take considerably less than the 50 percent Aristotle received. The rule seems to be that if the developer or syndicator gets his "goodies" concomitantly with the investor, there is no way he can receive more than an amount considerably under 50 percent.

developers versus syndicators

In actual practice, there is a definite distinction made between benefits to a developer who creates a new building as opposed to a syndicator who acquires an existing building. Most of the successful real estate developers who specialize in the development of income-producing properties rarely receive more than 25 percent of all the benefits connected with owning of real estate. These benefits include receiving approximately 25 percent of all the tax losses attributable to construction as well as 25 percent of the cash flow, most of which is not subject to federal taxation in the typical venture during the early years. The developer also receives 25 percent of the proceeds of refinancing and receives 25 percent of the cash proceeds distributed at sale. The interest belonging to the developer, oddly enough, at the beginning at least, is "tax deferred." There have been, of course, developers who wanted 50 percent of everything at the beginning, and most of these are no longer engaged in the development of income-producing properties. While a strong investment market exists for any well-located income-producing property, there is a limit to what the investing community will allow the developer. Restated, if you are developing, let us say an office building, from the very beginning with the acquisition of the land at cost and following it through until the building is ultimately completed, leased, operating, and producing cash flow, as a reasonably intelligent developer, you would seek 25 percent of the benefits of owning.

The benefits to the developer besides the tax-deferred piece of the action, in the case of the office building example, include leasing and management fees. The managing and leasing fees in the metropolitan area of Washington, D.C., in late 1978 are competitive at 3 percent of the gross income both for management and for leasing. You should not take a commission at the beginning with respect to the acquisition of the land and charge a development fee to the partnership. Everything should be done at cost. The benefits flowing to the developer include the tax-deferred piece of action plus commissions for leasing and managing the property. In the development process and included in the agreement by and among developer and investors is the exclusive right of resale of the real property. The goodies to the developer usually include in the partnership agreement the exclusive right of resale of the real property for a commission at 5 percent of the gross selling price of the property including mortgages assumed given, or taken back. It is always specified that this fee should be paid in cash. In addition, there is a cost to the partnership of 1 percent of the amount of original financing and 1 percent of the gross amount of any refinancing that should occur at a later date.

The benefits to a syndicator acquiring property are lessened only to the extent that there are prior leasing fees to be paid to other brokers and that the management of a fully leased building generally does not command the same fee as a building that has to be opened and leased from the outset. However, the exclusive right of resale of the property at 5 percent of the gross of the selling price including mortgages assumed given and taken back, plus refinancing fees, are an important consideration.

non-real-estate goodies

All of the benefits from developing and acquisition heretofore mentioned naturally relate to what is known in the real estate community as "pure real estate goodies." Most successful developers avoid taking for themselves such non-real estate goodies as fees from parking operations in an office building, for example. At the outset and until you have many, many buildings under your wing, it is far better to have this function contracted out to a third party. One of the problems involved in trying to operate garages is the rapid turnover and, indeed, the disappearance of personnel who are at the low end of the income scale, such as car jockies. Another problem involves knowing how to handle customers who are incensed because their cars have allegedly been damaged by people in your employ. There are so many other goodies to be obtained that non-real estate operations such as parking should not be considered.

The same could be said for obtaining income from owning and operating your own washers and dryers in apartment complexes, or owning your own coin-operated vending machines, or from obtaining income from managing and directing a "char-janitor" service. It is also unwise, even if you have many buildings with swimming pools, to form a company to operate these. All of this income, including income from perhaps a hospitality or recreational room in an apartment complex, belongs to the owner, and the owner is generally the partnership that you, the developer or syndicator, have organized.

There are several reasons why the developer should avoid being in the parking operations business or the coin-operations business, or any other such business. This distracts the developer from his real job of striking the best bargains he can for his investors in the successful leasing and management of the real property. Moreover, considering the developer's share of 15–25 percent of the future profits of a venture, plus the leasing and management fees, the financing and refinancing fees, and the exclusive right of resale of the real property, any more fees that were to go to the developer appear excessive.

In time, and in some instances, the developer or syndicator may wish to become a casualty insurance agent. Through the years, this can develop into a fair amount of money, and generally speaking, the developer has to do just about as much to obtain the insurance as he has to do to actually have the policy written under his own agency name. Most casualty insurance companies are delighted to have real estate entrepreneurs as casualty agents because the nature of the business underwritten by the insurance company is generally quite profitable, and the companies are very helpful and happy to assist realtors and developers in obtaining casualty insurance licenses. At any rate, it is an additional source of income and should be thoroughly investigated.

forming a corporation

The developer should seriously consider forming a corporation that will receive all of the emoluments from the development or acquisition of the real estate except that portion of the real estate in which he has a financial interest. It should be said here that it makes no sense whatever to put income-producing real estate in corporate form. Many real estate counselors frequently discover that owners needing real estate counseling assistance never received decent representation in the first instance because the real estate, or part of it, was owned by a corporation.

Real estate owners and those contemplating real estate ownership should have originally been counseled by a qualified tax attorney or real estate counselor. It seems almost unbelievable that some otherwise intelligent investor would not seek such advice initially, but many such persons have not done so.

One day, you may wish to join with a larger organization and have such an organization acquire the corporation that obtains the leasing and management fees, the exclusive right of resale fees, financing and refinancing fees, and possibly, the casualty insurance commission fees. If the developer is operating as an individual rather than a corporation, he really does not have much to offer a large corporation who is seeking to acquire him. If these benefits are in corporate form, he may, under current tax law, be able to exchange on a tax-free basis the stock in his corporation for the stock of the acquiring corporation, which may be traded on the New York Stock Exchange.

The thrust here is to put all of the developer's goodies, except the piece of the action, in a corporation. In other words, all of the goodies with the exception of the developer's interest in the profits and losses should be in a corporation, and the developer's interest should be in the developer's name by himself. Later on, we will explore all the benefits we are discussing now and consider how to protect them from someone who wants to take them from you. At the moment, it is only important that you know that these profitable benefits, with the exception again of the piece of the action, should be in corporate form. Your attorney will tell you what kind of a corporation will save you from double taxation.

So far, we have briefly outlined the benefits to you as the developer. All of the benefits flowing to the developer are available because there are also inherent benefits to the real estate investor that are so compelling, the benefits you receive are perfectly acceptable.

becoming a developer: a case history

Every few months I am questioned as to how I became a developer. It was a happy accident or more precisely a combination of fortuitous circumstances. From 1946 through 1950 I was in the residential kitchen remodeling business and it was during this period that I purchased my first home. The kitchen remodeling business was very competitive so I was surprised and amazed at the lack of sales skill demonstrated by the real estate salesman who sold me my house. In fact he didn't sell me the house, I closed the transaction myself as soon as it became evident he would not or could not close the transaction by his own actions.

At the same time I was becoming disenchanted with the kitchen business because of the inordinately long hours. Work began at 7:30 A.M. and often ended at midnight. I supervised the workmen in the morning and did the selling and planning in the evening. The business also required a six-day week leaving only Sunday to spend with my family. Under these circumstances, I couldn't be a decent father or husband, so demanding were the time requirements.

I called the owner of the real estate company from whom I purchased the house and asked what his top salesman earned. When he replied his top man earned $25,000 annually (1951 dollars), I sold my one-half interest in the kitchen business and entered the real estate field as a house salesman.

My earnings the first year were slightly in excess of $20,000 and I have remained in real estate to this day. One of my first real estate assignments involved sitting on a subdivision sample home. On dull days I played with the mathematics of the results of an investor purchasing the house and keeping it as a rental property. The return was very good, about $200 yearly for a down payment of $1,000, a neat 20 percent cash-on-cash return. I sold quite a few houses on this basis and for a while everything looked rosy. The risks involved were disregarded by both me and the purchaser. We totally disregarded the rather obvious fact if the house was not rented the investor was holding property for rent that was 100 percent vacant. To make matters worse, the rental market became very soft and vacant houses found few renters or no renters at all. About this time it occurred to me that there was an imaginary great scale in the sky which was in balance only when the risks and rewards were equal. This was a real revelation to me and it has helped my decision making in all areas of real estate investment ever since.

The next move was to concentrate on small apartment houses. My first syndicate involved a down payment of $8,100 for the purchase of an eight unit apartment house. I sold one percent units of participation for $810, which was the minimum participation amount. In 1975 minimum units of participation in a large downtown office building at 2020 K Street., N.W. in Washington, D.C. were sold for $175,000 each. Many things happened to me between 1951 and 1975 and I will list a few highlights which may give you an insight as to how to start your own development business.

The problems found in syndicating and managing a small apartment building are the same as in a large one except that in a large one the problems are far less costly. This sounds screwy but the reason is simple. If you own an eight-unit apartment and one unit is vacant you sustain a vacancy loss of $12\frac{1}{2}$ percent ($88\frac{1}{2}$% occupancy). If you own a 441-unit garden apartment with one unit vacant, your vacancy loss is less than one quarter of one percent (99¾% occupancy). If you place a classified advertisement in the local newspaper your cost to advertise can be spread over eight units in the first syndicate whereas you can spread the costs over 441 units in the latter.

At that point a course I had once taken in economics suddenly made sense to me. The economy of scale (size) now became clear. Applied across the board for all expenses, the unit cost of operation was and is much smaller in the 441-unit garden apartment compared to the 8-unit apartment building. I also learned that the larger projects were safer because they could afford resident managers and resident engineers on the site. This helps tremendously during times when the apartment rental market is soft, i.e., demand is light and there are many apartments available. There is always someone to show the apartments to prospective tenants and maintenance is always better than in smaller projects, unless you plan to live in the smaller project and act as owner, rental agent, engineer, and on-site handyman.

My first development project started through a land purchase by the owner of the real estate firm for whom I worked. He offered me a chance to own one-half interest in a 43-unit apartment project which he planned to build on the site. Neither I nor the owner of the firm knew anything about developing income-producing real estate. The general contractor who now heads the largest development company in the Washington, D.C. metropolitan area, Charles E. Smith and his son Robert H. Smith both implored me to change the plans which consisted of 43 identical units all of which were efficiencies. Being young, stubborn, and stupid, I didn't listen. The contemporary architect that I hired I naïvely assumed was also the one to supervise construction.

The economic result of the project was a disaster, showing little or no return on our combined investment. We sold it after a few years and were lucky to recover our original capital. Curiously, the project won an architectural award! While the experience shocked and frightened me from immediately developing another project, I learned several lessons that has helped prevent me from doing another loser.

Now the first thing I do is research the market. The location of the first apartment development could not support a 43-unit apartment building of only efficiency apartments. Had I researched the project in advance, this would have been apparent. I now hire only speculative architects, not award-winning institutional architects. I now organize a limited partnership wherein my risk is much smaller and I receive an interest in future profits for acting as the developer and general partner. From 1952 to 1956 I spent most of the time syndicating existing properties. During this period my employer designated me as head of the commercial investment department. Looking back, that took a lot of courage on both his part and mine. Neither he nor I knew a lot about investments, but I was learning.

In 1956 I left the firm to open my own business and within three months my friend, Herb Blum joined with me. Within that year (1956) we joined together and founded Swesnik and Blum. We rented one room in the Tower Building at 14th and K Sts., N.W., bought two desks and one typewriter. We had no employees and I acted as secretary for both of us. It wasn't because we couldn't afford a secretary, although our resources were limited, it was a backlash from watching our former employer literally throw away money, to massage his ego. To this day we are careful of hiring bodies, and although we administer real estate holdings totaling nearly $150 million, our firm has only eight persons in our offices and that includes Herb and myself. There are no chiefs, we are all braves. Everybody works!

Because I couldn't find quality income-producing properties to my liking, I again decided to become a developer. Learning several lessons from my first almost disastrous experience, I set about seeking a positive strategy. The late Morris Cafritz, the largest and richest developer in the greater Washington area at that time, helped me in a most positive way. He made suggestions as to what to do and carefully pointed out the risks and rewards of each strategy I could follow.

Clarence Johnson, a real charmer who had "done it all" including selling lots in Chicago during the Depression in the 1930s was working for the Prudential Life Insurance Company and at that time (1956) was the loan manager for the District of Columbia. Curiously, I never made a loan with the Prudential. I wouldn't make a purchase of land without first seeking advice from Clarence Johnson. He vetoed developments which could have been disastrous as his comments and suggestions were made from a lender's point of view. I clearly owe a debt of gratitude to both Cafritz and Johnson who helped me develop both positive and negative real estate strategies.

Thus, I became a developer by backing out of residential selling into investments requiring syndication. When quality properties in good locations, getting better, were not available for purchase, I started to manufacture such projects. To this day Herb Blum and I tend to view our work as the manufacturing of quality real estate investments.

federal bar building west, washington, d.c. 1968, cost $6,500,000.

them:

the investors

chapter 2 outline

One of the most attractive features of investing in a real estate project is the federal income tax consequences of such an investment.

investor benefits over the life of the venture

In the initial phases of a real estate development, certain items are partially deductible in the calendar year of the investment. Let us suppose you plan to develop a new office building in the city in which you are active, and your owning vehicle is a partnership. Further, let's assume the project is in the $5 million range and you plan to borrow about $4 million from a permanent mortgage lender. It would be "standard practice" for you to employ a mortgage broker to obtain such a permanent commitment from an insurance company, a savings institution, or a pension fund. It is not uncommon for a mortgage broker to charge one point (a point means one percent of the gross amount of the loan) to obtain such a long-term commitment. It is also not uncommon for the lender to charge you, the borrower, one point for making such a commitment.

Because you are paying these fees for financing your project over the life of the loan, most tax attorneys will not allow partnerships to deduct these brokerage fees all in one lump sum in the first year that the partnerships pay them. The attorneys insist that long-term financing fees should be amortized (deductible) only over the life of the loan. This means deductions of long-term financing may be charged as an expense for federal income tax purposes on an annualized basis. Chances are you also will be paying your broker one point for obtaining your construction loan. This loan will probably be obtained from a commercial bank, which may also charge you a point for the loan. These fees should be deductible ratably over the term of the construction mortgage.

Let us assume that each of the ten investors who had each committed $100,000 had **split** their contributions to the partnership over the first two years: $50,000 payable each year. This is quite common because the total cash investment of $1 million would not all be necessary during the first year of construction.

No well-informed investor will purchase an interest in your real estate development without first considering the effects of the investment on his personal income tax return. Therefore, before organizing the partnership, it will be obvious that any sensible developer will necessarily have an expert tax attorney assist him in determining the lawful deductions available to the partnership.

capitalization and amortization

Before the Tax Reform Act of 1976, real estate taxes and interest (subject to limitations on prepaid interest) attributable to the construction period could be either deducted currently or at the taxpayer's election, capitalized and depreciated over the life of the property to the extent allocable to depreciable improvements.

Under the Internal Revenue Code as amended by the Tax Reform Act of 1976, construction period interest and taxes on real property that is or will be held for business or investment purposes must be capitalized in the year in which the interest and taxes are paid or accrued and amortized over a 10-year period. Ten percent of the amount capitalized may be deducted for the taxable year in which paid or accrued. The balance must be amortized over a 9-year period beginning with the year in which the property is ready to be placed in service or is ready to be held for sale.

If the real property in question is sold or exchanged, the unamortized balance of the construction period interest and taxes is added to the basis of the property for purposes of determining gain or loss on the exchange. If the real property is transferred or exchanged in a nontaxable transaction, the transferor is to continue to deduct the amortization allowable over the amortization period remaining after the transfer.

In lieu of the new capitalization and amortization rules, the taxpayer may elect to capitalize construction period interest and taxes as a carrying charge under Section 266 of the Code. The amortization rules of Section 189 of the Code apply to all noncorporate taxpayers and to Subchapter S corporations and personal holding companies.

Different effective dates and phase-in schedules are provided for nonresidential real estate, residential real estate, and low-income housing. The phase-in of the new rule for nonresidential real property began in 1976. The full 10-year amortization period will not apply to construction period interest and taxes paid or accrued before 1982.

The phase-in period of the new rule for residential real property (other than low-income housing) begins in 1978. The full 10-year amortization period will not apply to construction period interest and taxes paid or accrued before 1984.

The phase-in period of the new rule for low-income housing does not begin until 1982. The full 10-year amortization period will not apply to construction period interest and taxes paid or accrued before 1988.

The phase-in periods are as follows.

If the amount is paid or accrued in a taxable year beginning in—

Non-residential real property	Residential real property (other than low-income housing)	Low-income housing	The percentage deductible for each amortization year
	1978	1982	25%—4 years
1977	1979	1983	20%—5 years
1978	1980	1984	16-2/3%—6 years
1979	1981	1985	14-2/7%—7 years
1980	1982	1986	12-1/2%—8 years
1981	1983	1987	11-1/9%—9 years
After 1981	After 1983	After 1987	10%

the partnership's tax advantages

Organizational expenses incident to the creation of the partnership must be capitalized and may be deducted ratably over the first 60 months of the partnership's business activity. Expenses incident to syndication of the limited partnership interests must be capitalized, but these expenses may not be amortized as long as the partnership remains in business. Upon liquidation of the partnership, any unamortized balance of the organizational expenses and all of the capitalized syndication expenses may be deducted as losses.

If the partnership is properly organized, it will not be a taxable entity. Each item of income and each deductible item is allocated among the partners in accordance with their partnership interest as reflected in the partnership agreement. In the illustration we are using, let's say the developer is entitled to a 25 percent interest in all profits and losses. If the ten investors invested equal amounts of $100,000 each, then each of the limited partners would be entitled to $7\frac{1}{2}$ percent (10 percent × 75 percent) of the partnership's profits and losses.

Now let's look at the operation of these rules during the first three years of the partnership's existence. Let's assume that the partnership activities commence January 1, 1979; that the office building was completed at the end of the second year; that the permanent loan was closed at the end of that period; and that the building was fully occupied during the third year. The interest payable on the construction mortgage during the first year will be $100,000. The interest payable during the second year will be $300,000. We will also assume that the $4 million permanent mortgage is obtained at a 10 percent interest rate.

Under Internal Revenue Service guidelines, office buildings may be depreciated over a 45-year life. Using straight line depreciation, a $4 million office structure may be depreciated over 45 years at 2.222 percent annually. This returns to the partnership the cost of the structure (improvements) **equally** over a 45-year period.

Although the 150 percent declining balance method may be used (which means that more depreciation deductions—write-offs or charges as an expense for federal income tax purposes—may be taken in the early years), the depreciation is "on the average" 2.222 percent annually. Obviously, all the depreciation is not used up until the end of 45 years. Since 150 percent of 2.222 percent is 3.333 percent, this percentage may be applied each year on the then undepreciated balance. Using this method, our $4 million improvement may be depreciated at 3.333 percent the first year during which the building is ready for occupancy. This amounts to $133,332.

The second year, the same 3.333 percent factor again may be applied on the **remaining** undepreciated balance. The book value of the improvements after the first-year deduction of $133,332 will be $3,866,668. The second year's deduction would be $128,889 (3.333 percent × $3,866,668). Each succeeding year, the deduction would be smaller as the remaining book value of the improvements is decreased annually by the depreciation deduction.

Because there was no rental income accruing to the partnership during the first two years, the partnership deductions for the first two years are as follows.

1979

Mortgage interest	$140,000	
Real estate taxes	40,000	
Construction period interest and taxes	$180,000	
Amount allowable in year incurred	14-2/7%	
Subtotal		$25,714
Organizational expenses	$30,000	
Amount allowable in year incurred	20%	
Subtotal		$ 6,000
One-half of brokerage fee		$20,000
Insurance expense		$ 4,000
Total first year deductions		$55,714

1980

Mortgage interest	$300,000	
Real estate taxes	40,000	
Construction period interest and taxes	$340,000	
Amount allowable in year incurred	12-1/2%	
Subtotal		$42,500
1979 organizational expenses allowable in second year		$ 6,000
Insurance expense		$ 4,000
Total second year deductions		$52,500

If we assume that the gross rents received by the partnership in the third year are $900,000, then the partnership accounting for the third year is as follows.

1981	Taxable Income (Loss)	Cash Flow
14-2/7% of first-year construction period interest and taxes	($ 25,714)	$
12-1/2% of second-year construction period interest and taxes	(42,500)	
Organizational expense allowable in third year	(6,000)	
Mortgage interest	(390,000)	(390,000)
Real estate taxes	(175,000)	(175,000)
Insurance expense	(4,000)	(4,000)
Depreciation	(133,332)	
Management fee	(24,000)	(24,000)
Utilities expense	(160,000)	(160,000)
Mortgage amortization		(40,000)

	Taxable Income (Loss)	Cash Flow
Total third-year deductions	($960,546)	($793,000)
Gross rents	900,000	900,000
Net loss	($24,999)	
Cash flow		$107,000

In our example, the profits and losses of the first three years would be allocated as follows.

	1979 Loss	1980 Loss	1981 Loss	1981 Cash Flow
General partners (25%)	($13,928)	($13,125)	($15,136)	$ 26,750
Limited partners (75%)	($41,785)	($39,375)	($45,409)	$ 80,250
Totals	($55,714)	($52,500)	($60,546)	$107,000

Each of the limited partners is entitled to 10 percent of the losses and cash flow allocable to the limited partner group. Therefore, each limited partner will be entitled to a loss of $4,178, $3,937, and $4,541 in 1979, 1980, and 1981 respectively, and he will be entitled to $8,025 of the cash flow to be distributed. All of these cash flow distributions are sheltered from current income tax by the partnership deductions described above. However, the cash flow distributions reduce each partner's basis in his partnership interest, which becomes significant only at the disposition of his partnership interest or in the liquidation of the partnership. An analysis of the above figures discloses that cash flow is tax sheltered to the extent that depreciation and carryover amortization deductions exceed the mortgage amortization.

more ways to improve tax posture

In our example, certain unimportant factual details have been deliberately omitted to keep the example simple. Sophisticated developers are well aware they can "break-out" tenant improvements and depreciate these items over the life of the tenant's lease. Additionally, certain items included in the improvement costs, such as elevators, are eligible for tax credits. Tenant improvement depreciation along with tax credits would dramatically increase the tax losses in our example.

Let's look at another facet of structuring the investment to maximize tax losses. In the example of the $5 million venture we have been using, $1 million of the total was allocable to the land, which, of course, may not be depreciated. Having the unequivocal use of land is what makes the development process possible. Notice the word "use." This does not necessarily mean "ownership." Unequivocal use may be obtained through leasing the land, let's say, for 99 years. The annual rental of the land is deductible, as an expense item for federal income tax purposes and this technique makes for even greater deductions, and, thus, losses to the partnership. A useful rule of thumb on land leases is that they make good sense when the **ratio** of the cost of improvements to the cost of the land is **lower** than five to one. In other words, if land costs $1 million and improvements cost $4 million, the ratio is four to one, and if conditions favor it, a land lease or sale-leaseback makes good sense. It tends to reduce the number of dollars expended annually on mortgage payments and land rent combined.

While making a speech to real estate executives in Tokyo, Japan in the early '70's, I was amazed to discover the Japanese had never heard of the term "leaseback." We Americans have so much land for our population compared to the Far East and Europe that we treat land as an asset we want to **control** not necessarily **own.** This is unthinkable to a Japanese developer, mainly because land is so scarce they wish to pass it on to future generations through their inheritance laws. Our federal income tax laws do not allow depreciation or other deductions for the use of land we own. So developers frequently sell the land to an institutional investor (lender) and lease it back for as long as possible— usually for 50 to 99 years. The lease payments are rentals and are thus deductible as an expense for federal income tax purposes.

Americans understand that the desirability of locations change because we have so much land mass and have a highly mobile population. Ownership of land does not have the same emotional effect on an American as a foreigner, especially in those cities where land is at a premium such as Tokyo or Hong Kong. Later on there is a discussion relating to the appropriate time and conditions when land should be sold and leased back.

It should only be used, however, if the partnership has the right of repurchase and the land rent is not only fair, but tied to the actual gross income of the building. No-No's to avoid in creating land leases and sale/leasebacks are:

1. The absence of right to repurchase (this may jeopardize your ultimate ability to refinance or sell).

2. Rent tied to the Consumer Price Index (the CPI may at times rise more rapidly than the building's gross income, thus putting your profit in an economic bind).

3. Too short a lease term (anything under 80 years for an office building is foolish. You need to plan for at least two 40-year-life office buildings).

tax sheltered is not tax free

If your office building venture rents up and you have not miscalculated expenses, the investor benefits of tax losses during construction have not only been realized, but cash flow commences, and depending on the speed of depreciation, some, all, or **more** than all of the cash flow is not subject to income tax. Some unsophisticated lawyers, developers, and investors call the tax-sheltered income "tax-free" income. Writing in the **Washington Post** on Saturday, May 15, 1976, one real estate writer who should know better called the tax-sheltered income "tax free". Every time I read something like this I get angry. This type of incorrect information causes consumer groups and others to scream against real estate owners and to demand that the government change our tax laws.

Inasmuch as tax shelter occurs whenever depreciation (and other amortizable items) exceed amortization the following example may be helpful.

GROSS INCOME:	$100,000	
All cash expenses including mortgage payments	60,000	
CASH FLOW		40,000
Add back mortgage amortization		1,280
		41,280
Deduct non-cash expenses (depreciation and other amortizable items)		39,280
Taxable Income		2,000

Note that as the owner of the real property you received $40,000 in cash in the year just ended. Your taxable income is $2,000. Thus $38,000 of the cash flow was tax sheltered. Whatever bracket you are in will determine your tax on the $2,000. If in the 40 percent tax bracket, your total would be $800. When one owns income-producing real estate, he **knows** there is no such thing as "tax-free" income. The ultimate payment of taxes to the federal government occurs when the property is sold. Tax losses reduce the book value (cost less depreciation) of a property. They also reduce each partner's basis in his partnership interest. Taxes are paid at sale on the difference between the book value and the sales price. So, all that can be said about tax losses and tax-sheltered income is that it is tax deferred. It isn't "tax free."

refinancing proceeds

Sooner or later, the property can be refinanced. If the planning was sound, rents will have been increased to keep pace not only with increased operating expenses but also with newer competitive buildings that have been built at a higher price (because of scarcer land and inflation). Newer buildings necessarily will have higher rents than older ones, but may not be in a better location nor have more to offer the prospective tenant. Amortization is increasing and interest is decreasing monthly, while depreciation decreases annually. Between the eighth and twelfth year, amortization may be higher than depreciation, and therefore, your tax-sheltered income will have become not only fully taxable, but there may be more taxable income than cash flow. This is the time to refinance.

A new loan not only means a fee for the developer, but it also makes for happy investors. None of the net monies the partnership derives from refinancing is subject to federal taxation. Remember that the ultimate sales price minus the book value is the taxable gain. If the sales price is less than book value, there is a loss from the sale.

Although the proceeds of a mortgage refinancing are not taxable income, the distribution of such funds reduces the basis of each partner's interest in the partnership. After all negative adjustments on the basis of a partner's interest equal or exceed all positive adjustments, distributions of cash are taxable as gain from the sale of the partnership interest.

tax formulas

It will help you to understand the taxable consequences of real estate investments held while the investor group owns the property if you accept and understand the following tax formula:

Cash flow + amortization − depreciation = taxable income or loss.

Inasmuch as a properly organized partnership pays no taxes itself, each investor is responsible for his proportionate share of the taxable income or loss. Every developer should always explain the investing results of income-producing real estate to potential investors by using this formula.

You can see that whenever depreciation is greater than loan amortization, tax shelter results. If the depreciation is great enough, all of the cash flow is tax sheltered because there is no immediate federal income tax liability. When the depreciation is greater than the cash flow and the loan amortization, the result is not only fully tax-sheltered cash flow, but additional losses that, under current tax law, may be used to **offset** other income. Since the enactment of the Tax Reform Act of 1976, the amount of losses available to shelter income from other sources has been greatly reduced.

proceeds of sale

After a property is refinanced and the monies distributed, it may be a good time to consider a sale. Sales should be timed by the developer not only to make a profit, but also to prevent future operating losses. Everything that goes into a building depreciates or wears out, and much of what goes into a building will one day have to be replaced. Technological changes in heating and air conditioning are surely going to occur as well as changes in the building's "atmosphere," a function related to its location. The developer's job is to see to it that his investors are not locked in to a deteriorating situation.

One of the factors you should take into account in determining when to sell is the tax status of the property. At some point, taxable income from the property will exceed the cash flow. In addition, the taxable gain from a sale will usually exceed the net cash proceeds from the sale. This is so because the basis of the property declines faster than the principal balance of the mortgage. In any case, the taxable gain may be partly taxable as ordinary income (i.e., to the extent of depreciation recapture). The balance of the taxable gain will qualify for the favorable tax rates applicable to long-term capital gain.

My own strategy is to sell the building at the point of its "prime," a point in the ownership life where cash flow could diminish. This differs, of course, from building to building, but I think it falls generally between the tenth and twelfth year of ownership.

Sell it while it is still desirable—buyers who will pay decent prices for distressed properties are hard to find. When you think it is time to sell, describe to your investors all the factors you have considered and stand firm. One of the paradoxes in this business is that investors only seem to want to sell when the property has already begun its downward slide. "Sell," they say! "To whom?" You might well ask. Serious investors seem to fade away when property has begun to be troubled, consequently very few sales are made or capable of being made at this point.

You are the sole judge as to when to initiate the sale. You are the expert. Use your expertise; do not be intimidated by wealthy investors with no expertise in making real estate investment decisions. If you are right, you are expected to be right. If you wait and are wrong because of waiting, you will have a very short business life as a developer. This is true even if the investors voted not to sell. "Why didn't you tell us there would be no cash flow, and worse, there would be negative cash flow?" "Why didn't you advise us!" Indeed, insist that they sell.

Make up your mind early in the development process that you will be making important decisions as to refinancing and sale. You will be well-compensated, but included with the monetary goodies comes the responsibility for these decisions. If you need professional help in your decision making, get help by employing a member of the American Society of Real Estate Counselors, especially one who has specialized in what you are doing. But for your own peace of mind, do not let the investors' dollars or the investors themselves guide you. The lesson here is that as you progress through the development process, you will not have all the answers. Remember, though, some other developer or counselor has faced a similar problem and solved it!

Don't be afraid of making an investment decision because you haven't done it—just locate another professional who has. The fee charged to you will be peanuts compared to the result of a poor decision.

Ignorance is charging ahead with foolish arrogance—intelligence is understanding you don't know the answer, but discovering who does. Be assured it is rarely an investor. Something about real estate investments makes quite a few persons feel like experts. How foolish they become when up against a learned person with twenty-five years of precise expertise in a highly specialized field such as developing and leasing a new office building.

When it is time to sell—**sell.** Go on to the next venture.

lack of liquidity

During the investing life of a new typical income-producing real estate development, an investor can have his funds tied up for as long as ten or twelve years. Certainly as a developer, you should be aware that at least in terms of liquidity, the investor is taking a risk peculiar to income-producing real estate.

There is no market for an individual's participation in a venture, except your office or other investors in the venture. Should an investor really need cash, he will find it difficult or impossible to find a buyer. My advice to an investor is that if he thinks he may need his money before the project is ultimately refinanced and sold, he should not invest in the first place. If the project is going well, one of the other investors might be interested, but a profitable sale of his fractional interest is unlikely. And, if things are not going well, there will probably be no interest in acquiring someone else's participation.

The first thing an investor should be told is how illiquid he will become. Unsophisticated investors never know this. Your task then is either to educate the unsophisticated investor (later on in the book you will find this is a very difficult task indeed) or preferably deal only with sophisticated real estate investors.

Illiquidity has its rewards, too. Although it is not a very pleasant social conversation, should an investor die during the life of the investment, the estate will never be taxed on the future worth of the investor's participation. The Internal Revenue Service only need know the then current worth. The courts have long held that 10 percent of the whole is not worth 10 percent of the **total value** because of the fact that such participations are rarely sold, and if they are, it is usually at a reduced price.

major advantage

Obviously, the major value of owning income-producing real estate is that it is one of the few investments that moves up with inflation. If you accept the premise that inflation is a fact of life in our economy, then the easiest path for an investor to follow is to invest in income-producing property. If he cannot afford to own one building by himself, or does not want the bother of management, or wants the diversification of owning parts of several properties, and sees the advantages of being in different classes of properties (office buildings, shopping centers, or apartments), then he needs a developer in whom he has confidence.

More people probably have been made millionaires through real estate than any other form of investment. Even William Shakespeare made more money from his real estate investments than he made from the production of his plays.

safety, appreciation, and cash flow

We in the business of real estate investments preach safety, appreciation, and cash flow. But the investor, while cranking into his brain safety, appreciation, and cash flow, really tends to make his investment decisions on the basis of tax considerations: tax losses and tax-sheltered income. He loves to receive tax-deferred refinancing proceeds and ultimately, all the sales proceeds. He also wants all these goodies at little or no risk to himself. The brighter investor knows there is a risk-reward quotient, but investors are very much tax oriented. Once in a speech about real estate investments to a group of lawyers at a state bar association convention, I said I was going to write a book dedicated to the Internal Revenue Service called "Up Your Bracket," and I made a simultaneous obscene gesture at the same time. It tore the house down—300 attorneys stood up and applauded for about a minute. I was embarrassed by the whole thing. When I returned home, I chatted with a psychiatrist investor friend of mine who told me why in an attempt at humor I had hit a nerve.

After high school graduation, usually at age 18, there are four more years of college "pre-law." A student who wants to go to law school must consider at age 22 and after graduation from college whether to devote three more years to a legal education. He will be about 25 years old when he graduates, and then must pass a stringent bar examination before he can begin to earn a living.

If he is very bright, attends a fine law school, and graduates in the upper 10 percent of his class, he may start earning some serious money at about age 30. At this age, he learns that if he really is a success, he will have to pay the Internal Revenue Service up to 50 percent of his income after certain more or less standard deductions. I have heard lawyers really "smoke" about this. Things used to be worse. Uncle Sam used to tax the earned income up to 91 percent before 1964 and 70 percent until 1969. Thank goodness, Congress has put a limit of 50 percent on earned income.

Just a word about "tax loopholes" and "tax preferences." From time to time, Congress has used our income tax laws for purposes other than to impose taxes. Certain preferences were enacted from time to time to stimulate the flow of funds in one direction or another. For example, deductions are allowed to increase contributions to charity. Others were created to stimulate the construction industry, especially during difficult years. Still others were enacted to help mining, oil, and other mineral exploration. These include the depletion allowance applicable to mineral-extracting industries. Further, to encourage industries to invest capital in new plant equipment, investment tax credits were enacted. These cannot fairly be called "loopholes." They were made a part of the tax law for a purpose. Politicians who desire to eliminate such tax preferences call them "loopholes" because everyone should be against "loopholes."

Congress has shaped our tax laws to help our economy, to keep employment high, and to help see that our citizens have a place to live (citizens who own houses may deduct interest payments and property taxes. Is this a loophole?), a place to work, and a place to shop. Tax preferences, or tax incentives, then are the tools of our lawmakers who in good faith are striving to keep our American system of free enterprise going. Tax incentives are changed from time to time to accommodate our nation's needs. There is a small, but vocal, group of people who keep up constant pressure because they want to see our tax laws "fair" to everyone. This will never be. No single law can cover every single person or every single transaction. Our income tax laws work better here in the United States than in any other free country in the world. Surely they can be improved, but let's never forget the tax laws are **not just to collect taxes evenhandedly.** Whether we like it or not, they are social and economic tools that must be constantly updated and improved. And, one final question: Who would invest in a speculative, unleased apartment house, shopping center, or office building if there were not special tax incentives for taking such enormous economic risks? Who would incur such risks with the federal government as a partner who shares in profits only?

To quote the late, eminent Judge Learned Hand, "Any one may so arrange his affairs that his taxes shall be as low as possible; he is not bound to choose that pattern which will best pay the treasury; there is not even a patriotic duty to increase one's taxes."

the world trade center, new york city. ten million square feet of office space.

both you and them

chapter 3 outline

developing winning ventures

Let's assume you want to try your hand as a developer. What kind of real estate should you develop? At any given time, there may be a surplus of either shopping facilities, apartments, or office buildings. For that matter, there may be a surplus of hotels, motels, industrial parks, and warehouses. Fortunately, it is rare indeed (only in the early 1930s) that **all** of the various kinds of real estate are surplus for which there is no market.

If the apartments are nearly 100 percent rented in your community, think of developing additional apartment units. This assumes that there are no rent controls in the community in which you live and work and that the possibility of such controls being enacted by your local government is remote. With today's cost of construction, you may effectively rule out building high-rise apartments. If you live in the South, or Southwest, you may wonder why there are so few high-rise apartments, and those you may see are struggling for tenants or their developers have gone "belly up." Land for apartments is relatively inexpensive in the South and Southwest. A developer does not need to build a high rise, he can build garden apartments which are much less expensive to build. Developers have gone belly up because they tried to obtain higher rents required from a more costly type of construction and the renting public simply would not pay the higher rents.

There must be a compelling emotional and economic reason for the development of high-rise apartments. In larger cities where people want to live close to work, there is no alternative to going up. Land is so expensive that you cannot build sideways. With the exception of a few cities of large populations in the South and Southwest, such as Atlanta, Georgia, and the large cities of Houston and Dallas, Texas, you may see only a few high-rise apartments. Yet, from time to time, some developer "feels" like building such a building in areas where there is no shortage of good land priced within reach so that he could build a garden or low-rise apartment. Strangely enough, he may find a lender who may commit a loan to him. This occurs because two or more stupid people come together: the developer (usually a fledgling) and some young person in a lending institution who can sell his superiors on the idea. The result is usually predictable: a terrible economic mistake. It is not necessary to do anything spectacular, such as building a high-rise apartment in a market that does not call for it, to go broke. It is possible to go broke by developing an otherwise winning venture by borrowing too much, by not putting your skills into the specifications of the building, or by poor leasing and management.

I was once called upon to give some real estate advice to an acquaintance. Being a member of the American Society of Real Estate Counselors, I charge a fee for counseling. The situation was this: an important investor who had done very well through the years in buying garden apartments in the West was interested in acquiring an office building in the mid-South. The couple (a man and wife team) who had developed this office building that my investor friend was considering had built a few one- and two-story office complexes and for some reason known only to them, they decided to branch out and **up** by building a ten-story office building. They had obtained a construction loan from a large real estate investment trust without having a permanent commitment. As it turned out, the real estate investment trust ultimately was the permanent lender. But, I don't want to get ahead of the story.

Upon arrival at the city, I had the opportunity to lunch with my investor friend at the top of one of the newest and most modern office buildings in the downtown area. The top floor was a private daytime club and had an exquisite view. Following lunch, we visited the office building which he was considering. In the first place, the office building was in a suburban location, and although once we got close and we could readily see it, we couldn't drive to it for about ten minutes because we were driving around in circles, which tells you immediately how I liked its marketing potential. As I had guessed, only the first lower level, the main floor, and a few suites were rented. To make matters worse, the building was built for midgets, who apparently never had the desire to relieve themselves. Are you ready for this? Each floor was about 20,000 square feet; this means that approximately 175 to 225 people would eventually occupy each floor. The men's room had one toilet! Since the ladies room was unoccupied, I visited it too. Would you believe there was only **one** toilet there too?

The ceiling height was about eight feet clear, just right for midgets. Any office building with a clear floor to ceiling height of less than 8 feet 6 inches could make persons of average height emotionally uncomfortable. The desirable ceiling height in most cities with high-rise office buildings is usually 8 feet 8 inches. And, here's a word of caution. If the room size gets over 20 feet long, a lower ceiling makes you feel like you are standing in a tunnel. When I asked the then owners of the building who had designed the building, I found out that they had merely hired an architect to get their plans through the phase of obtaining a building permit. In fairness to my client, he had not seen the building before, but had been intrigued with the "numbers," assuming full occupancy.

It is important, therefore, to study your market with a view to discovering its special characteristics and what it needs, but it is of paramount importance to diligently follow the checklists that are furnished in this book to avoid mistakes. Honestly, before I visited this mid-South city, I didn't think it was possible to create such an abomination of a building. But I have seen this many times, even with people involved that at least **seem** to have the proper credentials. Imagine a high-rise apartment house in Dallas (there are very few in that lovely city), with 8-foot ceilings too, and imagine this—there are no trash chutes. All trash must be manually picked up. Don't think this mistake is terribly uncommon. In Chicago, there is a lovely high-rise apartment project on Lake Shore Drive, overlooking Lake Michigan, where the developer also forgot to put in a trash chute. The world-famous architect, the developer, the lender, and the city inspectors all overlooked this important sanitary fact as well as the horrendous cost of collections several times daily. Note: several collections daily—if not, who could stand the odors?

Developing winning ventures assumes not only those positive aspects of site selection, design, and construction, but **avoiding mistakes.** I call this negative strategy, and as mentioned before, I have developed extensive checklists that are reminders of what to do correctly, but perhaps more importantly, to avoid catastrophies along with huge out-of-pocket losses.

tailoring types of investments to your background

In almost thirty years of lecturing, making speeches, and teaching about acquiring or developing income-producing properties, someone invariably asks the question: "It's no problem for you, but how can you expect me (or us) to develop properties when we have no background to draw on?" I always respond by asking how many parents have ever heard their children, either in grade school or at the preschool level, state that when they grow up, instead of being a doctor, policeman, or fireman, that they have thought their occupational future through and have decided to become real estate developers? It happens that this particular fashion of making a living calls for hard work, imagination, research, and good judgment. You need no college degrees, and developing income-producing properties is a business and not a profession. The purpose of this book is not to give me status or wealth, but rather to show how easy it is to gain wealth, a good reputation in your field, and a chance to make a serious contribution to what your town or city looks like. While some persons in the income-producing business would like to call what we do professional, this is only so because they wish to be called professionals. Somehow, this is supposed to make them feel better. There is nothing scientific about what we do, but neither is there anything scientific done by an economist, statistician, or lawyer, all of whom are professionals. My latest definition of a real estate "professional" is "anyone doing anything whose earnings are in excess of $50,000 annually (1979 dollars)."

You will begin the development process or acquisition process only if you are emotionally comfortable with what you are about to do. If you are intimidated by the prospect, you'll be comforted to hear that hardly anybody knows much about developing income-producing properties, but you can learn. In addition, there are no tests to pass. To become a developer does not even require a real estate license in most states. In addition, this business is as honest as any other. The developers who have not gone bankrupt, have not been sent to jail, or have not had their licenses suspended are in the majority. When you consider that some one-half million people earn their living at real estate, the bankruptcies or unscrupulous persons represent a tiny minority.

Most developers became so by accident. You can become one by desire. Let's take this example. You are a house broker; you know better than anyone else in your community what people look for in seeking homes. By extension, I would prefer that you design an apartment building, however small, for me if I were to live in your community. You would probably include all of those things one would expect to find in a well-designed home.

I'd wager that you would include a washer and dryer right in the confines of my two-bedroom and den apartment. I wouldn't have to leave my apartment to wash and dry my towels, sheets, and other laundry. You'd probably include a master TV antenna system that gave me an outlet in each bedroom and den, and perhaps include one in the kitchen. Incidentally, it occurs to me that if 94 percent of all TV being watched in America is done in a room **other** than the living room, why are there not many TV master outlets in the bedrooms and dens of new apartment homes? Admittedly, some developers have awakened to this fact and are now moving in the direction of putting outlets everywhere imaginable, including balconies.

You would probably include an abundance of good closet space, and I'd bet you'd have the kitchen designed so that I could have breakfast, lunch, and informal dinners there if I wanted. You'd give me some decent sized medicine cabinets, and probably design the washer-dryer ensemble to fit near the source of dirty laundry, one of the bathrooms perhaps, or off the master bedroom. Not that there is anything wrong with doing laundry in the kitchen, but perhaps the new tenant or owner should have a voice in the location of the washer-dryer ensemble.

You are my developer because you know **how** people live. I would trust you rather than anyone else to develop an apartment building for me.

If you are working in an office building, I'd trust you to think through some of the desirable (and undesirable) features you are now working with. Honestly, couldn't you develop a better building? The same thing applies if you work out of a shopping center. If you have occasion to travel frequently, jot down all the good and bad features you encounter in your travels. I'll bet you could someday build the nearly perfectly designed motel or hotel with the most livable and comfortable layouts and equipment features. It doesn't take anyone smarter than you to know that in Washington, D.C., where it can be hot and humid in the summer, that your halls must be air conditioned and your ice machines must have enough capacity on each floor to serve ice to each occupant. One of the newest hotels in Richmond, Virginia, has an ice machine on each floor for the use of its guests. After a very warm round of golf, my buddy and I couldn't find enough ice on three different floors to prepare one drink, let alone cool a bottle of wine we had brought along.

This single example should teach you that the development field is wide open to you. **God knows, you couldn't do worse!** Tailor your first development (however small) to your own life experiences. If your location is good, and you follow the precepts explained here, you've got to be a winner. One strong note of caution: Do not do anything spectacular. Your task is to develop a property that has the **least** amount of negative criticism. The moment someone "loves" your development, someone else "hates" it. This is always the predictable result of "spectacular" design.

A good example of this love-hate ambivalence occurred in the exterior design of the Forum Apartments in North Bethesda, Md. One Sunday morning I was having breakfast at my golf club when a fellow developer complimented me on the action of the flaming urns at the entrance to the apartments. This was in our pre-energy conscious days and I had installed a gas flaming urn mounted on a pillar on either side of the driveway entrance. My fellow developer felt all apartment buildings needed some form of action, either flames or perhaps fountains and in our climate he "loved" the flames.

Five minutes later the wife of another friend haughtily told me the flaming urns turned her off because they seemed too contrived. She refused to examine our sample apartments even though she was considering a move, because of the flames.

structuring the legal owning vehicle

Quite early in your thinking about the development process, you will concern yourself about how to take title to the property you are going to develop or acquire. If you are going it alone, and you know that this is not what I would recommend, you will have no problems with titling the property. It will merely be conveyed to you in your name. Should you title it with your spouse, your attorney may advise you there may be legal problems later on if either one of you dies, or if you split or if one wants to sell, while the other doesn't want to buy or sell. Lots of ugly things can happen, so no matter how long you may be in the real estate business, the best advice I can think of is to properly organize your team, starting with an attorney thoroughly familiar with SEC and Blue Sky Laws (state securities laws) as well as joint ventures, general partnerships, corporations, and limited partnerships.

pros and cons for joint ventures, general partnerships, and corporations

Because you may be a beginner, your attorney will briefly discuss with you the advantages and disadvantages of each of the possible forms of ownership of the income-producing property you may wish to develop. As a practical matter, he will show you that it is very difficult to administer a **joint venture,** how it may foul up the title at a later date when you wish to sell or refinance, and how **all** of the joint venture parties have exposure to liability. Chances are you will not opt for this method of ownership unless there are only three or four close family members in the venture with you.

He will also tell you that in a **general partnership,** you will have difficulties in getting decisions as **all** partners have equal liabilities and each are responsible for the others' actions. You will probably not opt for this method either.

He surely will explain the horrendous tax ramifications of owning income-producing properties in **corporate** form. Unless you will be gigantic in size (City Investing Company, Arlen Realty and Development, The Rouse Companies), which really present different organizational and administrative problems than you would encounter in a relatively small syndicate, he will advise you against forming an owning corporation. Tax losses will not pass directly through to the shareholders as sooner or later, your corporate earnings will be taxed twice: once at the corporate rate and once when each individual receives dividends. There are a few tax techniques that will delay the day of reckoning, but no tax technique will allow you to postpone indefinitely paying corporate as well as individual taxes. The worst advice you could get would be to incorporate as an owning vehicle. Those of us who do counseling are frequently called upon to try to solve the problem of double taxation resulting from corporate ownership of income-producing properties. We can't, of course, and neither can anyone else. It is difficult to sell a corporation (sell all of the corporate stock) to someone who really only wants to buy the real estate. There are a myriad of tax problems that foul up the process of liquidating a corporation which has as its sole asset an income-producing property.

your attorney will probably advise you to organize a limited partnership

Your attorney will most likely advise you to organize a limited partnership. This owning vehicle has numerous advantages and only a few minor disadvantages. By now, most of our states have passed legislation enabling adoption of the "Uniform Limited Partnership Act." Under this act, title to your property can be held in the name of the partnership itself.

So long as the partnership is properly organized so that it conforms to current tax law, you (and your investor partners) can rely on the fact that the partnership itself will not be treated as a corporation for federal income tax purposes. If the partnership were treated as a corporation, the losses would do neither you nor the investors any good, and eventually you would bear the burden of double taxation.

Under our tax laws, if transfer of limited partnership interests is restricted except by approval of **both** general partners (we always use two general partners although sometimes there are more), thus, admitting or not admitting a substituted limited partner, it does not have the corporate characteristic of freely transferable units. Therefore, the partnership is not taxed, only the partners.

Another corporate characteristic that is avoided is the continuity of life of the limited partnership. Usually, the death of both general partners terminates the partnership. Our limited partnership agreements generally provide that if both general partners die, the limited partners may meet to either liquidate the partnership or transfer all the assets of the first limited partnership to a second limited partnership, naming new general partners. The important thing to remember is that upon the death of both general partners, the partnership is **terminated.** If the board chairman and president of a corporation were to die, the corporation would legally continue, merely electing a new board chairman and appointing a new president.

These two keys are the difference in the tax treatment of a limited partnership from a corporation:

1. Limited transferability of units of ownership.
2. Limited life of the partnership.

Your tax attorney will no doubt know all this, but it is important that you understand the different characteristics of a limited partnership compared to a corporation.

The limited partnerships that seem to work the best (and avoid taxation problems) are those in which the limited partners **have no active part in administering the affairs of the partnership.** The active day-to-day affairs of the partnership are administered by the general partners. The limited partners vote only on two key issues:

1. To refinance or not to refinance.
2. To sell or not to sell.

Partnerships organized this way avoid the corporate characteristic of "active shareholders." This also follows partnership law (having nothing to do with federal income taxes) in that the limited partners are indeed passive, usually voting only twice during an eight- to twelve-year period of ownership. In Chapter 4, we will really get into limited partnership agreements to ensure that **both** you and your attorneys use clean and concise language in order to spell out clearly what the goodies are that are received by the developer or syndicator, and most importantly, to **protect** these emoluments.

doing only winners

If you follow a strategy of development that considers what important activities people **must** do, you will develop or acquire places where people **live, work,** or **shop.** If you choose housing, then do apartments, because single family homes, unless your goal is to own over a hundred, are not great investments. The economies of scale available in large apartment developments; the opportunities for amenities such as swimming pools and tennis courts; and on-site resident managers, engineers, and porters are just a few examples of the kinds of service and benefits available to apartment dwellers that cannot economically be made available to renters of homes.

In large metropolitan areas, people work mainly in office buildings, hotels, banks, and shopping centers, where the people who work in office buildings eventually go to shop.

Even in large cities, certain areas seem to be "set aside" for shopping, either by zoning or restrictive covenants, such as in Houston, Texas, where there is no zoning. The Galleria shopping center in Houston, Texas is probably one of the most attractive shopping centers in the U.S. Its anchor store is Neiman Marcus—a truly fine store. Certainly everyone is familiar by now with the large, regional shopping centers, the relatively large community shopping center, or the smaller "strip" center where generally food, drug, and small service stores such as dry cleaning or fast-food stores do business.

Here is a strategy you may follow in this business of developing and acquisitions:

Apartments:	The larger the number of units, the better, 150 or more.
Office Buildings:	Economies of scale make it tempting to develop or acquire large ones at least over 150,000 square feet of rental area.
Shopping Centers:	Try to acquire or develop units of 125,000 square feet or more.

During a lecture, someone will invariably ask what about ground as an investment? Or a factory, or a warehouse, or a hotel or motel? Because by now you may be forming a positive investment strategy, let's look at some of these other "investments."

less attractive investments

land

Unless you are a civil engineer **and** have a great deal of money, investing in land is not appropriate because **it does not produce income.** You may acquire land upon which you may erect an income-producing property, but this will be part of your ongoing investment strategy and certainly you will not be foolish enough to "stockpile" land. Being a civil engineer and having a great deal of money does not mean you should invest (speculate?) in land, it merely means you will be able to research the land properly. You could readily see where the sewer lines are (you can read blueprints) and are intelligent enough to check the zoning; availability of electricity, water, gas; and other facts that could affect land values. They include, but are not limited to, population growth, area trends, appropriations for new roads, highways, rapid transit lines, and a myriad of other things that affect the land values. Proximity to fire stations, police stations, and hospitals has a bearing on land values.

Having a lot of money helps, too, as you will need to "carry" the land for some length of time. Because vacant land produces little or no income, you will have to reach into your pocket to pay **interest, principal,** and **taxes.** Don't forget to get a **liability insurance** policy as well.

Professional land speculators can do well because they **understand the risks** in acquiring land, and they know all the things we have been discussing. Include in your negative strategy the acquisition of land as an investment. In other words, **don't!**

factory, warehouse, or free-standing fast-food building

These "investments" should also be included in your negative strategy. If your tenant (and you usually have only **one**) gets into financial trouble, you could own a building that is 100 percent vacant. Many persons do not seem to understand that unless your tenant is GM or GE or IBM, there is no such thing as a **guaranteed** income even if you build a factory or warehouse and lease it to some other "AAA" tenant.[1] W. T. Grant Company, which went bankrupt, was a AAA tenant. So was Franklin National Bank in New York and so was C. Arnholt Smith's banking empire headquartered in San Diego. So was the Robert Hall clothing chain.

the federal government as a tenant

There is no such thing as a "guaranteed" investment in real estate unless you are dealing with the federal government as a tenant, and they are not much fun to deal with. The late and highly respected Morris Cafritz (a developer in Washington, D.C.) once reminded a congressional watchdog committee investigating windfalls in the old FHA 608 programs that the monies he received were loans, and only if the loans were not repaid, were he to be admonished. The loans were ultimately repaid, but he was personally quite upset at certain members of the Congress and the press because he felt they were attacking his integrity. I was fortunate enough to lunch with Mr. Cafritz shortly thereafter when

---

[1] AAA tenants are those deemed of worthy of the highest credit as rated by Moody's Investor Services, a securities analysis firm.

he gave this advice: "If you do business with the federal government (or any government for that matter) and you make money, you will be investigated and tried and found guilty by the press. If you should **lose** money, no one will investigate you—not the government, not the press. So it really doesn't make sense to do any real estate business with the government, does it?" I got the message! I hope you do too.

Hotels and motels will be discussed later, but for now, include them in your negative strategy—**don't get involved with hotels or motels as an investment strategy.**

location

For your development strategy, you may not want to acquire land or buildings in the **very best** locations. While this may sound paradoxical, it really isn't. Almost always, the very best location is fully built-up and is at least ten years old. The chances of it staying as the very best location are dim. Most real estate experts agree on one axiom, "**Locations change.**"

When I first arrived in Washington, D.C., in 1940, the very best location was 13th and F Streets, N.W. Two decades later, it was Farragut Square (two miles northwest). By 1970, it was 18th and K Streets, N.W. (one block west of Farragut Square). And so it goes.

Even if you were fortunate enough to locate a parcel of ground in the very best location, you would do well to avoid it. As long as real estate is trendy, you should analyze the direction of its movement and try to forecast where you think the best location will be ten to twelve years hence.

The importance of this location guess will manifest itself when you ultimately want to sell your building. Wouldn't you like at that time to be merchandising your building in the **very best** location?

You may be sure the very best location today may very well be the next best ten to twelve years hence. To quantify this strategy: buy or develop in an 85 percent to 90 percent location. But, make certain you have done your homework so that your 85 percent to 90 percent building will be a 100 percent location when you wish to sell.[2]

market forecasts

Sooner or later, you will come to the conclusion that the investment decisions you have made and will make are nothing more than guesses about what the market demand will be at some future time. For example, if you are getting

---

[2]There are no mathematical location ratings for office buildings. I made this "rating" system in my imagination. Anyone with a few months experience in real estate will know a 100 percent location when they see it. They will also be able to "rate" less exceptional locations.

ready to develop an office building, the acquisition of the land should represent your best guess of not only what the market demand for office space will be two years later, but also if your building will be gradually acquiring a 100 percent location.

Most developers have very large egos, but in lucid and honest moments, they will tell you that they really cannot **forecast** a specific market demand for office space. The more honest ones will also tell you that nobody else can, either. While we can hire a real estate economist to make "market absorption" studies, they are not valuable. All they are generally used for is to support, in an objective manner, the developer's purchase of the land.

Let's understand how market forecasts are made. An economist studies what has occurred in the past, then forecasts by interpreting historical data. We know, for example, that an area delineated by 16th Street, N.W., on the east; 21st Street, N.W., on the west; Pennsylvania Avenue, N.W., on the south; and Massachusetts Avenue, N.W., on the north; roughly 35 square blocks in downtown Washington, D.C., has on the average absorbed 1.7 million square feet of office space each year from 1966 to 1976. What does this tell us about the future? Not a thing! Markets are notorious for misbehaving. Four buildings, with a total of 1 million square feet of rentable space, may have extreme difficulty in renting up in 1978, or even 1979.

You may have a $20 million construction loan, interest at 9 percent amounts to $1.8 million per year. Add to that operating expenses and real estate taxes, and it is easy to understand what a risky and financially scary business this can be. But what about the market studies? Well, what about them? No study actually said that because we have used 1.7 million square feet of office space each year that this absorption rate will continue.

Phrases like "it appears likely" and "based on the analysis of historic data" and "100 percent location" and the "statistical averages" are all doubletalk if you are betting a wad of money that a building will rent up fast. To paraphrase somebody who thought about this long before most of us were born, "A statistician who has his head in a hot oven and his feet soaking in ice, **on the average,** feels just right." In truth, you will either rent up quickly or slowly, not "on the average."

I find some humor in the idea that I know what I'm doing when I start a $25 million office building. What is really even funnier is that the lenders (mostly insurance companies) truly believe they know what they are doing, too, when they make my partnership a $20 million loan.

A very real side benefit of a market study is that the lender (who cannot forecast the market either) must have some professional advice other than from the developer who is seeking a loan. A good lender, thus, is assured that he has done his homework.

One has to be just plain lucky if the building rents up fast. One of the amazing things about renting up an office building is that the price per square foot per year can be lowered in a soft (slow) market and nothing much happens. You don't get any more tenants, just a few more "lookers."

In New York City, where an estimated 30 million square feet of new or relatively new office space was going begging in early 1976, virtually every builder and lender had market studies that indicated the demand for office space in the city was virtually incapable of being satisfied. How financially devastating it is to own an attractive, new, and well-located **empty** office building. Some developers blamed the World Trade Center, owned and developed by a quasi-government-owned agency, with murdering the New York City office building market by dumping 10 million square feet on the market in one shot. Naturally, this is an immense amount of space for any market to absorb at one time, but you must remember that the twin towers of the World Trade Center were additions to some 20 million square feet of existing uptown newly developed space.

You soon learn in this business that you must eliminate certain words from your vocabulary. Of necessity, they are "always," "forever," and "never." Yet, some developers have said that all of the space on the New York City market may **never** be rented, but I know better. Sometime, somehow, those buildings **will** be occupied. When? How could a professional answer the question any other way—"in a few years."[3]

should you leave your own territory?

In lectures to real estate brokers attending classes in some real estate trade associations, usually at the state level, I caution would-be developers that they are limited to developing what their local areas can absorb. If they want to be really big in the business, my advice is to move to a large city. The economies of scale obviously preclude certain developments in relatively small towns. Who would rent a 200,000-square-foot office building in a town of 25,000 persons?

Because most developers do not relish the thought of leaving their homes and moving their families to a much larger city, they frequently ask if they could develop in some larger city while they continue their home and family life in the town in which they now live.

If you can imagine how difficult it is to develop in a city where you **know** the market, you must conclude it is nearly impossible to do so in a strange place. **Very few** persons have made a success in real estate development outside their own backyards. A major exception to this rule are the national developers of regional shopping malls: Taubman, DiBartolo, Rouse, and a few others. In reality, we now know far more about shoppers' habits than we probably will learn in the next forty years about office building markets.

---

[3]The New York City office rental market recovered in 1978. Space is now getting scarce. How about that?

american railroads building, washington, d.c. anodized aluminum with tinted glass—contemporary, elegant and not extravagant.

4

organizing the venture

chapter 4 outline

should you invest?

Frequently, I am asked if I (my partner and I) invest in the properties we are about to develop or acquire. Sometimes we do, and sometimes we don't, the decision being relative to our own cash position at the time. If we have surplus cash, we will certainly invest, but if we do not have sufficient surplus to invest, then we don't. The same rule certainly should be (and indeed is) the rule for outside investors. Yet, I am asked this question frequently by would-be investors. They seem to be emotionally more comfortable if they know that my partner and I are investing right along with them. The truth is just as I have stated it. Sometimes it is imprudent for my partner and me to invest at that particular time. Somehow the investor is not satisfied that we are not financially able to invest at that particular time and feels that we **select** which ventures we choose to enter. Nothing could be further from the truth. We have no more prescience than they, and if we were to invest in every venture, then most of our time would be spent with our bankers reorganizing our personal debt. Occasionally, I tell the following anecdote to an investor, especially if this is the first time he might have an opportunity to invest in my partnership.

"Mr. X, I feel like a composer directing my very own symphony orchestra. I have personally selected and have exposed myself to considerable financial liability by acquiring the site (the land). I have spent umpteen hundred hours working over the design and specifications with the architect. I have worked closely with our general contractor, eliminating, adding, and changing; and finally, I have gone to the permanent lender seeking the loan. I have had to put up between one and two points, in advance of their commitment to me, and finally after the permanent loan was committed, I obtained the construction financing—also putting up one point in advance. I may have as much as $6 million 'up front.' Now that the job is ready to start, we will start a leasing program and will supervise the venture until ultimately it is producing cash flow. At some later date, we will refinance the project, and with the investor's permission, we will negotiate a sale and the partnership will terminate." Now you recall that I said I felt like a composer and director. Do you know any objective reason for me to buy 200 tickets to watch myself perform?

first outs, or priority rights

If you recall the Aristotle story, you will remember that he agreed with the parents who were putting up the money that he would take a small salary for his teaching and give them **all** the profits from the building until they had recouped their original investment. It was agreed that from that point on profits would then be shared: 50 percent to the investor-parents and 50 percent to Aristotle. The point to remember here is that Aristotle wanted to own 50 percent of the land, building, and the school. As a consequence, he gave a "first out" to the parents. A "first out" means that instead of simply dividing the cash flow, say 25 percent to the developer and 75 percent to the investors, the **first** 'x' percent cash-on-cash return goes to the investor. If the project has a total cash equity investment of $100,000 and the cash flow is $10,000 and a 10 percent investor priority right were given, then **all** of the cash flow would go to the investors and none would go to the developer. A first out, in essence, means the financial or investing partners receive a predetermined percentage of the cash flow, based on their investment, prior to any distribution to the developer. Some lawyers like the term "priority right." I have no quarrel with the term "priority right," but because most real estate people use the words "first out," most investors are more familiar with this term. In contemporary real estate transactions, when the developer is obtaining as much as a 50 percent interest in future profits and losses, it is often common to offer the investors, as a group, a first-out provision especially as it relates to the cash flow.

Up to this point, there is no logical argument to the rationale. We no longer use first outs because it is a bit of "con" when it relates to a specific cash-on-cash return. For example, to state to the investor that he has a first out with respect to the cash flow in the amount of 10 percent per year, then, 10 percent to the developer, then, a 50/50 split, is to imply that there will be at least 10 percent cash-on-cash return to the investor. This, of course, is untrue. There may never be any cash flow; indeed, the project may develop negative cash flow. Will the investor assume a first out or priority right in putting up 10 percent of his investment to cover such negative cash flow? Of course he doesn't, and that is why while it may not be dishonest to speak of first outs in this fashion, it is definitely misleading when it is done as an annual percentage cash-on-cash return for his investment.

A true first out would be stated over a period of years, just as Aristotle had done. It would be fairer to say to an investor that if the cash-on-cash return to the investor is not (let's say) 10 percent per year upon refinancing or sale, if **available** from such refinancing proceeds or sales proceeds, the investor would receive a first out equal to a cumulative 10 percent cash-on-cash return on his original investment. This would occur before the remaining cash would be split 50 percent to the investors and then 50 percent to the developer. The facts here as now stated do not imply a guaranteed 10 percent return, but give a first out equal to that amount accumulated, **only** if the cash received from cash flow, the refinancing, or sale would so allow. It is not my intention to imply that other developers who use first outs as sales tools are dishonest, it is only to state they may not know they are engaging in a little "con."

There are some other important facets to the first-out right to an investor. First, since an investor is an investor, do not be confused with nor allow the investor to be confused with the fact he is seeking profits. We all should be aware that in an investment (as distinguished from a loan) the investor has three main risks:

1. **Financial Risk.** He might lose some, all, or more than all of his investment.

2. **Liquidity Risk.** He might not be able to convert his equity investment into cash without loss of some or all of his investment.

3. **Purchasing Power Risk.** He might get his investment back and perhaps more at a future date, but with dollars that are highly inflated and, thus, will not buy what they could or would have at the beginning of his investment.

As a developer, you cannot, indeed should not, seek to moderate the liquidity risk. The purchasing power risk is or should be understood as a function of inflation. We all know that real estate, in general, moves up with inflation.

First outs are, therefore, a mutation of the financial risk whereby the developer seeks to "soften" risk by allowing a first out. It may be that the fledgling developer is unaware that

1. It is hardly necessary to attract capital to a decent real estate investment.

2. It is a weakness, perhaps, in the selling arena, and the developer wishes to make raising capital more certain. As an example, a new or young developer who is unaware of the seeming limitless amounts of equity money available might think a first out is necessary. It isn't.

Two ways of answering the request for a first out are as follows:

1. OK, you win. You want a first out. You take the first 10 percent cash flow; I'll take the next 20 percent cash flow—thereafter, we split 50/50. This makes the investor **pay** for a first out.

2. You can get a first out in any amount, but after you have recouped your capital without imputing interest, I'll take **half** of whatever you then own.

Strangely enough, if you are asking for 25 percent instead of 50 percent, first outs rarely are mentioned.

The rest of this chapter is a partnership check list. It will help to make your business life profitable and enjoyable.

assign contract to partnership for an interest in profits

Assign **anything** relating to the development process: contracts to acquire the land, loans, contracts with the general contractor, **anything** to the limited partnership you are forming for a future "interest in profits" or percentage of the future profits of the venture.

What is meant by a future interest in profits and losses? By definition as stated in your partnership agreements, "profits" are defined as cash flow for this one single purpose: explaining the distributions of cash, whereby so much cash goes to the limited partners and so much to the general partners.

If you are getting, say, a 25 percent interest in future profits or losses, you receive 25 percent of the cash remaining after cash expenditures—from cash flow, refinancing, or sale. Your 25 percent interest in future profits and losses allow you to deduct partnership losses in the amount of 25 percent.

At the beginning of the project there is an assortment of losses: construction loan fees, real estate taxes, construction interest, and other such deductions. The deductions you are allowed as a general partner are the same pro rata deductions the limited partners are taking. You are getting 25 percent of such losses, and they are getting 75 percent. When the project is finished and occupied and producing cash flow, the investors (the limited partners) receive 75 percent of the cash flow and the general partners 25 percent. Do not confuse the 25 percent interest held by the general partner(s) as an equity interest, which it is not. It is merely a 25 percent interest in future profits and losses. Because nobody can predict what such an interest is worth in the hands of the general partner(s), the Internal Revenue Service has not taxed the **act** of assigning contracts to a limited partnership in return for a "25 percent future interests" in profits and losses.

Naturally, during ownership, the general partner(s) is reporting a 25 percent interest in profits and losses as they actually occur. If they report profits, they pay their taxes on their 25 percent interest. At the beginning, especially if a project is being developed rather than acquired, there are nothing but tax losses. Even when cash flow commences, much of it in the early years is not subject to federal income taxes. Only when the amortization of the loan is **equal** to the depreciation charge is the cash flow all taxable.

If you remember the basic tax formula, C.F. $+ A - D =$ T.I., you will see that if A and D are the same, then the cash flow is the taxable income. With the use of accelerated depreciation and understanding the interest and principal combinations involved in loan amortization, it becomes evident in the early years that some, all, or more than all of the cash flow is not subject to federal income taxes. This comes about, in the main, because depreciation is usually always greater than amortization especially during the early years of any real estate development.

capital accounts and cash distribution

You must understand the basics of capital accounts accounting to understand how to protect yourself from getting a tax clobbering at **sale** of the project. Basically, this is how the capital accounts work. Suppose ten investors with $75,000 cash each invest in your project, which requires $750,000 cash above the mortgage to complete. You get a 25 percent "interest in profits" as outlined above for assigning your ownership in the land contract, the general contractor building contract, as well as the loans all to the limited partnership. This is how the developer receives his interest in profits there being no other legal and tax deferred method.

One hundred percent of the capital gets 75 percent of the benefits of investing: construction write-offs, cash flow, tax shelter, and proceeds of sale. Assume in the first year, $200,000 is attributable to interest and real estate taxes while the project is under construction. (See Chapter 2 for a discussion of construction period interest and taxes.) The limited partners (100 percent of the capital contributed) are allocated $150,000 in losses (75 percent) while the general partner(s) receive $50,000 in losses due to their 25 percent interest in profits and losses.

Each investor (ten investors invested $75,000 each) has a capital account of $75,000. Does the general partner(s) who has a 25 percent interest in profits and losses also have a capital account? Yes, he does, and here is where you (in the partnership agreement) should provide for some "cushioning effect" at sale. Here is why. In the first year of our illustration, the general partner(s) deducted $50,000 from taxable income. Assuming two general partners (each deducted $25,000) then each of their capital accounts are **negative** to the extent of the $25,000 deducted. The ten limited partners who started with capital accounts of $75,000 each are deducting their share of the losses ($150,000 ÷ 10 = $15,000) so that each limited partner's account is as follows: invested $75,000, deducted $15,000, balance $60,000. Note that each limited partner has a positive $60,000 in his capital account, while each general partner has a negative account of $25,000.

If a gain is realized at sale, it is taxable to the extent that the sales price is greater than the book value. Book value is cost, less depreciation during the owning period. If the sale were to occur early during the ownership period, the general partners could be in the position of paying taxes on the gain more **heavily** than the investing limited partners. This occurs because the capital accounts of the general partners are negative, while the collective limited partner accounts are still positive. If one were to add all of the limited partner capital accounts in the example cited above immediately after the first year, they would be $750,000 less $150,000 deducted as construction interest and taxes. They would total $600,000, while the general partners would total a negative $50,000.

The book value on the above project would be its original cost reflected as loans (mortgages) and capital contributions. If one adds the debt (the mortgage), and adds up the positive and negative capital accounts, the result is the cost **less** depreciation. If the sale were for the exact original cost and were for all cash, at the end of the construction the **gain** would be the total deductions, or in this case, $200,000. If you were one of two general partners and were to pay your proportionate share of the taxes, you and the other general partner would each have a gain of $25,000 or a total of $50,000, while each limited partner would have a gain of $15,000. All the limited partners would collectively have a gain of $150,000. All the partners, both general and limited, would have a taxable gain of $200,000.

Now let's see what the distribution of cash has to do with the capital accounts. If your partnership agreement has provided that the limited partners are to receive cash distributions up to the amount of their original investment before cash is divided between the general partner and the limited partners in accordance with their partnership interests (25 percent and 75 percent), on the facts stated above, all of the cash proceeds of $750,000 would be distributed to the limited partners. There would be no cash distributable to the general partners, while the general partners would have incurred taxable income of $50,000, on which income taxes must be paid.

While there are many variations that can avoid this event, the best form of agreement for the general partner is to provide that net cash proceeds from the sale of the property will be distributed in accordance with the partnership interests without regard to the respective capital accounts. In this case, the general partners would receive $187,500, and the limited partners would receive $562,500. In this case, the general partners have taxable income of $50,000 (their share of the gain from the disposition of the property), which brings their tax base for their partnership interests back to zero. The general partners have additional taxable income in the amount of $187,500: the cash distributed in excess of the basis for their partnership interests. (Additionally, the cash distributed may qualify for long-term capital gain.) In this case, the general partners have a total taxable income of $237,500.

A common middle ground found in many limited partnership agreements provides that net cash proceeds will be distributed first in liquidation of any positive balances in the capital accounts with the balance shared by the general partner and the limited partners in accordance with their partnership interests. On the above facts, this would provide for a distribution to the limited partners of $600,000 and the remaining $150,000 would be divided 25 percent to the general partner(s) and 75 percent to the limited partners making a cash distribution of $37,500 to the general partner(s) and an additional $112,500 to the limited partners who would have received $712,500 ($600,000 plus $112,500). The difficulty of this for the general partner is that the general partner will have taxable income of $87,500 ($50,000 plus $37,500) and will have received cash of only $37,500. The imbalance of cash and taxable income in these cases can be minimized by providing that instead of allocating the taxable gain from the disposition of the property in accordance with the 25 percent–75 percent interests, it shall be allocated in whatever proportion the general partner and the limited partners share in the distributable cash.

In the last example given above, where the cash was distributed $37,500 to the general partner and $712,500 to the limited partners, the taxable gain ($200,000 on disposition of the property) would be shared 5 percent by the general partner and 95 percent by the limited partners. In this event, the general partner will be charged with taxable income of only $47,500 ($10,000 plus $37,500), while his share of the distributable cash remains $37,500.

You and your tax attorney may select one of the three basic examples given, depending upon whether or not the control of when the property is sold in fact rests with the general partner or in fact rests with the limited partners.

management and leasing

Although our office prepares management and leasing agreements by and between the partnership and our management and leasing companies, the authority for "dealing with ourselves" is part of the original partnership agreement. Because an outsider may consider this to be a conflict of interest, be certain your partnership agreement is explicit that you are authorized to deal with companies you own or control in providing management and leasing. How much do we charge? In an office building, the fee is usually 3 percent of the gross revenues for leasing and 3 percent for management. This is our current fee structure for office buildings. Shopping centers should be the same. Management fees for apartments, depending on the size, would be at least 4 percent of the gross receipts, but usually 5 percent.

protecting management and leasing fees

The only fees that provide steady income to a developer are his management and leasing fees. This is steady because fees are collected monthly, regardless of occupancy. Unlike management and leasing fees, income from interests in profits and pieces of several ventures is conditioned upon the level of occupancy, lease rates, and expenses. Some shrewd developer, probably in the late 19th century, decided to get his first and get it "off the top." All promoters from time to time dream of getting theirs first and getting it off the top. Management and leasing fees are terribly important because these fees are deducted **first** from the gross income.

Any promotional scheme involving money usually is loaded with financial restraints to ensure fair treatment for those putting up the money. These restraints have come about as a result of financial abuses in the past in various promotions. Laws have been passed by the Congress. Regulations have been issued by regulatory bodies.

How nice it is to have some of your fees, specifically management and leasing fees, conditioned on nothing but the fact that your management company has collected the rent. After rent collection you get your fees **first!** This is the only area, i.e. management and leasing, where you receive your fees prior to the partnership itself. This is the stuff promoters dream of. It is truly "off the top."

Because these fees are so highly coveted and are indeed the backbone of the developer's office structure, everybody (at one time or another) may be called to defend his fee and the validity of his management and leasing contracts.

provide for management in the partnership agreement

One certain method of protecting the management fees is to provide in the management agreement for your management corporation to provide all the necessary management services for at least a decade. Because your development or acquisition strategy may require your project to be sold after ten or twelve years, you should be certain that your management agreement covers a minimum of ten years and is thereafter renewable for one year at a time.

Your partnership agreement should state that "... the general partners may provide for management services with any accredited management organization, including any organization controlled or owned by the general partners." It is also an excellent idea to state what the management fee will be: 3 percent or 4 percent of the gross rentals including any ancillary income such as that derived from coin-operated machines (laundry and vending) as well as commissions obtained from public pay telephones situated on your project.

can "they" buy you out?

The only way that management could be wrested from you (against your will) is at sale or for "willful malfeasance." Willful malfeasance is a deliberate act, in clear violation of the trust imposed upon you, such as pocketing[1] some of the cash from operations of vending machines (soft drinks, cigarettes, washing machines and dryers). It is any violation, willfully or knowingly done, of the public trust imposed on you in any agency capacity such as in management or leasing contracts. On the other hand, should one or more of the partners in your syndicate desire to purchase the property and either manage the property themselves or give management to another organization, then your management agreement should provide for a buy-out. Inasmuch as we write our management agreements for ten years and thereafter from year to year, any remaining years under your contract could be bought out. Let's assume a buy-out of your management agreement comes about with four years remaining. Assuming current annual management income of the year immediately past of, say, $40,000, you are looking at $160,000 loss if there is no buy-out. Your agreement could provide for a buy-out of the full amount: 4 years at $40,000 a year is $160,000. This may not be considered fair by some outside source, say a court, and therefore, you may wish to consider a discount of 5 percent per year for each year your management contract continues in effect. In the example we are using, the $160,000 would be discounted by 20 percent (5 percent per annum

---

[1]Pocketing cash by reporting less than that actually received is also called "skimming."

for 4 years), and thus, a cash settlement of $128,000 would be paid to your management company.

As you can see, if you develop or acquire several good-sized properties, the management fees provide very important steady income in good and bad times. These fees should **always** be payable to a corporation that you control or own outright. Under current law, management corporations with ten stockholders or less are eligible to be "Subchapter 'S' Corporations." Your attorney can explain to you in detail how such corporations work, but if properly organized, such corporations pay **no** federal income taxes. Taxes are due on the **earnings** of such corporations allocated among the stockholders in accordance with their percentage of ownership in the corporation.

provide for assignment of the management

Putting management (and leasing commissions) into corporate form also has some other advantages. For one thing, we provide that management agreements can be assigned as long as the assignee is an accredited management organization as defined and accredited by the Institute of Real Estate Management (I.R.E.M.) of the National Association of Realtors. Because you cannot anticipate how long you will live, having such management rights in corporate form means that income can continue after your death. One day you may also consider a merger into another company or may wish to sell your management business outright. Properly written management contracts can thus make a substantial contribution to your business net worth. Remember to show this portion of the book to your attorney to ensure that he will crank in the necessary things that will protect your management fees from outside or (heaven forbid!) inside raids.

When the property is finally sold in an arm's length transaction to an outsider, your management agreement will terminate. This fact does not automatically mean you cannot obtain a management agreement from the new owner. You may **not,** however, make the retention of management a condition of sale as this is a gross conflict of interest. Remember, your fees and commissions are paid by your partners, and you are ethically, morally, and legally bound to obtain the highest and best price for the property. If management is offered to you by the new owner, you must disclose this to your selling partners, whether such an offer is in writing or is agreed upon orally.

If all our discussions relating to the management agreement seem "strong" to you, they are. And, do not let anyone attempt to weaken your rights. If you are ever going to succeed as a developer or syndicator, your rights must be protected, and only you can protect them. Furthermore, you can only learn from your mistakes and **you must manage** the properties you are developing or acquiring. Farming management out to another organization, while retaining some of the commission yourself, may seem like a tempting idea, but don't do it. Another organization will not tell you where you have made development errors. They do not want to criticize their customers, including you. They will remain silent about your errors and in the long run, this will hurt you. Your own people will criticize what you have done, and you will love them for it. We make it a point to ask our management personnel what we have done wrong so we can design out mistakes in future buildings.

Another point to remember is that you need **negative** feedback from each person on the development team, including your investors. In order to do this properly, you may **never** again want to screen your incoming phone calls. You will discover that truly important and successful people in the development field are readily accessible. Don't let your personnel screen you from grief, because grief provides important learning experiences. One of my early jobs in real estate was with an organization whose president was encapsulated by both an administrative assistant and a secretary who shielded him from grief, and other feedback that would hurt his ego. As a result of this, he never really learned the development business. His company is no longer in business. Contrast this behavior with the availability of **successful** developers. You can be certain that if your receptionist, secretary, or administrative assistant asks "Who's calling please?" or worse yet, "What is the nature of your call!" you cannot properly learn this business.

In our office, if you ask for me over the phone, the next voice you hear will be mine. If I have visitors or if I'm in a meeting no matter how important, the caller is told what I'm doing and is asked if he/she deems it important enough to interrupt. Note, **they** make the decision to interrupt, I don't. Should they choose not to interrupt, we return their calls as promptly as possible.

Inasmuch as management personnel do make a serious contribution to the development team, hire only professionals in this area. When our construction plans are drawn, our management personnel review the plans in detail and suggest additions or eliminations that will either make the structure more efficient or reduce the owning cost, or both.

provide for leasing not only in the agreement, but also in the lease document

With regard to leasing, we do not provide for buy-outs because such fees are included in the lease document itself and are collectible as the rents are paid. Such fees, then, are only terminated when the tenant moves out. While some landlords try to prevent you from doing so, ensure that your fee is spelled out in the lease itself.

We endeavor to collect our leasing fees over the life of the lease, including any renewals, extensions, or modifications so long as the tenant, or his successor, remains in the building. If you do not insist on this, then somewhere down the line you can be cheated out of your leasing fee.

When the building is ultimately sold, properly written leasing fees remain in full force and may be considered to be a "lien" on the property. One reason you must protect your leasing fees is that you may not have procured the tenant in the original instance, and thus, may have to pay all or part of the fee to another broker.

provide for a 51 percent vote at sale

We provide that at least 51 percent of the partners in interest (this means the general partners, too) authorize a sale or refinancing of the property. It is interesting to learn how after more than two decades in business, we finally arrived at the 51 percent number. Earlier in our business careers, we used a substantial majority concept and in a sincere desire to have the limited partners actually make such major decisions, we decided on a two-thirds majority, $66\frac{2}{3}$ percent.

When we had a proposed sale of one of our syndicated properties under this earlier formula, we sought our limited partners' approval. We had acquired the property originally as an already built and 100 percent occupied apartment development. We were going to cast our 15 percent interest as general partners in favor of the sale, and thus we needed $51\text{-}\frac{2}{3}$ percent of the remaining partners to vote "yes" in order to consummate the sale. We sent out letters and ballots to all of the partners but could not obtain the necessary votes because one party owned 40 percent of the venture. He didn't cast his ballot either for or against the sale, and after waiting a respectable ten days, we called him.

He responded that he would dearly like to sell the project, but insisted he would only vote his 40 percent interest in favor of the sale if we split our real estate commission with him—60 percent for us, and the remaining 40 percent to him! We were flabbergasted inasmuch as we were dealing with a very wealthy investor who did not need the money, but felt that because the project wasn't a run-away winner, he was entitled to special consideration. We carefully explained that the license law specifically prohibited our sharing a real estate commission with any person other than a licensed real estate broker "who had actually helped in making the sale." He ignored this argument, however, and insisted upon **his** 40 percent share of the commission. We knew we were legally correct, but without his vote, there could be no sale. We discussed our problems with our attorneys who suggested we write to each and every limited partner who had voted to sell and truthfully point out our dilemma. (We did not do this.) Our attorneys also suggested we phone our 40 percent limited partner and explain we had no alternative but to point out to our other partners that we were asked to do something illegal and because of our refusal to be unethical, one man was frustrating the sale. Additionally, we hinted that on behalf of the other investor partners, we would hold him legally accountable if at a later date the property were to be sold for less money. We also advised him that our attorneys also felt we would have to initiate action against him at some later date should the tax laws be changed to produce a less favorable financial result on sale.

After waiting for about another ten days, during which time we almost lost our buyer, we finally received his signed ballot, and the sale was successfully consummated.

provide for a 51 percent vote on refinancing, and cover what happens if there is no response

Our recalcitrant investor partner taught us a good lesson that has made for fairer and smoother partnership decisions. First, we now only require 51 percent of the partners, in interest, to decide to either refinance or sell. Second, we also provide that in case of a potential refinancing or sale, the limited partners **must** respond within fifteen days or we (the general partners) are authorized to vote their interests. Your attorney may provide that the general partner(s) may be the attorneys-in-fact for the limited partner. The main point is that no one can just sit on the decision. For some strange reason, quite a few investor partners do not vote on any matter. So, it is very important that the general partners vote the interests of the limited partners if there is no response.

Let's consider the 51 percent rule again. As already explained earlier, on acquired properties, you may only own 15 percent of the interest in profits so you will still require 36 percent of the 85 percent remaining partners to vote "yes" on a sale or refinancing. If you develop the property, you may own between 25 percent and 40 percent of the venture, so, for all practical purposes, if 51 percent of the partnership is required for a sale or refinancing, you may be more than one-half of the vote yourself.

provide for a precise fee

Regarding the future sale of the property, I make certain that our partnership agreement contains very specific language relating to the commission. Whenever you or your attorney is not specific, a foul-up may occur. One of our company's early agreements stated we were entitled at sale to 5 percent of the "gross sales proceeds." A couple of our major investor partners considered this to mean 5 percent of "gross equity proceeds." Of course, this isn't what our attorney or we had in mind, but careless drafting created another major problem we had to solve. Our agreements now are quite specific, "5 percent of the gross selling price, including mortgages given, taken back, or assumed."

It is also important that you provide the commission be in **cash.** This forecloses the possibility of a partner suggesting you defer some or all of the commission if you have taken back a mortgage.

No investor objects to any of this when he originally invests. So, you might as well protect yourself at the beginning. There may be some screaming at sale, but this is hardly the time for an investor partner to object.

provide for assignment and buy-out commission

One of the most important benefits to you is the real estate commission at sale. Because the amount is generally quite large (usually 5 percent of the gross selling price including mortgages given, taken back, or assumed), someone within your partnership may covet your fee. This could happen at or about the time you are seriously negotiating the sale or may have tentatively consummated a sale. You want to make absolutely certain that this goodie cannot be taken away from you. One positive way is to allow you to assign your rights of resale to either a corporation controlled by you or to another corporation that may one day hire you. By providing for the assignment in advance, you will not need the consent of the other limited partners. Language which says that the real estate commission may be the exclusive right of your corporation could also provide that the commission right may be assigned to another corporation if you are employed by it or, at your option, the resale right may be assigned to you as a real estate broker, but not in your capacity as a general partner. This language is quite necessary because most partnership agreements state that as a general partner you may not receive fees or salary on an individual basis.

Our companies were acquired through merger and an exchange of stock by a listed company (American Stock Exchange) in 1972. Two of our earlier partnership agreements were silent on the transferability of the sales commission. As a result of not having an assignment clause we were virtually forced into a concession we would never ordinarily make: we agreed to defer certain management fees for a ten year period. Incidentally, we had a divestiture of our companies in 1978, and now we own all of our own stock again. This taught us the realities of needing an assignment clause in our partnership agreements.

Because I think it is also an excellent idea to provide for the buy-out commission, your attorney should definitely include in the partnership agreement a statement covering this. In the event one or more persons acting together plan to buy out a large number of partners in excess of 51 percent, you will need such a buy-out. Without such an agreement, a sale could be stymied by these persons by their refusal to vote "yes" even though a sale might be for a most favorable price, terms, and good conditions.

Although this has never happened to any of our partnerships, I know of one organization where a raid on partnership interests occurred for the sole purpose of seeking to avoid paying a bona fide real estate commission to the general partners at sale. By providing for a sales commission, if more than 50 percent of the **partnership interests** are sold, you are at least throwing up a substantial road block in the way of a raider. My partner and I provide for the buy-out of the commission at 5 percent of its appraised value should a large number of limited partners, that is, any group controlling over 50 percent of the partnership interests, seek to trade the property and try to avoid a commission. We usually provide what we call a standard appraisal method. The general partners appoint one appraiser, the limited partners appoint another appraiser, and the two appraisers together appoint a third appraiser. The high appraisal and the low appraisal are then thrown out and the remaining appraisal is used as a basis for computing the commission. You may wonder why all this protection for you is necessary if the property is a success. People tend to misbehave when serious amounts of money are involved, and they seem to misbehave more intensely in direct ratio to the amount of commission involved. It is probably normal that a person who can never obtain a commission or a fee (let us say) in excess of $1 million, probably becomes extremely envious and consequently intensely disturbed over the prospect that you, as the developer or syndicator, may receive such a large commission. The facts are that there is no way you can lose your sales commission. Of course, you must effectively and honestly find the highest price obtainable in the market place and present it fairly to your limited partners. They may not want to vote "yes" but their options will be effectively closed if you follow the precepts outlined in this chapter. It is important to remember that they may wish to sell the property for a favorable price, but they cannot stand to see you make what seems to them to be an enormous commission.

casualty insurance

Very early in my real estate career, I learned that the most desirable form of casualty insurance (at least from the insurance company's view) is insurance that covers new income-producing property. Fire insurance and extended coverage is usually very profitable business for an insurance company to write. Because this is so, I was canvassed by several insurance companies to serve as a company agent. The commission fees were between 20 percent to 30 percent of the premium written. The company I selected was one of the top ten fire and casualty insurance companies licensed not only in the District of Columbia, but in almost every state. The company even provided me with a brief training period so that I became familiar with the jargon used by the insurance industry so that I could be articulate in discussing insurance matters. There are certain licensing requirements that must be met, but these are not difficult. There is usually a study book available from the insurance commissioner in the state in which you are doing business, which is generally furnished free or for a small fee. The examinations are given frequently. The examination, at least in my opinion, is not nearly as intense or difficult as the real estate examination. I urge compliance with the state licensing requirements and ask you to seek a major company who will assure you of their continuing interest in writing fire, casualty, and extended coverage on the properties that you develop, lease, and manage.

To give up the potential commissions involved is rather senseless because you will necessarily have to perform all of the various requirements on request from another insurance broker, and you will not be paid for doing all this work. So, it is best that you select a good company, certainly one of the top fifteen or twenty in the United States, because they generally have excellent reputations, then see if they won't take you on as a "company" agent. It is not necessary to do any other insurance business other than the projects that you acquire or develop. It is highly unusual for an insurance company based on a portfolio[2] of office buildings, apartment buildings, and shopping centers to sustain losses in

---

[2]Insurance jargon for the entire group of policies in force at any given time.

their overall portfolio because as mentioned earlier, this is prime business for most insurance companies. This means they will love your business and do anything in their power to aid you in writing your policies.

At the beginning of your development career, this may not seem to be meaningful, but when insurance premiums aggregate in excess of $100,000 per year and are constantly increasing, you can see the benefits of being your own company agent. Being a company agent means that the insurance company's local office actually writes the insurance policies for you. All you do is sign them and collect the premium. Just to keep yourself on the competitive side, you may want to do this for more than one company, but certainly for not more than two.

The way most developers or owners of income-producing properties judge insurance companies is to inquire among their fellow developers or owners as to which gives the best hassle-free claims service. The fact that you are a company agent gives you no special rights in collecting claims, although it doesn't hurt. So, it is important that the company you select has a claims policy that is prompt and fair. By discussing this with other owners and developers you will at least learn with whom you should not deal. Sometimes, a negative strategy, such as whom not to deal with, may in fact be very valuable information.

You may be aware that in the event of a fire or other casualty there are people who specialize in claims adjusting who do not work for the insurance company for whom you may be a company agent. These people are more or less in an adversary position when you agree to let them represent you for a fee in claiming a maximum amount of loss so that they can participate in a larger reward. We have avoided hiring external people because we do not want to be in an adversary position with a responsible insurance company, and because we have no need for that kind of service. We provide that our management company acts as the general contractor to repair whatever damage has occurred.

provide for management company to act as general contractor in the event of casualty

One of the reasons you should act as the general contractor is not because it is such a profitable thing to do, but in the last analysis, you want to insure that your property is properly repaired by responsible personnel. This will mean that either you or your property manager, not to mention your resident manager if it is an apartment development, will have to spend a lot of time on the site coordinating the various subcontractors and trades that may be involved in the repair and restoration of your project. The number of tradesmen who are involved in this project may be enormous, such as painters, electricians, carpenters, plasterers, carpet installers, air conditioning mechanics, and others. One of the reasons that we act as the general contractor is that our insurer need not concern himself with getting "ripped off." Also, it guarantees us that we will get a first-class restoration and repair job. You may not be aware of the fact that there are some business people who are rather unscrupulous and seize every opportunity to perform work for an insurance company because they feel it is an opportunity to make a lot of money.

To avoid this and insure that we are not doing work for nothing, we write into our partnership agreement that in the event of a fire or other form of casualty that we will act as general contractor for a fee. We charge 10 percent for overhead and 10 percent for profit. In the construction industry, this is considered quite acceptable in terms of profit, but if you total the 10 percent for overhead and 10 percent for profit, you will discover this comes to 21 percent. We learned this early in our development career because our general contractor frequently does change orders for 10 percent overhead, 10 percent profit. As an example, if he does something for $100.00, we receive a bill for $100.00 plus 10 percent for overhead, the total is $110.00. The next sentence says 10 percent profit. Thus, they make a new computation using $110.00 as the basis. It comes out to be $11.00 for profit—making a total of 21 percent. There is nothing phoney about this; apparently it has been done for many, many decades, but on first hearing it, I assumed the general contractor would be receiving a total of 20 percent for overhead and profit. This is not true. Because you will be spending a good deal of time organizing the various trades and coordinating them, you will discover this is not a very profitable way to spend your time, but on the other hand, it is a very good way to establish rapport with the insuror who knows that any claim you submit is not only legitimate, but he is being protected from the possibility of dealing with an unscrupulous contractor.

protect management, leasing, and sales commissions

It may be advantageous for you at sale for your partnership to sell the partnership interests rather than to sell the property itself. This can occur when there is an inordinately high transfer tax involved with the sale of real property. In most jurisdictions, this tax can be avoided merely by selling all the partnership interests. The problem with this is that you may not be able to obtain 100 percent affirmative votes from your partners with respect to the sale. Your attorney can write appropriate language that will cover either unwillingness or inability of the minority limited partners to join in the sale or refinancing plans. It is also important that your attorney protect you against the partnership being reformed because of the death of one or both of the general partners. It is not that you want a new partnership to be formed in the event of the death of one or both of the general partners, but you want to ensure that you are protected for the fees that you originally set up and that may now be in corporate form. These fees could outlive your own life.

auditing of partnership books and records

The American Institute of Certified Public Accountants has a rule that prohibits your regular accountant from certifying the annual statement. For example, if he audits the books and records of your management company and assists in some way in the preparation of monthly or quarterly reports to your limited partners or in fact does anything in connection with the partnership books, he is specifically prohibited by the AICPA from certifying and performing an audit. To conform with the highest degree of integrity with respect to reporting to your limited partners, it is a good idea to have a clause stating that there will be no certified statements except at a requesting limited partner's expense. This will not offend anyone if you are using a nationally known accounting firm for your regular reports to your investors, especially your annual reports. The hiring of an outside auditor to audit that which your professional accountant has already done is not only an additional expense to the partnership, but an exercise in futility.

You will, of course, want a top accounting firm to assure that there is no "tomfoolery" going on within your own organization in accounting for the money or funds. You must be absolutely certain that there is no mingling of your partnership accounts one with the other, and you must also ensure that there is no mingling or co-mingling of partnership funds with your operating funds. Most developers have gotten into difficulty with the various regulatory bodies, such as real estate commissions, state securities commissions, or federal securities commissions, by not following the simple rules that have been laid down to them by their accountants. Most of us do not need such rules laid down for us because as general partners you are acting in a fiduciary capacity anyway, and you must be certain the partners' interests are protected in every way. If your accountant is not of the stature and does not have superior real estate accounting background, you should be hiring another major firm to do your work. Inasmuch as the partnership pays for the attorneys, accountants, and all other professionals you retain during the entire development and owning process, it really is short sighted to employ someone other than the best. In my business, we have conducted our business so as to avoid the slightest conflict of interest by adopting a no-nepotism policy. This means that no person in our organization can be related by blood or marriage to anyone up to and including a first cousin. There is no question in my mind that you lose credulity with your banker and with your investors if your brother-in-law, no matter how qualified he may be, is your accountant or your attorney.

partners' meetings

When a property is not doing as well as you expected in terms of cash flow, or when there are cost overruns, or when any other negative factors affect the property, it is very important that you communicate with your partners. Try to make it a habit to prepare quarterly reports. Report, but **never,** repeat, **never, forecast** results either in the near or long term. When we sent out regular quarterly checks we put a legend on the checks stating, "Cash Flow from Operations during the Period beginning January 1 and Ending March 31." We send no letters if we are sending checks. The money speaks for itself. If we are unable to send a check, we send out a letter stating the reasons we are not sending a check and give all the reasons, especially those that are negative to the partners.

If you do not do this, and things are not running along as well as you had hoped, you could be called to try to arrange a meeting on behalf of the calling limited partner for all the limited partners, which you would be expected to attend. My partner and I attended one such meeting many years ago. The meeting deteriorated into a shouting match in which the basic feeling of the crowd was to lynch my partner and me. There is a peculiar psychology particular to groups, and as you are probably aware, groups do have personalities. Because it is impossible to have a lynching one-on-one, it makes good business sense to conduct all of your business by scrupulously avoiding group meetings.

There are three basic reasons why, aside from the possibility of a lynching, you should not conduct your partnership business in open group meetings. The first reason is that there should be a written record of everything the partnership does in terms of major decisions, such as voting on a refinancing or sale. Second, business cannot be truly accomplished with discourse running back and forth through the general partners and limited partners on an oral basis. Third, there is the possibility that the Internal Revenue Service may view such meetings as mimicking a corporate shareholders meeting.

Inasmuch as the Uniform Limited Partnership Act provides that the limited partners shall remain inactive, they are only called upon to vote on two basic issues. The first has to do with refinancing and the second has to do with sale. In this connection, do not forget to obtain from your tax attorney the tax consequences of either the refinancing or the sale, as this information is important input for your partners in making an intelligent decision. You will note before that if there is no response in writing that the general partners are entitled to vote the shares of the non-responding partners. Make sure that your attorney includes these provisions in your partnership agreement.

If it appears to you that I am suffering from paranoia (maybe I am) the avoidance of group meetings is nonetheless a must. There is an adversary relationship that quickly develops in a group meeting situation between the investor limited partners and you. Aggression from one or more of the limited partners in the form of an unfriendly question is extremely difficult to handle. There are really only two options. You could (if you have the smarts) cut him up in little pieces. The moment you do this all or most of the other limited partners will want to strike because you have wounded one of them. You could ignore the unfriendly question and cause some of the limited partners to think either you don't want to answer the question—or worse—that you can't answer because you don't know the answer. As you can see, neither alternative is acceptable. Pretend you are a little boy or girl again. Remember your parents' admonition when encountering superior forces or numbers: retreat, it is the better part of valor. You'll live to fight another day.

Doesn't it make more sense to avoid a no win or can't win situation? Forget group meetings. I know your ego may be such that you consider facing a group a challenge—forget it—go to a gym and let off steam by banging a punching bag, play tennis, golf, handball or anything **wherein you can deliver a forceful blow** to a ball. My psychiatrist friends and investors recommend any of these activities as a marvelous method of relieving tensions and frustrations. Conducting group meetings is a marvelous way to develop tensions and frustrations. Take your choice.

Everything relating to the business of the partnership should be conducted through the mails, and you should specify in the partnership agreement that this should be by written notice.

payouts to the partners

If our companies manage properties for an individual owner, we remit monthly to the owner all the cash flow. Escalating postage rates and accounting costs have caused us to adopt a policy of quarterly payouts. Remember, you need not "propagandize" your partners when you are sending checks. It is only on a quarterly basis when you cannot make a cash disbursement that you must write a letter explaining your inability to do so. Again, scrupulously avoid forecasting. It is important that you set up adequate monthly reserves for such sporadic items such as your annual accounting fees; your real estate taxes, which in some jurisdictions are paid annually; your casualty insurance, which is usually paid annually; and if you have an apartment building and you live in a northern climate, an adequate reserve should be set aside for the operation of the swimming pool during the summer.

bank accounts and cash reserves

If you do not decide where to keep your partnership bank records, there will be a strong temptation on the part of possibly one or two of your limited partners or potential limited partners to make a commitment to you based on the fact that the money is to be kept in a bank in which they have an interest either as a shareholder or officer or director. Like every other facet of the development business, the decision as to which bank will hold the partnership account is decided by the general partners, and, consequently, by the management company they so designate. **It is also very important that the reserves be kept in cash.** This is very important because if you attempt to buy short-term certificates of deposit, treasury notes, and other forms of short-term securities such as commercial loan paper, any of your investors could be constantly second guessing you as to what you should have done to maximize the earnings. Because most of your reserves are utilized as soon as the full amount has been attained, it seems foolish to place yourself in the position of being an expert in short-term securities where you could be easily criticized by an investor with sharp hindsight.

unless otherwise provided by law, the security deposits should be kept in cash

There are some valid arguments that security deposits, whether they are for tenants in an apartment development or tenants in an office building, should be earning some interest. Such deposits will be maintained for relatively longer periods of time—anywhere from one to five years, and in some cases, up to ten years. In some jurisdictions, there have been laws at the local (city or county) level, and in some cases the state level, requiring that apartment security deposits be kept in an interest-bearing account in the state in which the development is located. The law generally sets a minimum, usually 3–4 percent per year, and the monies are shuttled in and out of the security deposit account on which the management company could be earning gross interest of between 4–5 percent on such deposits.

The amount earned in excess of that provided to the tenant is profit for the partnership or owner of the property. Generally the amount of security deposits, especially if there are few or no apartments in the management portfolio, amounts to such little profit that we prefer to keep the security deposits that could be called prior to one year in a separate checking account, in cash, with our bank. Long-term deposits, such as those accepted in shopping center developments and office buildings, are kept either in certificates of deposit or long-term interest-bearing accounts with United States government insured savings and loan associations. We have always felt that such interest income properly belongs to the owners of the property, and that the expenses involved, including record keeping and accounting, should be borne by the management company.

provide for possible negative cash flow

At the beginning of my development business, it was not uncommon for an attorney or an investor to ask, "What happens if it doesn't rent up quickly?" I find this an interesting way for an attorney or investor to obtain information which I have failed to disclose or failed to communicate properly. It always starts as "What happens if?" You could supply the questions by using your imagination and answering them too.

> **Q.** What happens if I die?
> **A.** In all probability they will bury you.
> **Q.** What happens if there is a construction strike?
> **A.** Repeat after me: "Our father, which art in heaven."
> **Q.** What happens if you do a terrible job of leasing and management and we have a half empty building?

A. Repeat after me "Yis-gadal v-yis-kad-dash sh'meh rab-bo. . . .

So starts the ancient Hebrew prayer for the dead.

The best and most appropriate way to avoid such questions is to have the answers provided to any questions in the partnership agreement at the outset. One of the things that could possibly go wrong is the property may suffer a negative cash flow. If more dollars are flowing out than such property takes in, obviously there is a need to replace the negative funds. I have always found it prudent to establish an order of priorities which the general partners must follow to remedy the negative cash flow situation. This is the order the general partners usually follow:

order of priorities

1. We seek to defer the interest and/or principal on our long-term, amortizing first deed of trust. We are required by the partnership agreement to either visit our mortgage or first deed of trust lender or visit with his correspondent giving all of the facts and figures concerning the property, including the amount of capital that has been invested and a forecast sheet as to what will happen under **varying** conditions. One of the reasons we do not like to forecast is because most developers are optimistic, including ourselves. But, in dealing with lenders, we merely forecast a set of conditions based upon varying levels of occupancy and varying levels of expense. If the lender does not wish to defer the interest and/or the principal, we ask him to state the reasons why, and preferably to do this in writing in a letter to the general partners. Some lenders are reluctant to do this because of fear of some legal action that a general partner may initiate on behalf of the partnership that is being treated cavalierly by a lender.

   It is common knowledge that a well-financed property (by well-financed, we mean good, solid equity financing) is a factor generally in favor of any borrower. There is probably no major lender in the country who has not at one time or another deferred the interest and/or principal to help a well-capitalized project. If they have done it in the past, they will do it again, and if they do it again, they will do it for you. If they don't, they are guilty of economic discrimination, and there may or may not be some cause for legal action. In this connection, our organization has never instituted legal action against any lender. We do maintain a "naughty" list of those lenders who, either from our own experience or from the experience of fellow developers, seem to be imperious, capricious or worse. Other developers have often told us not to deal with "so and so," because, "If things get tough, the lender will not help you." Therefore, avoid the problem in the first instance by dealing only with those lenders who have a reputation for treating gently those borrowers who are known for putting solid equities into properties.

I have had very good rapport among several of the larger lenders. When difficulties have arisen they have been most helpful in their relationships with me. Because of my proximity to their headquarters, I have had occasion not only to obtain loans from Jamaica Savings Bank of Lynnbrook, N.Y. (assets: $1\frac{1}{2}$ billion) but have been an equity partner with this bank. The Equitable Life Assurance Society (assets: Ungawa!) is very active in the making of quality office building loans. Equitable is a prime example of the white-hat type of lender with whom we have several loans. I can't list all of the acceptable and non-acceptable lenders but the two lenders just mentioned are and have proven themselves to be most acceptable, at least to me.

2. If we are turned down by our lender, and he will not defer either the interest or the principal, we must then seek a commercial loan from one of our banks. In this sense, we are referring to our lead bank and our secondary banks. All Americans refer to banks, lawyers, and doctors as "my" bank or "our" lawyers as if they do not work for others. As you are no doubt aware, most bank loans are for relatively short periods of time. Yet, under certain conditions, some bank loans with adequate curtailments can be extended for as long as five years. If the response is negative with respect to our request for borrowing from our bank for a project that is suffering negative cash flow, we are then directed by our partnership agreement to proceed further.

3. The general partners may make loans at 1 percent over prime to the partnership and have the power to execute such loan agreements. If the general partners are unwilling or unable to make such loans, we then proceed to the next step.

4. We offer the limited partners the opportunity to make loans to the partnership for the purpose of covering the negative cash flow at 1 percent over prime on a pro rata basis. If we are unsuccessful in borrowing from our limited partners or still need additional financing, we are then authorized to proceed with the next step.

5. We are authorized by the partnership to borrow money needed because of negative cash flow from the secondary market. The secondary market is the market made up of institutions and individuals who specialize in real estate loans at rates anywhere from 4 to 8 percent over prime. Whatever the market happens to be at that time, we must seek to get such funds from secondary marketing. As an aside, we have only had one occasion to do this and certainly do not want to be in a position to do this again. This can be avoided, of course, by

allowing enough dollars in your individual projections when you are in the initial stages of a project to cover the rent-up time and possible rough sailing ahead.

no limited partners authorization necessary

Obviously, if we had to present each condition to our partners, as enumerated previously, we would be constantly sending letters and receiving ballots in the mail in the event of negative cash flow. So, we provide absolutely and concretely that the general partners must act and follow the procedures as outlined above and do not need any limited partnership authorization of any kind if the purpose of the borrowing is to provide dollars to service negative cash flow that the property is suffering.

legal expenses of general partners

Our partnership agreements provide that, except for willful malfeasance, the partnership will pay all legal expenses of the general partners in defense of lawsuits from any source, including those initiated by limited partners. As we have indicated before, the management, development, leasing, and insurance fees are all quite important, but nothing is more important in the last analysis than the exclusive right of resale. To avoid lawsuits from a limited partner at the time of sale, especially if such a sale has been approved by 51 percent of the partners, in interest, the partner so desiring to sue is saddled not only with his own legal fees, but also both his share of all legal fees paid by the partnership in defense of any lawsuits against the general partners.

provide for a transfer fee

After all the limited partnership interest has been marketed, and the day-to-day operations of management are going on, a peculiar thing happens. Some of the partners, only a few during the first year, desire to change the ownership as it has been recorded with the Clerk of the Court in the jurisdiction either where the partnership was formed or where the property is located. The charge for actual recording such changes is rarely more than twenty dollars. If your partnership agreement is silent about such changes, you will be spending more time than you want in signing "Amendments to the Certificate of Limited Partnership," which will include an amendment to the "Limited Partnership Agreement" and signature sheets that will require notarizing.

If you charge a fairly stiff fee, payable to the general partner(s), this will tend to discourage "impulsive" changes among the limited partners. Before we charged hefty transfer fees, one limited partner wanted his 1 percent interest divided among his 6 children and 11 grandchildren. Imagine dividing a limited partnership interest of 1 percent among 17 persons! Our new agreements not only charge a hefty fee (which does **not** include any tax levied against such a transfer) but also specifically prohibit the "breaking down" of the limited partner's interest except in case of death.

the forum—a luxury apartment with 227 units—example of a larger apartment development with lower per-unit cost of operation.

5

acquisitions

chapter 5 outline

going ahead if you acquire: a proven modus operandi

Probably the easiest way to begin as a developer is to acquire an existing improved property that is producing cash flow. Since developers come from varied backgrounds (no one I know has a master's or doctorate in the development of income-producing properties), it is important that whatever knowledge you have of the income-producing realty field be supplemented by that of the experts in their respective areas. Aside from a good real estate attorney who has a thorough knowledge of not only real estate law but also partnership law, it is important that you use him before you are committed to buy. The best way to react to various real estate proposals is to have in front of you a written strategy.

In our own office, my partner and I are following a written strategy developed in 1956. We only acquire or develop three main classes of property. Chapter 12 outlines in detail why you should not consider acquiring for syndication raw land, hotels, motels, industrial buildings, and other special purpose buildings such as automotive dealerships or funeral parlors. We are interested in development or acquisition of apartment houses, shopping centers, and office buildings. Because we are developing in a rather large metropolian area (over 3.5 million people), our strategy is dovetailed to the community in which we are working. For example, we are not interested in developing apartments that do not have at least 150 units. The economies of scale are well known to most investors, and we have learned that a smaller building is less economical to operate than a larger building. For example, we would not acquire an apartment development without a swimming pool facility. If it were large enough (say 400 units), we would be interested in having a building independent of the apartments that could be used for hospitality purposes, that is, as a club, as a recreation room, gym facility, or what have you. We would also like to have at least three tennis courts, and if we were catering to families with preschool and school-age children, we would also dearly love to incorporate a nursery facility. We have also learned that the per unit cost of operation of a larger apartment development generally is quite a bit less than for a smaller unit. Taxes per unit seem to be less, that is, the real property taxes per unit seem to be less and we can, of course, amortize the cost of the resident manager and resident engineer over at least 150 units as opposed to acquiring or developing say an apartment complex of 60 or 75 units. For those persons interested in the acquisition of income-producing properties who live in less dense areas of population, the size of the development will have to be scaled down. The economies of scale follow just as surely in an office building or a shopping center as they do in an apartment development. Our minimum size office building is 150,000 square feet of net rentable area. Our minimum for a community shopping center is 125,000 square feet of net rentable area. These economies of scale apply to those of us in population areas of anywhere from three to four million persons.

The first criterion for acquisition is size, as described above. When we are considering acquiring an apartment development, our next consideration is its age. We generally like to acquire a building that is in its first decade of use. We do this because we know the agonizing decisions we would necessarily have to make regarding replacements of equipment and appliances that will wear out sometime during the second decade of ownership. This limits us to the acquisition of relatively new developments. The next thing we consider after age is location. Our strategy has been to acquire in 85 percent to 90 percent locations after we have studied the population movement of the area. This is done with the thought in mind of the ultimate sale taking place when perhaps the area is a 100 percent location.

We are also very concerned as to who built the property. If it was put together by another developer, we would, of course, be familiar with his quality of construction. But if it were another builder, we would necessarily have to arrange for an inspection by a reputable general contractor and above all an inspection by a reputable mechanical engineer. More damage has been caused by water than by probably any other form of casualty. As a result of our own experiences, we would not recommend any apartment house that has a flat built-up roof no matter how excellent the quality of such a roof. If we did not have height restrictions in our area, you can be certain that all of our properties, apartments, office buildings, and shopping centers would all have pitched roofs.

In the District of Columbia all developers are subject to Congressionally mandated height restrictions. This law dates back to 1910. Personally, I believe it is a good law because it means that private industry cannot erect buildings which would dominate the federal buildings in our area. Our maximum height is 130 feet which means we can only build 12-story buildings. Since this is our maximum height, with a few exceptions, zoning to permit 12 stories is conditioned on the width of the street. Leonardo da Vinci is quoted as saying: "Let the house be as high as the street is wide." For practical purposes, that is the law in the District of Columbia. Unlike Miami Beach or Tokyo, nobody sues anybody in D.C. because their sunlight is shut off by another person building an extremely tall building that effectively leaves smaller buildings without natural sunlight.

The disadvantages of such height restrictions are many. Aesthetically, downtown Washington, D.C. has taken on a "boxy" look and many persons joke about our wall-to-wall buildings.

The **maximum** density allowed by zoning in downtown Washington, D.C. is ten times the lot size. If you have a site containing 10,000 square feet, your finished building may have a maximum gross area (above ground level) of 100,000 square feet. There may be other larger metropolitan areas where the downtown restrictions are even more stringent, but I'm not aware of them. Many cities do not have downtown height or density restrictions and for the most part skyscrapers are permissible, but this permissive attitude is rapidly changing. Citizens groups have banded together and working with city planners as well as local politicians have caused down-zoning (a legal act restricting density downward from its allowable zoning use) which the courts have held to be perfectly legal. This is just another hassle that developers across the nation are having to put up with. It seems crazy that you cannot buy land upon which to build and rely upon the zoning in effect. Local action that disposes of the zoning in such a way to cause a down-zoning and therefore a lesser land yield has happened frequently enough to make developers very wary of such possible political action. Informed developers work with local citizen groups to elicit their prior support for a project, thus forestalling possible down-zoning.

Those of you who are familiar with the Kennedy Center for the Performing Arts in Washington, D.C., will be amused by the fact that while attending a recent performance, my wife and I had to walk through this magnificent structure under temporary plywood walkways because, of all things, the ceiling was **leaking.** The Kennedy Center for the Performing Arts is a magnificent structure whose design was done by the famous American architect, the late Edward Durrell Stone, but apparently despite its enormous cost, somebody goofed. At any rate, this is something you want to avoid when you are acquiring less expensive structures than the Kennedy Center for the Performing Arts.

apartments

Going back to apartments again, and I'm referring mainly to garden apartments as opposed to high-rise apartments, it is important that your mechanical engineer advises you as to the condition of the heating and air conditioning systems. For reasons related to original cost and operational costs, most garden apartments cannot be cooled enough on the top floors or heated enough on the lower floors. Inadequate air conditioning or a poor distribution system is something that a trained mechanical engineer can spot quickly. The same can be said for the heating system. There have been arguments raging by and among developers for a long time as to whether it is best to have individual air conditioning and heating separately for each apartment or to go to a central system. Each has advantages and disadvantages. The most obvious advantage of individual units is that the tenant has them under his control. Whereas in central systems, generally speaking, in-between seasons present a problem both for heating and air conditioning because rarely are the systems sophisticated enough to provide heat or air conditioning at will. Generally speaking, the air conditioning is on, or the heating is on. A well-planned central system has the advantage of economy of operation. Its major disadvantage is that if it requires repairs either to the heating or air conditioning system, the entire apartment development is without heat or air conditioning during "down time."

During periods of escalating heating and air conditioning costs, the owners of apartment developments with tenants who pay their own utilities or owners who are managing apartments with individually controlled heating and air conditioning systems are lucky indeed. One of the major problems with providing air conditioning and heating self-contained units for individual apartments is that you will have extreme difficulty in finding high quality mechanical units. Some are better than others and your mechanical engineer will know this. You can get in a central system, however, quality equipment in both air conditioning and heating. Generally, the larger the air conditioning system, the higher quality equipment available. You, as the developer or syndicator, will, of course, have to weigh all of these factors and arrive at a conclusion as to whether or not to acquire based upon these mechanical considerations.

office buildings

What we look for first (after size) in an office building is age, and then its location. Here again, we are seeking an 85 to 90 percent location with the hopes that when we sell it a decade later that it would be in the 100 percent location. We also are in favor of free-standing buildings, that is, buildings that are open on all four sides. You will discover that when you are leasing an inside building, that is, any building covered on either of its sides, that you will have difficulty not only in attracting and keeping good tenants, but in competing with free-standing buildings. Men and women in the business world tend to have unusually high egos, and, for the most part, will demand outside offices. Outside offices naturally are brighter and will give tenants varying degrees of views.

After these two aspects, we look at structure. Here again, we do not rely on our judgment but seek a mechanical engineer who will assure us that the building has enough air conditioning and heating to serve its tenants. Beware of large office buildings that have only one air conditioning compressor. When it goes on the blink, you could have serious problems. Most modern office building developers are intelligent enough to have two units more or less the same size as a back up when, and if, one of these compressors would need to be repaired. One unit of, say, 500 tons capacity and another of 500 tons capacity make more sense than having one unit of 1000 tons capacity. If one unit goes bad there is some air conditioning while repairs are being made. It is also important that the building have decent elevators. Decent elevators are those that are tall enough to be used not only for passenger use but also for freight. Our latest elevator design includes elevators which have free, clear floor to ceiling height of ten feet five inches. You should not only observe the elevator if you are planning a building or syndication, but you should also go to each floor and press the elevator buttons to see how long it takes the cab to arrive. With the exception of rush periods in the morning and at the close of business, you should not have to wait long for an elevator to reach you in an office building. (See Chapter 6.) We have found that tenants will leave office buildings because of poor elevator service, poor mechanical service, or poor char service. The only other reason they would leave you is if you did not have enough room within the building for such a tenant to expand.

There is not much difference between one office building and another except that which we can see visually, so the developer surely must give serious consideration to the amenities of the building especially those in the lobby, elevators, and in the men's and women's rooms. Aside from the elevator lobbies on each of the floors, there is essentially not much difference from the point of view of the possible, future tenant. Here again, the tenant looks for decent location, a free-standing building, decent elevators, and good char and mechanical services.

shopping centers

As indicated earlier, we know a lot about American shopping habits, especially the shopping habits of women. It is definitely worth the money to join the industry association of shopping centers. They have delicious information about shoppers' habits, the size of centers, how far people will travel in a car to get to your facility, and how far they will walk to get there. Generally speaking, the community shopping center is anchored by a drugstore on one end and a food store on the other. These major, frequently AAA tenants, do not allow you to make any serious money. They simply will not pay higher rents. Therefore, you have to look for the quality of the local merchants in other stores. Again, you will want a location that is good and getting better, and you will want a thorough examination by a civil engineer and a mechanical engineer as to the pros and cons of the quality of construction.

If you stay with a written strategy, it will help you tremendously in avoiding mistakes. The worst thing you can do is to make an acquisition because "you need another deal." Reaching (paying a higher price than you would pay normally) for a deal because you need one will inevitably cause you to err. Acquire only if its fits your written investment strategy. In time, all income-producing properties are sold. Nothing is forever, especially real estate that has a good deal of mechanical equipment and moving parts. Therefore, you would do well to confine your purchases to properties that have been developed in the last decade.

how much to charge?

Generally speaking, we have found that if the property cannot accept a load of 15 percent then it is hardly worth acquiring. Aside from all of the professionals who will need to assist you in your acquisition, all of whom will be paid by the partnership that you will be forming, you must remember that the property will be subject to your getting at least 15 percent of the future "profits and losses." This means that if the property is currently enjoying a cash flow of $100,000 per year, your general partnership fee of putting together the venture will be in the neighborhood of 15 percent, and as a result, the investors will be obtaining approximately $85,000 based upon your projections. If $1 million cash equity is required to acquire the property, then such investors will be getting a cash-on-cash return of approximately $8\frac{1}{2}$ percent. In lectures throughout the country, I have been asked numerous times: "What is the minimum cash-on-cash return an investor will accept?" I do not know what the minimum is but I have heard some investors entering a venture where the sole benefit was tax losses because the property was producing a negative cash flow. Of course, these investors thought the property had a future, or they would not have made the investment in the first instance. We have successfully put together ventures where at the outset the investor did not receive more than a yearly 5 percent cash-on-cash return. Frequently, such properties are easier to syndicate because they may be properties to which you could bring some of your expertise to bear, and thus in time produce a higher cash flow for all concerned. Or, they may be properties that are getting better all the time.

On the other hand, we have acquired properties that looked like they would be returning as much as 11 percent to the investors. We have also developed properties where we have deliberately lowered the income and forecasted higher expenses just to keep down the amount of estimated cash-on-cash return to the investor. For some reason, which perhaps is known only to psychologists, property that can produce a return (or that looks like it can produce a return) of 15 percent or higher, tends to frighten off at least 90 percent of your potential investors. They reason, and perhaps rightly so, that such a property is risky. As we have stated before, a load in excess of 15 percent of future profits and losses must of necessity show enough cash-on-cash return to attract sophisticated investors. Obviously, the higher your percentage for putting the venture together, the less the investor will receive. To suggest that you do a venture for less than 15 percent is, in my mind, unthinkable. Your own time that will necessarily be required to successfully syndicate, manage, and ultimately refinance and sell is certainly worth at least 15 percent of profits and losses. There may be instances where you could go a little higher, but we have found that investor resistance builds at the moment you go over 15 percent.

what about a brokerage fee?

There are two major reasons why we do not accept a brokerage fee on acquisitions. The first is that if you are aligning yourself with the investor's interests, it is difficult for you to determine what such a fee should be, and you can be assured the potential investor will look askance at your requiring a brokerage fee on entry. Most investors do not like to come into a venture where the developer or general partner is taking a fee off the top of the investor's money. Another reason, and equally important, is that in order to be offered properties by the brokers in your area, be assured that if you advise them all that you are not interested in participating in their commission and that you are acting as a principal for a group to be formed that you will be among those who will have the first shot at the fine commercial properties that are being offered in your area. There is enough money to be made in this business without denying the broker his fee for his work in finding the property for you and in participating in the negotiations with you and the seller. If the venture cannot stand a brokerage fee, it obviously is not worth acquiring.

locating the "front money," especially for the larger ventures

A question frequently asked is, "How do you get started? I don't have the capital necessary to begin a syndication." We call the monies necessary to begin a syndication or acquisition "front money." Besides the money that you will need to pay your professional civil and mechanical engineers, you will be concerned with expert legal and accounting professionals, and you will need a deposit as part of your contract to purchase the property. Because the acquisition may be delayed for as much as six to nine months, you will have to explain the delay as the reason you cannot pay your professionals until you have received all the equity dollars from your prospective investors. If you tell this to your engineers, attorneys, and accountants in advance, for the most part, they will be understanding.

There is no doubt about your needing enough money for a deposit on the property. Your commercial banker is the first person to see **prior** to your looking at various properties. Your banker is interested in making short-term loans, and because your front-money requirements are relatively short-term (usually not exceeding nine months), you are the type of account your banker is looking for. He knows that you will promise him the management account once you acquire the property. Because we live in a quid pro quo economy, it is natural for you to offer the management account to the banker who is willing to take a short-term risk by lending you the deposit money (front money). Most bankers are aware that the average daily balances of a management account are fairly large. It will help if, well in advance of your financial requirements, you have a long talk with the banker of your choice and explain what you intend to do. It is important because later, as you will discover, you must be able to put up a sizable deposit in order to convince the seller that you do have the financial power to carry the contract to settlement. We always put up our deposit money in the form of a regular bank check made out to either our attorney or the title company which will make the settlement. Our contracts usually have language to the effect that the deposit will be kept by the settlement attorney in an interest-bearing account in an institution of our choice. If final settlement does not occur because of some problem, such as the title, for example, or any other condition that is the seller's fault, the cost for the deposit money becomes negligible. It is the difference between what you are earning on an interest-bearing account and what your borrowing rate was. It is not a bad idea to place your money in an interest-bearing account in the bank from which you originally borrowed it. This is simple to do because you can direct where the deposit will be held and you can direct whomever is holding it to put it into whichever bank or savings and loan institution you choose.

After you acquire your first venture and develop rapport with your bank, things will become a lot easier. After a few syndications, most banks that are seeking short-term business with quality people will appreciate the fact that you are maintaining rather substantial balances in your management checking account. The larger ventures seem to "turn on" the banks more than the smaller ones because unlike you, they are looking at the larger balances that you will maintain, whereas among other things you are looking at the other goodies that will flow from such an acquisition.

delaying the settlement

You will want to delay the settlement for as much as six to nine months in order to give yourself the necessary time to develop the partnership agreement and to locate and obtain the equity dollars needed from the prospective investors. It is common practice in the acquisition of larger income-producing properties that settlement is usually delayed for as much as nine months. If you can do it, it is a good idea to allow for an additional 90-day delay in settlement. If you offer to put up additional deposit money for each month of delay, this will sometimes result in the seller being more willing to wait for a somewhat longer period of time. You will need the time not only to set up your limited partnership, but to obtain accounting projections and legal advice on the necessity or non-necessity of registering your "offering" with the state securities commission and the Securities and Exchange Commission.

obtaining expert legal and accounting professionals

I frequently explain that the only "bum" in our ventures is me. The reason for this is that I feel my partner and I have selected the best legal and accounting professionals to advise us on our acquisitions. This is hardly the place for you to think about saving money. You will be saving money if you "sniff" around your local community and determine who is the best real estate attorney, the best SEC attorney, and the best partnership and tax attorney. It is doubtful that you will obtain these experts in one person. In this day of specialization, it is virtually impossible to find someone skilled in all of these fields. But, it is not unusual to find someone with real estate background who not only can write an excellent partnership agreement, but who has good knowledge of the tax laws. It is in the area of whether or not you should register your offering that some of your major problems could occur. In order to avoid these, you will necessarily have to find an attorney who is skilled in knowledge relating to securities offerings.

Something that has escaped me and that I will never understand, is why people go to accountants for tax advice. The accountants are necessary, and we use them on every venture with respect to the amounts we are allowed to write off as expenses, whether they be depreciation, interest, or what have you. But to go to an accountant for tax advice seems silly unless the firm has one person who specializes in the tax effects of these transactions. All of the tax laws seem to be written by attorneys, and they seem to be administered by attorneys not only at the Internal Revenue Service, but in the tax courts. It follows that you need a tax attorney to represent you in these matters. This is not to denigrate the value of the accounting professionals because very frequently they can point to problem areas that need to be clarified, and frequently our accountants spend quite a bit of time with our tax attorney. Many tax accountants know as much tax law as the tax laywers, but their skills and training differ. The top lawyer will help you create your partnership agreement and can plead your cause if you are audited by the IRS. Because the partnership is paying all the legal and accounting fees as well as engineering fees and all other out-of-pocket expenses that you will be paying, it is important that your professionals be well known and successful.

avoid taxation gymnastics

While my strategy is to take all of the write-offs that are allowed, I avoid what I call taxation gymnastics. It seems that both New York and Los Angeles have numerous legal and acquisitions specialists who apparently have brought to bear the most imaginative techniques designed to increase the write-offs for the purpose of postponing federal taxation. On more occasions than you would want, these plans end up in the tax courts. The present laws allow a fair and reasonable amount of write-offs so that it is really unnecessary to get into some of these esoteric techniques. For the most part, they will not stand up under a sophisticated audit and not only will you be embarrassed, but the Internal Revenue Service, once they find such a write-off not allowable, frequently will audit all of the returns of the investors in your syndication. This does not make for goodwill among your investors, and it does not make good sense for you. If your participations are not saleable because there is not enough tax shelter, then you have not thought the syndication process through to its ultimate conclusion. Most of the money that I've made and most of the moeny that has been made in investing in income-producing properties is not, nor ever has been, made through taxation gymnastics.

After all, there is no tax-free income in real estate. The best we can do is postpone taxation until some future date. When the tax for capital gain purposes was at a maximum of 25 percent, it seemed important to obtain the fastest write-offs of all kinds. This was so because at a later date when the property was ultimately sold, the maximum tax on the gain would be 25 percent, except to the extent of depreciation recapture. However, from 1972 to October, 1978, capital gain is now taxed at 35 percent at its maximum, plus a potential 10 percent minimum tax on one-half the long-term capital gain. Additionally, to the extent of one-half the long-term capital gain, earned income may have been disqualified for the 50 percent maximum tax on earned income.

For long-term capital gains realized after 1978, the deduction is 60% (up from 50%). None of the gains are tax preferences subject to the 15% minimum tax and none of the gains will disqualify personal service income for the 50% maximum tax rate. Instead, the 60% deductible share of long-term capital gains and the excess of certain itemized deductions over 60% of adjusted gross income (less deductions for state and local taxes, medical expenses, casualty losses, and estate taxes related to income in respect of a decedent) are added to adjusted gross income to determine an alternative minimum tax. The first $20,000 of alternative minimum taxable income is exempt from the alternative minimum tax. Any excess is taxable at rates from 10% to 25%. The alternative minimum tax is payable if it is greater than the regular tax liability, including the regular minimum tax. With the maximum effective tax rate on long-term capital gains at 28% (70% times 40%), down from 48%, the prospect of realizing long-term capital gains is again an important incentive for investment in real estate.

What has happened as a result of some taxation gymnastics was that the property was ultimately foreclosed. The investors were paying more attention to the tax losses than to the property itself, and the property could not have been developed or subsequently acquired if not for such liberal tax write-offs. The problem was that the "corpus" they had acquired was economically unsound.

All the taxation gymnastics in the world cannot make a winner out of a loser. You should take those write-offs you are allowed to take and save the imaginative techniques of the tax attorneys and acquisition specialists for those who can't create income-producing properties without tax gimmicks. Because it is entirely possible that many of your investors will be attorneys, be assured that they will look askance at some new imaginative tax technique that may trigger an audit because of its implausibility. The important thing to remember is that the property must be economically sound, have a growing economic future, and be well constructed. In the last analysis, this is the only way you are going to stay in business. There are times, of course, when I have increased our write-offs by selling the land to a major institution and then leasing it back. As you know, you cannot depreciate land, but you can write off, as a legitimate expense, leasing expenses on land. I have only done this when there is a disproportionate ratio of land costs to improvement costs. When land represents as much as 35 percent of the total cost, it seems to me to make good, economic sense to merely control the land, but not own it. As a caution, do not sell land and lease it back unless you have in writing the opportunity to repurchase it sometime in the future. I like three-year option periods beginning between the seventeenth and twentieth years. Later on, I will get into the length and terms of land leases.

public versus private offerings

A public offering is an offering in which anyone with money can participate. It is always registered and frequently advertised. A private offering is one in which entry is restricted to invited participants and is never advertised.

In the years following World War II through June 1974, developers and syndicators were really unsure of whether or not their offerings were public or private. Because there is not only good protection for the buyer of syndicated real estate offerings by registering such "securities" with not only the state securities commission, but also the Securities and Exchange Commission, it would appear to be a good idea to register all such offerings not only with the state securities, but the federal securities people. The problem was and is however, that it usually takes many months to process a real estate syndicated offering. This is not only very expensive from a legal standpoint but very few sellers are willing to sell their properties with a clause in the contract that the transaction would be called off if the purchaser could not get his offering processed through the Securities and Exchange Commission. There is always the possibility that it could languish at the Securities and Exchange Commission, and the syndicator or developer would have to forfeit his deposit. Therefore, a good many people relied upon the advice they received from their attorneys as to whether or not what they were about to do would require registration either at the state or federal level. Frequently, the advice was based upon various courts rulings rather than anything precisely defined by the Securities and Exchange Commission. My own definition of a public offering is a private offering in which the project is suffering negative cash flow and is eventually foreclosed.

While the definition is meant to be humorous, there is no humor involved when an irate investor either writes or visits the Securities and Exchange Commission and finds that the security was one that should have been registered with the Securities and Exchange Commission. If in fact upon investigation, the Securities and Exchange Commission determines that the developer or syndicator was not exempt from the laws relating to public offerings, that indeed the investor who complained was correct, then the Securities and Exchange Commission can do several things. First they may require the syndicator to return all of the monies invested by the investor with interest accrued at 6 percent, running from the time he put up his money. This is called a "recision" and to make matters worse, the developer or syndicator must make this same offer of recision to all of the participants in the venture. Second, the SEC has the power to haul the developer or syndicator into court and seek to prosecute under a criminal charge. This does not preclude investors from filing a civil suit for damages. The result for not registering an offering that was subsequently determined to have been non-exempt (that is a public offering) could result not only in the bankruptcy of the developer, but also a large fine, and if the violation were flagrant enough, could result in a jail term.

On June 10, 1974, the Securities and Exchange Commission in Washington, D.C., issued a ruling called Rule 146, which is 26 typewritten pages, spelling out quite specifically whether or not a transaction involves a public offering within the meaning of the Securities Act of 1933. One statement that preceded the rule itself and made by the SEC was that "the protection afforded by the rule, however, is available only to those who satisfy **all** its conditions" (emphasis supplied). Rule 146 is titled, "Transactions by an Issuer Deemed Not to Involve Any Public Offering." Even after your attorney has reviewed what you are about to do, and even if he feels that you are exempt as a result of the rules under Rule 146, he must still be concerned with complying with the laws of the state in which you are doing business. Most of the state laws are not too complex or difficult, except the states with large populations, such as California, New York, Texas, and others.

When I first started, I could not understand the concept of real estate partnership interests being securities. I soon was disabused of my feelings that real estate is not a security because of the numerous cases in local, state and federal courts in which it had been determined that virtually any offering could be considered public rather than a private placement. My thinking went like this: If I were to go to a grocery store, buy a loaf of bread, and have it sliced while I waited, I would merely be buying a loaf of bread. If I sold the loaf of bread in its entirety I do not suppose anyone could call what I had done a securities transaction. If, however, I divided the bread up half for my wife and half for myself, I do not suppose that would be a security transaction either. Taking it a step further, if I were to give it to my brothers-in-law or my brothers or sisters, I do not suppose it would be a security transaction either. But the moment I offered that piece of bread or one slice of that bread to someone with an indication that he could make some money by permitting me to manage the use of disposition of the bread, then I was treading on very dangerous ground indeed. Nothing is more critical in the development or acquisition process than your complying with federal and state rules relating to syndicated offerings.

The rule itself, while it is fairly precise, is nonetheless not clear in every respect. But it appears that the 1935 Release 33-285, 11 FR 10952 (1935) was far less precise than Rule 146. According to the early rules, what we relied on were the factors involved, such as the number of units of participation, the size of the offering, the manner of the offering, and the number of the offerees and their relationship to each other and to the offeror—my partner and me. Some of the concepts in Rule 146, which superseded the 1935 ruling, are in themselves nebulous and need to be clarified. Some of the requirements, for example, which would make one exempt from this offering would be that there should be "reasonable grounds to believe and shall believe that the offeree is either sophisticated or rich"—or probably both.

The offeror, which is my partnership, is supposed to have made reasonable inquiries and come to the conclusion that if the offeree, that is, the potential investor, is not either sophisticated or rich, he must have an offeree representative who is in fact sophisticated. By sophistication, the SEC indicated the potential investor must have had "knowledge and experience in financial and business matters and he is capable of evaluating the merits and risks of the prospective investment." If he is deemed to be wealthy, he is supposed to be "able to bear the economic risks of the investment." You will note that the SEC required that the purchaser not only be rich, but also be sophisticated, or alternatively, hire an "offeree represenative." You are bound by law to make absolutely certain that the prospective investor is indeed sophisticated and that he could afford to lose all of the dollars he is placing with you, and he would not be seriously damaged economically. Even if you feel you are exempt because the investor is not only sophisticated, but has the ability to bear the economic risk, in no way are you allowed to advertise or generally solicit. It is extremely important, of course, that the potential investor has access to every possible aspect of risks and rewards relating to the investment. What the SEC was trying to do was to insure that the prospective investor had as much information available to him and perhaps more than he would have had if you had undergone a full registration with the Securities and Exchange Commission. It is important to note that even if you are exempt from Rule 146, this has no effect whatsoever on possible violations of the anti-fraud provisions or any civil liability provisions of the Securities Act of 1933.

Generally speaking, under Rule 146, there is a limitation as to the maximum number of purchasers in any given year, and that number is 35. There are, however, some exemptions to the 35 maximum requirement. For example, if the minimum participation is $150,000, even if it is payable in installments, these people are not counted as being among the 35 persons, the maximum allowed under this numerical test. But even the large investor has to be sophisticated, rich, and have unlimited access to any information relating to the potential investment. As your attorney will probably tell you, when you get into numbers, you are kind of in a "game." If an investment group, let's say made up of ten social acquaintances, forms a partnership, and the partnership itself decides to invest in your partnership, then you may have to count the ten persons under the 35 maximum test. You also have to be careful that the investor does not reoffer the unit of participation among some of his friends. If this occurs, you may not rely on the maximum number of 35 as an exemption from having to register with the SEC under this Rule 146.

Do not rely on anything you read here as being explicit without first going over things very carefully with your attorney, who in fact should be sophisticated on securities matters, and who will advise you **before you contract to buy** the property. You may have to lose your deposit if you go ahead without proper advice from your securities attorney or you may have to file a registration statement, which is not only very, very time consuming, but your attorney's fees could also get very expensive because of many hours of conferences generally necessary before a securities offering involving real estate is released from the SEC in final form. Of course, you are aware that the SEC neither approves or disapproves your registration, but merely ensures that all pertinent information has been disclosed. Of course, if all of your offerings were limited to individual participants who were investing $150,000 or more, and who were sophisticated, rich, and had total access to what you were doing, I believe your attorney would still advise you to do certain other things so that a registration may not be required. I believe Rule 146 is a good rule. It clarifies whether or not the offering need be registered. Since the investors themselves would be paying for the registration expense, which can be considerable, it tends to reduce the cost of syndicated acquisitions. I am relying now on Rule 146 to ensure that everything I do in the syndication field is exempt from federal registration.

determining a unit of participation

My experience has taught me that to exceed 20 participants in any one venture does not make for good business. This is true because whether the amount of money you are about to raise is $100,000 or $3 million, it will serve your interest and the best interest of the project to have a maximum of 20 partici-pants wherever possible. Naturally the preparation of your full disclosure state-ments, which are required under Rule 146, will contain voluminous information. A recent private offering by our company weighed $3\frac{1}{2}$ pounds and contained over 160 sheets of paper. The production costs of, let us say, 100 or 200 of such full disclosure statements can be quite expensive, and we feel it is totally un-necessary to produce more than 20–25 with a maximum of 35. Once you begin operations and the syndicate is fully closed, you will discover that communication with more than 20 persons becomes very expensive. Not only will your mailing costs and reproduction costs escalate constantly, there is either something wrong with the venture or your sales technique if you need over 20 persons. If you are in a relatively small jurisdiction, and your requirements are $100,000, there is nothing intrinsically wrong with having 20 participants at $5,000 each. The amount of the unit of participation really has to do with the wealth and sophistication of the investors with whom you are dealing. To exclude persons with a fair degree of sophistication, who have decent net worths, and who are enjoying good incomes makes no economic sense. So you may have to lower your unit of participation. As long as your attorney approves your method of presentation, and you can and will abide by all the rules required, not only those of the SEC in Washington, D.C., but your local and state securities commission, I do not see why units as small as $5,000 could not be easily marketed.

The last offering that we did relying on Rule 146 involved minimum participations of $175,000. We could do this because of the size of the offering was $3.5 million, and we did not want more than 20 participants. As an aside, when I first started in syndications in 1951, I was asked by some of my friends, "Why sell the same building over and over again? Why not just sell it to one person?" Well, the answer is relatively simple. If you look at all the substantial financial benefits that flow to you as a result of either acquiring or developing income-producing properties, you will see that such benefits would not flow to you if you made a sale to one person. By opening up the market to more than one person, and by going the limited partnership route, you have security and sufficient economic rewards to make the process worthwhile. When you offer participations to more than 20 people or the participation amount is quite small, I think you run two basic risks. First, you may not qualify for an exemption under Rule 146, and second, the level of sophistication not only required by Rule 146, but also which you yourself would desire in an investor simply may not be there. Therefore, we have concluded that a minimum participation in a medium-sized town should be in the area of $25,000. In the larger cities, a minimum participation of $100,000 is usual. Smallish towns of 100,000 population or less could have minimum participations as low as $5,000.

In determining the unit of participation amounts, remember that you will not only need the equity required under the contract to purchase the property, but you will need to add in legal and accounting as well as engineering and other "expert" costs, costs of the settlement, and costs for insurance and real estate tax escrows, which may have to be paid either at settlement or escrowed on a monthly basis. Therefore, you will find that even though your contract calls for an equity of $500,000, it is quite possible for you to raise as much as $650,000 to cover all possible contingencies, which may or may not occur. It is much easier to return capital to your investors if it is not needed than it is to try to obtain more capital when your syndication has been closed. I have read quite a few private offerings and have noted that not enough money was being raised to cover future cash requirements. The time to raise the money is at the outset—not at some later date when you must follow the conditions, outlined under the partnership agreement, that deal with negative cash flow. As a real estate counselor, I have been employed to review submissions of others. I have also been employed as a counselor after the person has entered the venture, and it is not doing well. In both instances, the major cause of the problems was the inability or unwillingness of the developer-syndicator to raise the appropriate amount of money in the first place. I suspect that some of the reasons for not raising that kind of money was to try to show a greater cash-on-cash return to the investor. This is not necessary as you will discover when we discuss marketing the equity participations in Chapter 7. It is not the cash-on-cash return that will determine whether an investor comes into your venture. That is just one factor, and probably the least important factor, among all of those a sophisticated investor will take into account when he makes the decision to participate with you. He will consider the tax effects, namely tax shelter, and if truly sophisticated will try to assess the economic future of the project. He will also consider your "load" to determine its fairness.

managing the offering time for easier equity participations

One of the most important things you must do is have enough time to not only develop a clear and understandable private placement memorandum if you are exempt from Rule 146, but also you may require this time so it is easier for you to obtain all the investors necessary to fully fund the equity requirements. There is no point in putting yourself under needless pressure at the outset. Any venture that has to be done quickly may often be done shoddily. There is no need for this kind of pressure to be put on you especially since you can get enough time in the initial phase. As you may know by now, any real estate decision that requires an "instant" decision to buy on your part should be passed up immediately. More syndicators or developers have gotten into difficulty because of making purchases under pressure than they have for a variety of other reasons. The quality property that is for sale will find you a willing buyer provided the seller is willing to give you the time necessary to settle. As indicated before, that should be a minimum of six months. We prefer nine months with additional deposits for each month thereafter for a maximum of 15 months. That gives you plenty of time to manage the offering. Never let yourself be saddled with a 90- or 120-day settlement. The longer marketing periods will please your attorneys and accountants who will have a lot of work to do. Your banker also will be more emotionally comfortable if he knows you will have ample time to successfully conclude your offering.

Most developers have started their development careers by starting to acquire, usually with partners, existing structures. There is something to be said for evaluating a projects' preceding five years performance. Certainly there is less risk in comparably sized projects if you acquire the property fully leased. You will pay a higher price because all of the development risks have already been faced and are history. Because the price you pay will be higher than if you were to develop, your "load" or fee will necessarily be lower.

Don't be afraid of not being spectacular—lots of spectacular syndicators and developers have gone bye-bye. Stay with apartments, office buildings and shopping centers—none of which are as risky as investments in land or single purpose buildings. Do not be afraid to charge a decent fee for your work. A sophisticated investor may consider you to be a dummy or a fool by not charging enough of a fee. In any case he won't have any confidence in you. The sophisticated investor, more than most folks, knows there is no such thing as something for nothing.

Forget about a brokerage fee except at sale. You are a principal, acting together with other principals with whom you are financially, ethically and morally bound. As a general partner you are also a fiduciary. Consider every action you take as an action you may have to defend against law suits or governmental charges.

Your banker and the bank with whom you deal is a tremendous asset. This is where your front money, at least in the beginning, will be found. Remember that acquisitions are not accomplished overnight. You will need lots of time, a very good reason to plan to settle well into the future.

You will need lots of professional help from attorneys and accountants as well as appraisers and even real estate economists. Don't let your attorneys or accountants get too creative. One day your partnership financial affairs will be audited by the Internal Revenue Service who frown on taxation gymnastics which are not quite in line with the statutes, rules and regulations. This may trigger an audit of each partner's individual tax return, a condition which will positively make you personna non grata with your investors.

Consider whether or not your offering is really a private offering or whether it should be registered. Rely heavily on your securities attorney on this matter. He may have to defend either choice some time in the future.

In determining the smallest unit of participation, make sure you are not treading close to the number (35) which could require a full registration.

Above all, don't allow yourself to be boxed in to a limited time to raise your equity monies. You may be so enthusiastic about acquiring the project that 9 months seems forever. It isn't forever and besides, you can always settle on the project earlier.

You should hire attorneys and accountants on a time basis. This is simple enough and all the higher class firms prefer to charge you by the hours worked. Just ask what the hourly fee will be; the professionals will love you for asking. They know that those syndicators who never ask how much the fees will be may not pay or be very slow in paying the bill. This also avoids acrimonious discussions later on over what you may consider to be an onerous fee. This summary relating to acquisitions should be borne in mind should you decide to develop. It is riskier to develop, but more rewarding financially. I have always had more fun developing income-producing properties, because the challenges are more stimulating than those found in acquisitions.

WEIHE BLACK JEFFRIES & STRASSMAN   ARCHITECTS

artist's rendering of 2020 K street, washington, d.c. attractive renderings are needed to show potential investors and to give newspapers for their stories on a project.

6

developments

chapter 6 outline

going ahead if you develop: a proven modus operandi

Making a decision between acquisitions and developments is generally forced upon you sooner or later. The fact that your goodies are far more attractive in developing income-producing properties rather than acquiring them will probably not enter into your decision. What forces the decision is your belief that you can build, or cause to be built, a better income-producing property. If you stay with a strategy of acquisitions you will find that it is, or will become, increasingly difficult for you to find excellence of design, proper selection of materials, adequate mechanical systems, properly designed elevators, and a host of other quality features you will want in a building that you are acquiring and will be owning for probably at least 10 years. Aside from the quality features just enumerated, you will also discover that your 85 percent location, which you hope will become 100 percent in a decade, is not readily obtainable in existing buildings. You will discover a trend toward the west or north (or whatever) and in order to position yourself with a winner a decade hence, you will be necessarily drawn to the newer locations. It could be that you may assemble the land for the project or that you will find adequate land available nearby the newer and hopefully "better" projects.

determining the amount of equity needed

Sometime during the development process, you should have some general talks with some reputable general contractors. They will tell you the latest building costs related to what you are contemplating developing. Any certified property management (C.P.M.) will give you the latest operating costs. All you need to compute in your pro forma operating projections is the size of the loan and your annual constant. The annual constant is the percentage of the original loan amount that has to be repaid annually and includes the interest and principal. Generally, on commercial properties, you can borrow up to 75 percent of the **value** of the property. You can compute the costs both hard (actual building costs) and soft (interest during construction, points, taxes, and insurance during construction, and other items such as ground-breaking ceremonies, topping-out parties, and opening ceremonies). Don't forget to include your legal, accounting, and other administrative costs in your soft cost computations. By subtracting the anticipated loan from the total costs of construction and allowing appropriate rent-up periods that frantically add to the cost because during this period your interest costs are the highest, you can readily determine the amount of equity needed.

real estate specialists

Remember that as a developer you need the real estate community and you need them desperately. In the first instance you will need a commercial real estate broker who specializes in what you are looking for: apartment ground, office building ground, or shopping center land. Until someone proves to the contrary, your real estate broker **is** the market for these ground acquisitions. Here is the place to pretend you are without greed. Steadfastly maintain you are not interested in sharing in the broker's commission. Protect your commercial real estate broker in any way possible, including having his precise commission spelled out in the contract to purchase. You will not only need a good commercial real estate broker, you will need dozens of other people in the real estate community. You will need design input from property management. You will need leasing brokers if your project is a shopping center or an office building. You will need a mortgage broker or mortgage loan correspondent to help you obtain your financing, both construction and permanent. As part of the preparation for your presentation to a lender, you may want to employ either an appraiser or real estate economist, or both. These specialists are by no means the only outsiders you will need.

hiring the architect

Before you start to look for the land, you will have determined what your community needs. If you feel the office building market is ripe for another development, then that is the course you should follow. Perhaps your area could use more shopping facilities, or more apartments, or whatever; the initial decision as to the purchase of land will be yours. You need, first of all, an architect. He will tell you your yield from the ground in terms that should be quite precise. He will tell you the square feet of gross area in an office building, and depending on the method of calculating space in your community, the net square feet of rentable area. From his initial calculations, you can determine if the project is feasible, through analyzing a projected pro forma operating statement.

PRO FORMA CASH FLOW STATEMENT
WASHINGTON, D.C. OFFICE BUILDING
BASED UPON FULL OCCUPANCY

INCOME			
PARKING	71,163 sq. ft. @ $ 2.50 (includes 2,272 sq. ft. ramp 1st floor)	$	177,908
RETAIL			
Stores	57,441 sq. ft. @ $20.14		1,156,537
OFFICE			
Third Floor	28,714 sq. ft. @ $11.50	330,211	
Fourth Floor	29,362 sq. ft. @ 11.50	337,663	
Fifth Floor	29,362 sq. ft. @ 11.55	338,878	
Sixth Floor	24,129 sq. ft. @ 11.50	277,483	
Sixth Floor	5,233 sq. ft. @ 11.00	57,563	
Seventh Floor	29,362 sq. ft. @ 11.00	322,982	
Eighth Floor	29,362 sq. ft. @ 11.00	322,982	
Ninth Floor	29,362 sq. ft. @ 12.50	367,025	2,354,787
STORAGE	2,000 sq. ft. @ $ 5.50	11,000	
	500 sq. ft. @ 5.50	2,750	
	15,583 sq. ft. @ 6.50	101,289	115,039
GROSS ANNUAL INCOME			$3,804,271

EXPENSES

CHAR SERVICE	$ .70 per sq. ft.	$ 143,420
ELECTRICAL	1.10 per sq. ft.	225,375
HEATING, AC & PLUMBING MAINTENANCE		14,000
ENGINEERING SALARIES		30,000
ELEVATOR SERVICE CONTRACT		33,600
LEGAL AND ACCOUNTING		10,000
LEASING AND MANAGEMENT (3% + 2%)		190,214
INSURANCE (ESTIMATED)		30,000
REAL ESTATE TAXES*		311,100
SECURITY		11,000
TOTAL EXPENSES		998.709
CASH FLOW BEFORE DEBT SERVICE:		$2,805,562
DEBT SERVICE (INCLUDING 10% OF INCOME OVER $3,350,000)		2,017.447
CASH FLOW		$ 788.115

*Real Estate Taxes: Assume $17 million value (Current rate: $1.83 per $100 of assessed value).

A pro forma statement is an annual forecast which is a computation showing all cash rental income, usually floor by floor in an office building, store by store in a shopping center, and apartment by apartment in a residential rental property; all cash operations expenses are also shown and on the next to last line is shown the annual cost of the mortgage, principal and interest included. The bottom line is the cash flow. The preceding is an example of a pro forma statement.

There are a few important things to remember about the selection of your architect. In the first place there are two broad classes of architects: institutional and speculative. Developers use these terms, not architects. Just remember that an institutional architect is rarely into what anything costs. Institutional architects are the same architects that win all the architectural awards (the judges are mostly institutional architects). A test is this: if the architect has won many awards—don't hire him. Award-winning buildings have a propensity for losing money. The only loser I ever had won an architectural award! Of course, this is an oversimplification and admittedly a generalization but the only people that can usually afford the institutional architects are institutions. Because many institutions are building buildings for their own greater glory and frequently to massage the egos of the presidents and chairmen of the board, the finished buildings could **never** compete in the marketplace on a competitive basis because they cost an enormous amount of money to build compared to speculative buildings. So astronomical are the cost of most institutional buildings that they frequently out-cost quality speculative buildings by as much as ten to one! As an example, we developed an office building of good quality downtown in Washington, D.C., during 1958. Our hard cost ran about $16/gross square foot. I found out by meeting the head of an institution at a cocktail party that his building (the institution he headed) cost $135 gross square foot. They were both built at approximately the same time.

As part of your research for an architect, there are several positive things you must do. In your tentative selection of an architect, obtain from him the names of other local developers for whom he has done work. The key question to ask the owners is related to field changes or change orders (changes made after the building is under construction), as they are called in the industry. To the extent your general contractor can build the building without any field changes, then you have found your man. This is not possible, however, so you want the architect who's responsible for the least amount of change orders. No set of plans can be perfect. There being no such thing as perfect, your task is to seek out the architect with the least change-order record, meaning the **least number** of field changes.

Every time my partner or I must approve a change order we ascertain what caused the problem. We usually find that the design, on paper, seemed fine. But is the "little" things that can drive you crazy. For example, check closely the swing of the doors. Be certain which direction it swings and find out from the architect if it is a building code requirement or merely his design. Sometimes a tenant will desire and will pay for custom woodworking in his office. If you don't coordinate his interior custom work with your basic plan, you could be faced with changing the door to swing in, instead of out. While this seems minor, a solid core oak door costing approximately $450 without hinges, lock, and knob can cost as much as $1,250 to replace if all of the hardware is designed for the door to swing out and because of custom interior work it now must be replaced with one that can swing in.

Once we had designed a board room for a nationally known association that was virtually soundproof and would seat 32 persons. Special air conditioning and smoke exhaust systems were also designed and installed. Special acoustical ceilings were installed as well as sound deadening wall coverings. The room was a beauty. There was only one fault. The conference table was 24 feet long and we couldn't get the table in the building, much less the room. Guess what we had to do? Imagine virtually ripping out a finished exterior wall complete with windows, renting a crane for $1,250 and hoisting the table up to the floor and pulling it through the 12-foot hole we now had to refinish. The entire mess caused field changes which we could not predict at the outset. Who paid the $6,000 cost? Our partnership did because such foolish contingencies are always at extra cost to the owners. This is only one reason for continuous design input by your management and leasing personnel. We did suggest that our tenant saw the table in four separate six-foot chunks and install them once they had all been delivered. Obviously the tenant wasn't fond of the suggestion so the brouhaha just described developed into a $6,000 change order at our expense.

Stay away from any building shape that is not a rectangle or a square. Curvilinear buildings and odd-shaped setbacks are quite expensive to build. They will not reduce the owning cost nor will such buildings command higher rents. Avoid these shapes as you would the plague. Don't let the architect puff your ego so that you are conned into making a mistake.

Another rule to follow is to always employ a local architect. If there is no local architect qualified in your area, ask the most qualified local architect to assist you in your search for a relatively nearby experienced architect. If you make the mistake of not having a local architect, your job can be stopped completely because of an unsuspected field problem that could develop when your architect is unavailable. If your architect is local, at least he can help solve the problem on the spot.

searching for and acquiring the land

You will start with the land. This is the area wherein all of your expertise and intuition will be brought to bear. If you make a real mistake here you can get into serious financial trouble no matter what the quality of your development. First, understand that there are no bargains in real estate. You may overpay occasionally but if you think you are underpaying, you may be acquiring an inferior piece of land, even if the land is in exactly the location you desire. This is possible because the land may be "fill," and your contractor will have a very difficult and expensive time in his foundation work. You may also find a river or smaller body of water under the ground, which will make either for a serious design change (probably lessening your yield) or make for considerable expense in pumping out water. Remember, the largest single item of expense is your interest costs. Do nothing that would cause these interest costs to escalate.

Your designated architect will hire the appropriate contractor to test the land before you actually agree (or as a condition before you agree to purchase it). The tests can be done in many ways but the essence of these tests is to bore into the ground in more or less the same intervals (called a grid) and take a core sample of the ground (similar to oil well drilling operations). The core will be examined by either a local geologist, hired by the driller, or your potential contractor. The contractor, having looked at many samples himself, can tell you if you can anticipate any undue expense after he analyzes the foundation driller's report. Merely knowing about the possible underground problems can help you in any subsequent negotiations with the seller.

It is important if you are just beginning to be a developer to contract to purchase land that is already properly zoned. As stated earlier, this is not the time for a bargain. Trying to obtain favorable zoning for a tract of land is difficult and is seldom financially rewarding. Pay retail for the ground. Let the real estate speculators buy the bargains and obtain favorable zoning; then purchase the ground from them and pay retail. There is a surprising amount of pressure and in some cases outright graft in obtaining appropriate zoning. Because you may not know whether or not your city or county officials are honest, by the time you find out that some of them may not be honest you could, albeit against your will, end up being in the position of having to grant favors of some kind (money) or go belly-up (bankrupt) in your quest to do a development. Make no mistake about it, probably 99 percent of all zoning officials are "straight arrow." But if you happen to run into the other one the first time you want to do a development, you will have serious problems. At this point, there is too much at stake to gamble. Later on in your career when you are comfortable about your local zoning officials and the community in which you live has a fine reputation, perhaps then you may wish to consider buying ground that may have to be rezoned to accommodate your development. Even then you will need a competent zoning attorney and the process of rezoning is agonizingly slow. Because of these two problems (attorney's fees and the length of time such a process takes), you may not wish to buy unzoned land. Remember also that the land you are negotiating for must have sewer, water, utilities (gas, electric, or both), and telephone lines and must face on a street that is accepted by the local or state roads commission for maintenance. Your architect must check this out for you.

In negotiating for your land, it is not uncommon to allow time for the buyer to perform drilling and under-the-ground tests, and the time you may want to conduct such tests must not be unreasonably withheld. You should also have your attorney insure that all the zoning, utilities, and other things that you require including good and marketable title be included in the contract. If any of these items are fouled up in one way or another, the contract should call for the prompt refunding of your deposit. Additionally, if circumstances change relating to financing or market conditions, you may decide it is more appropriate to forfeit your deposit than to go forward with the purchase of the land. It is up to you to see that there is a clause in the contract that limits your liability to the extent of your deposit.

This is one more reason to try to hold down the size of your deposit. Beware of your ego. Frequently developers who have massive egos fall into the trap of putting up massive deposits (to match their egos) in order to titillate the seller into thinking how powerful and wealthy they (the developers) are. Save this type of ego massage and fantasy for your dreams.

And speaking of egos, here is a very important rule that will help eliminate your ego from investment decisions.

> **Never** select a material over the standard material if it costs more, unless (1) it reduces the owning cost so that your **savings** will pay for the item over the first six years, or (2) it will **increase** the rentals immediately.

advance talks with contractors

There is no way you will know what you are doing in terms of construction costs unless and until you have some serious talks with your general contractor. We do not use the term "builder" because we are not sure of what the term means. In the case of a general contractor, what he does is quite specific. He will execute as faithfully as he can the working drawings prepared by your architect after you have hired him to construct your building. His basic fee is rarely negotiable, the fee being in the 5-percent range above his costs. Long before you hire the general contractor, there are several things you must do.

You must check his performance record with the owners of his last three projects. Your inquiry will include how tenderly the owners were treated when there were changes (usually in the field) from the basic contract. You must understand that once your contractor is hired, he cannot be discharged. If he is a union contractor, he cannot discharge any of his subcontractors without a good deal of risk to himself, to the job, and to you. Inasmuch as a subcontractor will rarely come onto a job where a previous subcontractor has been discharged, you should accept some responsibility in the beginning in the selection of subcontractors, too. You should insist on the right to approve all the subcontractors who will be employed by the general contractor.

Prior to your specific contract with the contractor, it is he, not your architect, who will give you his best estimate as to what the "hard" costs will be. During periods of rapidly escalating prices, it is not possible for your architect to give you a reliable estimate. His pricing knowledge about costs are usually dated because his price information is generally gathered when the contract is originally let. Thus, the architect is not often informed of escalating costs due to changes in the field.

At any rate, your working with a general contractor, prior to his actually being sure of getting the building contract, is a usual and highly acceptable procedure. He can give you not only a general concept of hard costs, but also frequently can use his experience in substituting a different material that works equally well at considerably less cost. More on costs later on in this chapter.

At any rate, no matter how well your proposed contractor checks out through your inquiry regarding his past three projects, you **must** have your real estate attorney check the legal records in your community to determine if your proposed contractor has filed a law suit against an owner within the past five years. Your attorney will also tell you if any subcontractors or prior owners are suing **him.** The importance of this check by your attorney cannot be overemphasized. A litigious contractor must be avoided. Being litigious generally means your contractor is not tractable or is not amenable to negotiations.

Because negotiations continue well after the original contract is let due to changes you feel you must make and due to changes brought about through an error in design, your general contractor must be willing to bend a little here and there. He also must be willing to represent **you** when he deals with his subcontractors on changes. A litigious background reflects a costly inflexibility.

Once you are satisfied that you will be doing business with general contractor A, don't go to contractor B with the idea of beating A's price downward. There should not be a great difference in price among the two or three general contractors in your area who would be acceptable to you. Frequently, such contractors will know each other well and may indeed be friends. In order to avoid being known as a chiseler or a cheapie, do not play one against the other. A few owners have tried this technique only to discover that the contractor ultimately selected will know that you tried to get a better price through some form of deception. He may know that you were fibbing when you told him he was the one you really wanted to build your job but his competition came in with a better price. He will know you are lying if you suggest a price to him saying that if he meets it, he will then get the job. He has lowered prices before on this basis and the contract was given to another contractor. Therefore, don't quibble with your contractor once work has commenced.

Understand that a contractor can, if he so desires, make the job costs go out of sight if he merely **slows** it a little. If he does this at or near the end of the project, you could be in for some really hefty charges relating to interest alone. For example, if you are paying, let's say, $9\frac{1}{2}$ percent interest on a $20 million construction loan or $1.9 million annually, your monthly cost is $158,333. Considering that there are usually about twenty-two working days a month, your interest costs alone on this loan amount to $7,197 for each working day.

It is important not to knock heads with the general contractor you have tentatively selected, especially about his fee. There are many other ways your general contractor can "get even" if you are seriously trying to get him to lower a legitimate figure. There is no point going into this ad nauseum, just believe that he can hurt you financially if he so desires. Your task is to not force him to take advantage of you. I recently met a general contractor who told me his motto was, "Forgive and forget, but get even first." I got the message and hope you will too.

understanding the development process

At lectures and speeches throughout the country, I have been asked, "Where does one begin?" Although many things are going on at the same time, you will be overwhelmed unless you have established some definite order of things. The old aphorism, "First things first," applies in helping you understand the development process. You cannot begin the development process unless you either have the land upon which to develop your project or have in hand a contract (or option) to purchase a specific parcel of land.

Once you own the land or you have a contract or option to acquire it, the development process begins. You will need to have a **compilation** sheet prepared by your architect that will or should give you the maximum amount of net rentable space allowed by the zoning authorities for your parcel of land.

The next step is to prepare a pro forma income and expense statement. This is explained in greater detail later on. You will also need a general understanding of what such a project will cost. Without knowledge of the loan market, you cannot compute both your hard and soft costs. An assist will be given you by your mortgage broker or mortgage loan correspondent who, prior to reviewing your plans and specifications, can give you an informed guess as to how much the interest probably will be. He or your local banker can give you an estimate of your construction loan points and interest costs during the development period. Between your mortgage broker and your banker, you can easily figure out your soft costs.

In determining how much you should borrow, rely on the 80 percent borrowing test. Remember **you** are not God and **you** do not make the real estate markets—tenants do. We like to structure our permanent loans in such a way so as to break even at 80 percent occupancy. In other words, if you need more than 80 percent occupancy (office buildings, apartments, or shopping centers) to break even, you are either borrowing too much money or have to repay it back too soon.

The speed of amortizing a loan and paying the interest on the loan on an annualized basis is controlled by the **annual constant.** The annual constant is always expressed as a percentage of the original loan that must be repaid, including interest for one year. Keep the annual constant as low as possible; it is in your interest and in the interest of the partnership you will be forming. This is one of the most misunderstood concepts in the development process. For some reason, fledgling developers always want to borrow **too** much. This probably comes about because they have heard stories of developers borrowing out (a term that means that **all** the monies needed to successfully develop a project are obtained from a lender). They reason that if all the monies are borrowed and there is no personal liability for repayment, why should they not "borrow out?" A simple truism: if you borrow out and the rental process is slow, you will be "carried out." What will make matters worse is that a foreclosure is a sale under IRS rules.

You can understand more readily the reason for **not** borrowing out. A foreclosure is a sale. All the early write-offs and early depreciation allowances will have lowered the book value **below** the level of debt. By definition, profits at sale are subject to taxes, usually capital gains. Inasmuch as the sales price is the foreclosure price, the **taxable gain** is the difference between book value (cost less write-offs) and the sale price. Thus, the developer who borrows out and eventually is carried out, is subject to very large capital gains tax and usually has little or no capital with which to pay. A foreclosure sale generates taxable gains without generating any cash for the seller. Besides, 25 percent to 50 percent of nothing is nothing! Thus if you bring in partners and follow the 80 percent rule, you will be doing everyone a favor: you, the lender, and your limited partners.

Once you have obtained the commitment for your project from either an insurance company, savings bank, or pension fund, you can readily obtain a construction loan based on your permanent commitment. By this time, you will have obtained working drawings from your architect and will have worked out a definitive agreement with your general contractor. You must begin to work with your potential investors after conferring with your attorneys (real estate, tax, and securities), and your accountant for the financial and tax projections. More on the investors in Chapter 7. Once all the funds are raised and the investors are limited partners, construction may commence.

Be careful about trying to start construction too soon. All the money you will make in the development of new properties is controlled by all the work you do prior to the shovel hitting the ground. Once construction starts, it is too late to change anything. The time for caution is **prior** to construction. Once construction starts, the only real contribution you can make is to obtain the most favorable prices for your project from your future tenants.

At this point in the development process, the only serious risk left (aside from strikes and acts of God) is that you may have difficulty in obtaining tenants at the rents necessary to meet your projections.

research, research, research

One of the first things I observed in 1951 when I entered the real estate field was that real estate developers had sharply divergent backgrounds. The first few I met had been, or still were, speculative home builders. The body of knowledge required to be a speculative home builder is considerable. A home builder must know location, ground costs, the intricacies of subdividing land, design of houses, supervision of all the trades involved in the construction process, knowledge of interim and permanent financing, and ultimately the knowledge and skills to profitably market his finished houses. After the sale, he must work with his buyers, mollify them if mistakes were made, and continue to follow up complaints by ensuring his subcontractors return to the job to correct errors in their original work.

They must possess an enormous amount of knowledge and skills and in addition, have important amounts of their personal monies (or their families' and friends' monies) at risk. Successful builders are not rare, but be assured there are many losers. Goodness knows how many neophyte builders have not made it in the business of speculative home building and yet they keep coming back only to get walloped again.

After World War II, the group of home builders (collectively) were essentially former tradesmen: carpenters, plumbers, heating and air-conditioning contractors, and others already in some segment of the construction field. There were others too: former liquor store or grocery store owners or other small businessmen with some capital who sought to take advantage of the shortages and consumer demand for every conceivable kind of housing.

When these home builders had vacant ground facing a busy street or intersection, they did not build houses on such land. In the first place, most home buyers had school-age children and facing a busy street near a busy intersection was hardly the environment for raising children. Thus the former house lots, not built upon, remained in the inventory of the home builders. Nobody likes to service vacant ground with its interest and principal payments and property taxes. Even in those instances when the land was free and clear, the investment in the land produced no income and so a new industry and new tycoons emerged—the developers.

Once the land was rezoned to accommodate apartments, shopping centers, medical and dental office buildings, and suburban office buildings, many of the same speculative home builders became developers. Putting their home building knowledge to work, they anxiously had plans drawn and, union and nonunion alike, they started to build as soon as possible to stop the negative cash flow, which the empty land was then producing.

Let's say they decided to build apartments. Under then prevalent federal government programs, namely the Federal Housing Administration, hundreds of thousands of FHA 608 apartments were built. The problems of inexperienced developers building apartments manifested themselves quite quickly.

These same developers who were building tract housing (or subdivisions, if you prefer) were building for **resale.** Thus the primary consideration during the development process was **cost.** Because of a six or seven year pent-up demand for housing (especially inexpensive GI housing) the market was there. To maximize profits, builders used the cheapest materials and labor available. All the American tradition of excellence in design and pride of workmanship, which had been conventional wisdom before the war, went out while the making of a fast buck came in. It was then fashionable among builders, who naturally belonged to the same social groups, to discuss their profit margins. Profits could only come to those who built fast (interest costs were important then too), and who could build cheaply.

This is not to say that all tract houses were junk, they certainly were not, but there was no premium to the builder who built quality **especially** in houses that sold in the early 1950s for under $16,000. However 25 years later after the original apartments called 608s were built, it was indeed difficult to find any still operating. They are either abandoned or torn down—a miserable end to the federal government's dreams of decent housing for all. It seemed that whatever the minimum specifications established by the FHA were, these minimums came to mean the maximum specification (standard) to be incorporated in these early FHA projects.

During this postwar period, our highest institutions of learning together with the National Association of Realtors and its numerous affiliates began to give courses in real estate appraising, property management, and more recently, real estate investing. The National Association of Home Builders also cooperated with our learning institutions, junior colleges and universities all over the country. Courses were offered from design to blueprint reading, to cost estimating to fundamentals of home building.

As a result of these courses and the leaning toward professionalism among both the home builders and Realtors,[1] some college students had some general background in home building and at least an overview of the real estate industry. By the early 1960s, our best colleges and universities were graduating students with either bachelor or master's degrees in business administration, some with majors in real estate.

---

[1]Realtor is a **service mark.** The National Association of Realtors defines it as follows: "REALTOR® is a registered collective membership mark which may be used only by real estate professionals who are members of the NATIONAL ASSOCIATION OF REALTORS® and subscribe to its strict Code of Ethics."

While the emphasis was to upgrade or professionalize both the home builders and Realtors on an educational basis, the real estate industry decided to upgrade their own personnel through their state associations. The program of professional education sponsored by a state real estate association, usually in conjunction with a university, has developed into learning centers called Realtors Institutes in virtually every state. Even tiny Delaware (less than 750,000 population) has a fine annual Realtors Institute, which is offered in conjunction with the University of Delaware at Newark, Delaware.

What has come out of these Realtors Institutes educational programs are a group of very well-informed Realtors who have spent a minimum of three full weeks, generally a week at a time every four to eight months studying virtually every facet of the real estate business. These Realtors, after taking a specified course of study, receive recognition in the form of a designation called G.R.I. (Graduate, Realtors Institute). Most graduates, proud of their G.R.I. designation, usually wear a pin with the G.R.I. logo embossed on it.

More importantly, these Realtors have taken time off from work for one full week, three different times, have spent eight hours daily in classes, spent another hour or two nightly going over the material they learned each day, and finally at the end of each week, they have taken a comprehensive examination that they must pass before they can enroll in the next higher class in the future. They must pass all three week-long sessions in order to receive the G.R.I. designation.

The National Association of Realtors, which has approximately 700,000 members, has sponsored the Realtors Institute programs. Because the colleges and universities many Realtors have attended do not educate a person to become a practitioner, the Realtors Institutes endeavor to fill this educational void.

Here's an interesting sidelight about the Realtors Institutes. Each instructor is rated, individually, on his or her expertise in the organization (the outline) of the material, the presentation of the material, and, more importantly, whether the student believes the instructor should be invited to return as an instructor in the future. Unlike university lecturers, instructors, and professors, there is no tenure for Realtors Institute instructors. The old adage, "Those that can, do— those that can't, teach," does not apply at the institutes. Every instructor makes his or her living in a specific phase of the real estate business. On rare occasions, the institute may hire a college professor to handle a course in psychology or motivation, because many Realtors Institute instructors do not have the academic credentials to instruct in certain areas. The dull instructors (the droners and verbal cripples are weeded out after one session) are no longer on the staff of the next session; thus the longer the institute has been organized, generally the better the quality of instruction.

The Realtors Institutes of North Carolina and Virginia (in the mid-Atlantic area) are just two examples of fine Realtors Institutes both having been organized prior to 1955.

Because it is impossible to properly research what you are doing or contemplate doing without proper research tools, it is practically imperative that you attend the three one-week sessions provided by the Realtors Institute. You will not necessarily need to be a Realtor to enroll in these classes. Many state associations will also allow attorneys or accountants to attend. To find out if you are eligible to attend, you may call your local real estate board (listed in the white pages) and obtain the name and address of the education director of your state real estate association. The education director who is a staff person (their salaries come from Realtors' dues) in the state association are generally delightful and helpful people as they deal with a wide range of personalities. Get in touch with them. The courses offered are among the best research tools available in America today. After an individual has received a G.R.I. designation he or she is eligible to attend postgraduate courses offered by the state Realtors Institutes. These postgraduate courses are simply dynamite! They offer more "how to" knowledge in an ethical, concise, and precise way than any course in any university or college that attempts to teach a similar course.

One of the reasons the postgraduate courses are so alive and challenging is the average age of the student is around 42. These are not your typical postgraduate college students. They want to learn; they have given up their own time to learn and most importantly, their **own** money. Under these no-nonsense conditions (postgraduate students do not take examinations), the instructors teach virtually every major specialty that can be identified in the real estate industry.

Let's go back to the educated business administration graduates of the late 1950s and early 1960s instead of the typical builder of the 1950s. How did they do as developers? Not bad, but not well either. If you want to know how well they did, merely look critically at what was built in your town in the 1960s. If you find buildings that turn you off aesthetically, the developers made a mistake. If you see a commercial building such as an office building or a shopping center that doesn't please you in terms of function, then the developers probably made mistakes.

Let's examine some of the research techniques that my partner and I use prior to **every** development. Let's first go back to the early 1960s when we were about to develop our first high-rise apartment house project. By this time we had developed or acquired approximately 2,000 garden apartments.

Before we had even contemplated the purchase of land, we examined over 30 apartment buildings. They were located not only in Washington, D.C., and its suburbs in Maryland and Virginia, but in Philadelphia, Baltimore, New York City, Boston, Pittsburgh, and Chicago. Since my partner and I were active in real estate association work, both at the local and national levels, we had easy access to developers in all of the major cities in which were located the apartment houses we wanted to study. We didn't use these contacts, however, as we reasoned that the one person most familiar with the apartment's assets and liabilities (and from whom we could expect an honest answer) was the resident manager.

We didn't pretend we were trying to rent an apartment, we just showed up at the building and asked to speak to the resident manager. We presented our business cards and also a sample of one of my pictures. Years ago I had two-dollar bills padded together (45 of them) and then bound with a cover which reads, "Custom engraved exclusively for Richard H. Swesnik." Each bill was then fitted with my picture precisely over Jefferson's face. Since it is illegal to permanently disfigure or otherwise alter federal money, each picture was stuck on with temporary adhesive.

In order to spend the money, the recipient would peel off my picture and the crisp two-dollar bill was ready to go into regular circulation. Shortly after presenting our cards and the two-dollar bill, we would be speaking to the resident manager, or in his absence, to a rental clerk. We always asked the same question: "Can you tell us, aside from location, what are the five **worst** features of this building? Before you answer, let me tell you that I will give you a two-dollar bill with my picture on it for each **bad** feature up to five that the residents complain most about."

Some $300 later we had answers from approximately 30 resident managers and rental clerks. There was no hesitation from the personnel we questioned about what was wrong with their buildings. They hardly heard anything complimentary about their apartment buildings, except on rare occasions.

Many of the answers we received were duplicates of previous responses, and because our survey was conducted in the late 1960s, some of the responses are now technologically obsolete. For example, we usually found among the first two or three responses that the women hated to defrost their refrigerators. By the mid-1960s most manufacturers had eliminated the defrosting process. I take no credit for the technological changes that occurred in the manufacturing of refrigerators. Because it was the complaint that was most often registered, somehow changes did come about.

As an aside, I learned that **any** household chore that tied down the homemaker was unacceptable. Look at how many new apartments feature washers and driers inside the apartment. Many real estate practitioners feel that this change came about because women were afraid to go to the laundry rooms on their own floors because of fears of assault. This sounds like it should be the real reason to include washers and driers in the confines of one's own apartments. I don't think it is. Women still hate to be tied down while waiting for their wash to get ready. Our respondents all felt that large laundry rooms in one central location within an apartment building were acceptable if they did the laundry themselves. If a person was hired to do the washing and drying for them, they opted for smaller laundry facilities on the same floor as their apartment, ostensibly to keep an eye on their employee. No one back in the early 1960s suggested that washers and dryers should actually be in an individual apartment. Had they so suggested, we certainly would have incorporated washers and driers within each unit.

The other most frequent complaints were:

1. Lack of room, i.e., counter, eating, and storage space within the kitchen.
2. Not enough closet space.

3. Lack of medicine cabinet space in the bathrooms as well as counter space.

4. Lack of telephone or master TV outlets in the appropriate rooms, e.g., telephone outlets in the bathrooms, and master TV outlets in the dens or bedrooms.

5. Not enough electrical outlets, especially in the kitchens and bathrooms.

A lot of funny things happened when we took all of these complaints and (without architectural help) designed rooms and features to eliminate these negatives. The kitchens were designed so that even in a 500-square-foot executive efficiency apartment, there were not only enough cabinets and work surfaces, but we divided the kitchen from the living room-dining area by a half wall, which from the floor up allowed for storage and which was high enough to sit up to when using the top to dine on. In the smallest apartments, two persons could dine simultaneously. The half wall was made even more useful by hanging kitchen cabinets from the ceiling.

In the larger units, we designed the kitchens so every kitchen could hold at least a circular table and chairs for four persons. In the larger 3 bedroom, $2\frac{1}{2}$ bath apartments, the kitchens could accommodate as many as six persons for dining.

In relation to the total apartment space, the kitchens had a much larger square foot ratio than many of the buildings we had visited. We appropriated some of the space normally devoted to the dining room area to make for larger kitchens with extensive counter and cabinet space.

I have invented "Swesnik's closet axiom" that says, "No matter how large a closet can be built, any woman can fill it." When I built a new home, I had a $31\frac{1}{2}$ foot $\times$ $10\frac{1}{2}$ foot closet adjacent to the master bedroom. It took my wife only 11 short months to not only fill the closet, but she even toyed with the idea of moving **my** clothes to a different closet in the house.

What I'm really saying is there probably can't be closets that are too large. People simply have difficulty in giving or throwing away clothes that are no longer "chic." Remember Carmen Miranda shoes? Short skirts? Nehru jackets? Leisure suits? Pointed men's boots? Enough said. There are no good rules of thumb for determining the minimum closet sizes for a given apartment area but you cannot attract or keep good residents in an apartment or rental house that has too little closet space. On a recent trip to south Florida to inspect some condominiums, I observed that Florida developers are very good about designing lots of good, and more importantly, well-designed closets. You may wish to make a research trip to south Florida.

I really went to work in the bathroom areas. Since most of the bathroom complaints were about storage space for cosmetics, medicines, etc., I purchased extra long (from top to bottom) medicine cabinets and attached at least three of these extra long cabinets together. I not only provided for more cabinet space in this fashion, but because they were all mirrored, the rooms also looked brighter and larger. As an aside, we discovered that many developers were using fluorescent tubes above or attached to the medicine cabinets. This was not only an energy saver but fluorescents do last longer than incandescent lamps, thus costing less as well as not giving off heat. But most developers had paid no attention to the fluorescent tubes. Most gave off a bluish hue and people looked ghastly, ghoulish, or both, when the lights were turned on. This was easily corrected by ordering fluorescent tubes that gave off a pinkish hue. Even after a bad night, almost everyone looks rather decent under a pink light early in the morning.

I also tried to answer the bathroom storage problem by designing deep (front to back) floor cabinets and covered them with marble (elegant but difficult and expensive to maintain) or DuPont's Corian. Corian is not as attractive as marble but is easy to work with (cut and install) and is also easy to maintain. It is more expensive than the plastics (Formica, Micarta, etc.) but is well worth the difference because it definitely **reduces the owning costs.**

Whenever you ask either the architect or the general contractor to explain why, for example, the cast iron grate exhaust is above the tub in the bathroom, the usual response is that it is "standard." When my partner and I were doing our research we were told that the exhaust fan over the tub was standard. Whenever you hear the word "standard" from your architect or your general contractor, be assured the real reason is obscure or long forgotten.

I have reasoned that the exhaust over the tub has two purposes.

1. Since it is cast iron and has a painted surface, it is at about room temperature. When the hot water is turned on, tiny rivulets of water form on the grate. Some people call this "sweating." At any rate, in time the paint will be eaten away and the grate will rust. It will then need to be painted, which is time consuming and, as a consequence, expensive. The old paint is scrubbed off, red lead applied, and after it dries, then a base coat, and finally a finished coat of enamel. Therefore, its number one purpose is to **rust.**

2. If the exhaust system works at all it will have a tendency to suck or pull the shower curtain inward. When one takes a shower, filling up of the remaining air encapsulated within the shower area with cascading water causes the curtain to be sucked across your back. I have, therefore, concluded the second purpose of locating the exhaust system over the tub is to ensure **a wet shower curtain will be sucked across the user's back.**

This exhaust system is nothing more than an attempt to conform to a building code that says that a bathroom without a window must be mechanically ventilated. Neither you nor I have to be mechanical engineers to understand that moisture isn't what needs to be exhausted from a bathroom. Under most exhaust systems, moisture isn't exhausted anyway. What we want to exhaust out of a bathroom are odors. Anybody with a modicum of intelligence understands that a proper exhaust system would entail removing objectionable odors and surely would place the exhaust intake above the toilet. I did this!

On a trip to Jamaica (in the Caribbean, not Long Island) in the late 1950s, I was impressed by the fact that the developer of the resort at which we were guests had enough foresight to design the bathroom facility so that the toilet was in a small room by itself with its own exhaust fan located within the larger bathroom area. This meant that whenever the toilet itself was in use, the bathroom still could be used by another person for showering, shaving, putting on make-up, or whatever. If husband and wife occupying the hotel room were both leaving for breakfast or dressing for dinner, the bathroom was not paralyzed by someone using the toilet. This seemed to make such good sense that I incorporated the basic idea of an enclosed toilet within the bathroom area in the design of our new high-rise apartment house.

Because we wished to have our residents emotionally comfortable, we designed the toilet room so that it was approximately 4 feet × 5 feet. At that time, entire bathrooms were "standard" at 5 feet × 8 feet so this design represented a radical departure from the norm.

The toilet room kept expanding in size until at 4 feet × 5 feet it was large enough to install a companion bidet and thereby lies the setting for a funny incident that happened to me. When the building was first opened for future residents to inspect, I (personally) accepted all phone inquiries from the prospective residents. One beautiful spring morning the phone rang in my office and when I said "hello," the luscious feminine voice on the other end of the conversation stated that she couldn't quite fathom the bathroom layout. I reasoned that she was confused by the side-by-side toilet and bidet installation in a separate compartment or room. I told myself, "Swes, she obviously doesn't know what a bidet is, and renting the apartments is going to involve some educating of future residents," so I said "Do you know what a bidet is?" She immediately shot back, "If you can't do a handstand in the shower, it must be the next best thing." By the time I had recovered from shock and laughter, she had hung up.

People were "hung up" about discussing bidets. I looked at the written material available from the Plumbing Fixtures Manufacturers Association and found the written data on the bidet, "gross"—to put it mildly. The young lady who told me about doing a handstand in the shower really helped me tremendously in the writing of a brochure. Credit for producing 6,000 brochures must go to the American-Standard from whom we purchased the bidets. The brochure I wrote is as follows:

"The Bidet"
(pronounced bee-day)

In every metropolitan city throughout South America and the European Continent, the better hotels and a surprising number of homes are equipped with a bidet. Men and women residing in these metropolitan areas use the bidet as regularly as we Americans shower or bathe.

Because many Americans feel the function of the bidet is too indelicate a subject to discuss, some do not understand its function. Quite a few think it is used for purposes mysteriously or vaguely related to sex. Lack of understanding and unwillingness to inquire as to its real purpose are the main reasons the bidet has not been a standard fixture in American bathrooms. Recently some of the finer American hotels, motels, and better apartment houses have installed them in their luxury suites. Production and sales of the bidet are now at an all time high.

how it operates

The bidet is approximately the same height and width as a water closet. It is nothing more than an upside-down shower. It is no sense a toilet nor a douche. Like a shower, it has a hot and cold water valve. When the hot and cold valves are turned on, the water swirls downward through the drain. The user tests the temperature by feeling the downward flowing water and adjusts the temperature to suit. As soon as the temperature is adjusted, the user sits down facing the controls. The user gently turns the large center valve and the water is redirected through a series of tiny holes upward in a spray approximately the size of a half dollar.

The large center valve is essentially a "power" control; should a gentle spray be desired, the power control is turned on just a little; if a more vigorous spray is desired the power control is turned on somewhat more.

That is all there is to the operation of a bidet. It is a temperature controlled rinse action with varying degrees of rinse power. Because the intensity of the spray can be regulated, it is the most hygienic and sanitary method known to cleanse the lower pelvic area. Most persons are sensitive in these areas and because the power rinse can be most gentle, it is the most satisfactory method of cleansing oneself without irritation. As in a shower, the center valve is turned off and the spray of water is redirected downward into the drain. The hot and cold valves are turned off and the operation of the bidet is concluded.

there is no better way

Besides personal hygienic care, many men and women who have been directed by a physician to take "sitz baths" obtain special benefits from the warm and gentle spraying action of the bidet. Because removal of all clothing is not necessary, cleansing of the lower pelvic area can be accomplished quickly. Additionally, it is sometimes used for gentle rinsing of the feet prior to having a pedicure in order to soften the nails and cuticles.

Anyone who has ever owned a bidet will never be without one again . . . and oddly enough, it is the men who eventually become the biggest boosters of the bidet."

Other developers kidded me about building a high-rise that was all kitchens, baths, and closets (and bedrooms) and not much in terms of living room and dining room areas. Now really, when you live in an apartment home, how much time do you spend in the living room or the dining room? My partner and

I had the last laugh—we almost tripled our money (ours and our investors) during a three-year owning period after which we sold the project to a specialist who converted the building to condominium ownership.

It is so easy to incorporate accessible telephone, electric, and master TV antenna outlets in an apartment building prior to its construction. Generally, once the shovel hits the ground, it is too late (or too expensive) to change the specifications. Suffice it to say, phone jacks can be put almost anywhere and your local phone company will help you with this, if you but ask.

A recent survey showed that television is watched by 93 percent of the population in a room other than the living room. Yet, some developers put master TV outlets in the living rooms and bedrooms only. How about the kitchens, dens, and bathrooms? The Stanford Court Hotel in San Francisco, universally recognized as among the finest hotels in the Bay Area, not only has a TV outlet in the bathroom, it has a small TV! That's luxury! How about shaving in the morning while listening to and glimpsing "Good Morning America" or the "Today Show"? One day when perhaps neither of these shows are still on the air, the residents of a building developed by you will appreciate your developmental skills and thoughtfulness by having thought to put a TV outlet in the bathroom.

Another area where the developer can bring his skills to bear is the kitchen. Include enough electrical outlets! Consider that all of the following electrical appliances can be or could be plugged in on a more or less permanent basis:

1. refrigerator and/or freezer
2. electric stove (even gas stoves need an electric outlet to turn on the oven light and clocks, if any)
3. mixer, blender, or food processor
4. toaster or toaster-oven
5. electric can opener
6. coffee maker
7. electric knife
8. crock cooker
9. electronic oven
10. electric wok
11. electric coffee grinder
12. electric clock
13. auxiliary floor electric heater (in case the central heating is off)
14. radio or TV
15. electric fork

And how about enough electric outlets in the bathroom for the following:

1. electric shower
2. hair dryer
3. electric shave cream heater
4. electric toothbrush
5. electric water pik
6. electric shoe brush
7. electronic scale
8. sun lamp
9. electric iron
10. radio, TV, or clock
11. electric make-up mirror

The research required to make your development as good as you know how depends entirely on **you.** You alone must determine if a market exists. Real estate economists can only give you a picture of the past; they are not in the business of forecasting. Market absorption studies do not guarantee a waiting market, they only indicate what is probable based on historical data (usually the decade just passed). Can you change the market? Not really, but you can try to avoid failure by researching your brains out prior to committing to buy land. If you are too important or too busy to do your own research, you can and will make some costly mistakes. It's better not to develop at all than to contribute nothing to the development process.

Many earlier developers imitated their own successes. Once they developed something that was successful, they repeated it, almost to the last detail, the same thing they had done earlier even if in a different location. As a result of imitating their own or other successful developments and not doing any research designed to improve their product, much of what they developed is technically, economically, or functionally obsolete. The worst mistake you can make is to develop an obsolete building.

It is unfortunate that probably at least 40 percent of all new developments are obsolete in one way or another and should never have been started. Mistakes are too costly. No book could list every common mistake made by a real estate developer—there must be 10,000 ways to err. Nor will I try to make such a list. There follows, however, a discussion that shows how to develop a strategy for successful developing. In the last analysis, only **you** determine the specifications. This seems to surprise many seemingly well-informed people. Who do they think determines the specifications in any development? The architect? Are you kidding? The builder? You must be joking—he can only build what the plans call for. It's **you!**

If you decide to develop an apartment complex, you must decide the apartment mix: you must make the decision as to how many different sizes and type of efficiencies (one large room); junior one-bedroom apartments (no dining room but fixed or movable bedroom partitions); one-bedroom apartments (usually with eating space in the kitchen, a dining room or dining area, and usually 1 or $1\frac{1}{2}$ baths); one-bedroom-and-den apartments (same as one bedroom except there is a small additional room usually off the living room and up the size scale to 2 bedrooms (usually $1\frac{1}{2}$ or 2 baths); three bedrooms usually $2\frac{1}{2}$ baths; and three-bedroom and den apartments, with at least $2\frac{1}{2}$ baths.

The mix is absolutely and solely the developer's responsibility. If you need advice, and in this area we all do, your best bet is to check with resident managers in the area you intend to develop and in buildings with which your development will be competitive. They can tell you which apartments they manage seem to rent the fastest and which seem to move the slowest when vacancies do occur. Beware of the rental price structure if you hear, "Everything is always rented here," or "We never have a vacancy." These expressions obviously translate into: "Our rental prices are very low" or "We are too chicken to ask for rent increases."

Similar research can be done by others for you. It is never the same as doing the research yourself. Don't be too important to spend some personal research time before you develop a project of considerable value, which will probably be in place for forty years. Surely it is a matter important enough for you to spend the time researching it yourself. If you constantly ask questions of both your architect and general contractor and do your own research, it will be difficult to develop a loser. There are enough cyclical demand problems, strikes and acts of God that could slow you down, thus making the job cost more. Don't create more problems by merely duplicating someone else's past success. It is possible that a project rents up quickly because of its exquisite location or a combination of certain fortuitous circumstances. But your success odds will get better if you spend more time researching your proposed project.

you determine the specifications

As indicated before, you, as the developer, are responsible for making decisions regarding the design and specifications. Because any material can be bought for either more or less money, you must determine a standard at the outset.

You can have a high-quality building without high material costs. Your task is to ensure that your completed project is **concordant** with the other buildings in the area. If many people "love" your building, many will "hate" it too. Since you can't please everyone, endeavor to displease as few people as possible. This may seem to be a terribly negative strategy, but it **works!**

Part of your job as a developer, as displeasing as it may seem to be, is to know every kind of material that will be used in your building. Let's take some examples of the kinds of things you must do. Let's again use an office building as an example.

the building's exterior

You must decide on the material used for your facade. The cheapest thing to use initially is brick. It is relatively inexpensive in the initial installation. There are some beautiful brick buildings in existence virtually everywhere. The main problems with brick are:

1. It is porous—too much rain and it may leak.
2. The mortar will quickly become dirty.
3. As the building settles, some or much of the brick may crack along the mortar lines.

Only you can make the decision. Do not be influenced by your architect. How many buildings has he managed and for how long?

On the other end of the cost spectrum is marble. Aside from marble's tendency to absorb dirt at the joints, it is in the opinion of many a statement of quality. I do not argue with these opinions. I like the translucent look of marble. I especially am fond of Tennessee pink marble. Probably the best looking facade of any building in the metropolitan area of Washington is the Australian Embassy on Scott Circle. Its facade is Tennessee pink marble, and when wet with rain it takes on a pink hue that warms up a dark, cool, rainy day.

The major problem with marble is its cost. You are probably familiar with the Latin expression, "De gustibus non est disputandum," (matters of taste are not disputable). You cannot "turn on" everyone. Just don't "turn them off." Marble, especially Tennessee pink, is probably six to eight times as expensive as brick. Remember, if it won't reduce the owning cost or produce better rentals, you are making a mistake by using a more expensive material than standard. Unfortunately, marble facades do not increase the rent or significantly reduce the owning cost.

You are not settling for less if you use precast concrete aggregate for your facade. You are certainly using an acceptable material if you select anodized aluminum for the facade. This can be done effectively without driving up your energy costs. We merely make our windows smaller and recess them so as to reduce direct sunlight. You may use a tinted glass facade with anodized aluminum. Some persons feel that metal and glass buildings are not only contemporary but elegant too.

the building's elevator system

You are guaranteed vacancies in your office building, no matter what attractions it has, if your elevators are inadequate to service your office building tenants. Something is wrong with the speed of the elevators, their individual sizes, or there are too few, if waiting time exceeds 45 seconds. We are constantly striving for a maximum waiting time of 30 seconds.

Westinghouse and Otis probably make the most elevators for high-rise buildings; their representatives, usually sales engineers, will work with you, independently of your architect, if you so desire. Make sure you take into account "down-time"; the elevators all need systematic maintenance and it seems the more sophisticated the system, the more there is that can go out of whack.

Naturally, elevator sales engineers are proud of their product and down-time is hardly ever mentioned. Our own office policy dictates we are not interested in office buildings with less than three elevators. A common problem in two-elevator buildings is that one or the other may be in down-time. The resulting mess of waiting tenants earns your building ill will. The situation is exacerbating in one-elevator buildings, even if the buildings are only two or three stories tall. Some people are unable to walk up a flight of steps. They don't have to be crippled, or have heart or lung problems. Just try getting up or down a flight of steps when your leg is in a cast. The thrust of this discussion is to ensure there is **proper** elevator service. This means you need at least three cabs of decent width, depth, and height that travel at least 350 feet per minute in buildings not over 12 stories. Any building over this height may require faster cabs (500 feet per minute or faster) and faster cabs mean each elevator will be probably **gearless.** Gearless machines generally run at 500 feet per minute and faster and "feel" different to the passenger. They accelerate and decelerate much more smoothly than the conventional geared machine.

In planning the waiting time before elevator doors close, remember **you** determine the speed with which the doors will close after someone enters or leaves the cab. Assuming a gong sounds as each cab arrives to answer a call, be sure to allow enough time for a passenger to enter the cab. This will depend on where the cabs are located on each floor, whether or not they face each other, and how many cabs are available. I am not trying to be humorous, but I once fooled around with the timing of elevator door openings and closings until I had things so speeded up that only one person out of three could get to the cab before the door closed. The slower passengers finally discovered what was happening and barraged our management office with complaints. We finally adjusted the speed so that when the cab arrived on the floor that was calling, all but the slowest people could hear the gong and get in the cab safely.

Every once in a while, don't you get on a cab in an office building (on an upper floor) and it seems like you're waiting forever for the darn door to close so you can get moving? This can all be arranged **before** the shovel hits the ground by talking with the elevator people first. You must do your own research by visiting competitive buildings and taking a ride or two.

Elevator signs have always interested me because they all seemed so stupid when I first started to develop office buildings. In my first visit with a Westinghouse representative, I asked why the round button said, "door open." Before he could answer, I interrupted by saying that I didn't like "door open" because it sounded like Indian movie talk. He replied that it was the American way—wasn't it? Since he had a good sense of humor, we exchanged jokes for a little while, and then I asked if our elevators could say "open door" instead of the other way. "No problem," he said, and more importantly, no extra charge.

Almost everyone has experienced the frustration of standing inside an elevator cab with the doors open and just as the doors began to close, someone else tries to get inside, but they are too late and the doors close. Because a developer has the job of easing daily frustrations, it seemed rather easy to me to solve this little problem. The frustration of seeing someone racing to the elevator only to have the doors close is caused by the inability of those person(s) already in the cab to find the "open door" button. Inasmuch as "open door" is the same size as all the other buttons, it is not easily found. Our Westinghouse man was up to the task and for a few dollars extra, we could have "open door" at the bottom of the panel about four or five inches wide, constantly lighted, making it a cinch to locate. All in all, we stopped the Indian movie talk; the wording was changed to a command, "open door"; this sign was made larger than any other sign on the control panel; and it was always lighted. In our new office buildings, all our elevator signs must conform to these changes.

As a developer, in order to help relieve life's little frustrations, you should be very careful of other aspects of elevator signs. Recently my wife and I went shopping in a new facility. The signs in the elevator were so poor neither of us could figure out how to take the elevator back to our car. Using initials instead of words (each button should say something) makes for confusion. Does "G" mean ground floor, and if so, which ground level? The building may have two or three floors underground. Does "G" mean garage? If so, which garage floor? Does "L" mean lobby or loft? Some office buildings have a low ceiling loft or storage space on the level just above the lobby floor. This is especially confusing when the control panel also lists "l."

To redo the elevator control panels in a building after it is finished is almost unthinkable because of the tremendous cost involved. Do it right the first time. Have your Westinghouse or Otis (or whomever else you wish to do business with) understand that you want the lobby floor buttons to spell out "LOBBY." If there is a main garage level, where the cashier is located, your signage should say "GARAGE CASHIER." You can, and should, be very specific. Your elevator supplier and installer wants your building to do well. Let him help you.

A final word about elevators. It is very critical to have elevator heights at least 10 feet 5 inches clear from floor to ceiling. Acquisitions of office buildings (Chapter 5), has a discussion on elevator cab heights.

char service

Tenants move out of office buildings because of poor air conditioning and heating, bad char (janitor) service, or poor elevator service. You cannot effectively do your own char service unless you own or manage many buildings. It again requires your personal research to obtain the finest char service available in your community. This can be accomplished by discussions with competitive commercial property managers. They will level with you.

Incidentally, one of America's strengths, as distinguished from other western countries, is the honest and frequent exchange of relevant and important technical data among competitors. This is especially true among developers of fine real estate. Because of this, you will rarely find any resistance to discussions by and among your competitors. Because there is a real paucity of written data that you can rely on in planning your buildings, it is imperative that you visit your competitors. Some developers feel it is an example of their ignorance if they ask another developer questions relating to some phase of the development process. This is wrong, wrong, wrong. You can merely evaluate the definition of intelligence and see that it is wrong. Intelligence is defined as the ability to **learn.** Do not make the learning process more difficult than it need be. Be assured of one thing: no matter how difficult or complex the development problem— somewhere, somehow, some other developer has faced the problem and solved it. Find him. He's probably in your home town, county, or state.

the guts of the building

Among the other important considerations are the guts of the building: your heating and air conditioning systems. Even though your mechanical engineer (through the architect) proposes a certain system, it is up to you to determine where it has been done before. Nothing is more critical than this. Do not let anybody experiment with anything new in your building. Your research demands that you examine anything that is proposed to you to make sure it works. Remember, you are trying to develop positive cash flow, not win awards.

plans and specs

Because **you** determine the specifications, the plans and "specs" should be reviewed not only by you, but also by professional commerical property managers and whenever possible, by another developer. Your office should be a great source of design and specs review. Your money could not be spent better than the payment of fees to outside consultants, certainly on the mechanical and structural aspects of the project. All the big money you will make will be made ultimately at sale. Make sure you have an error-free building to sell some eight to twelve years hence. Poor John Hancock Insurance Company! Whoever was in charge of the development of their building in Boston has learned by now the wisdom of research. Imagine windows blowing out almost daily before they were replaced at a purported cost of $10,000 each.

seeking the permanent loan commitment

There are many insurance companies, pension funds, savings banks, and quite a few savings and loan associations that make first morgage loans on quality properties. The difficulty confronting the developer is to know which specific lender has future available funds to commit at the time he is seeking a future permanent loan.

The developing process can take quite a long time, and permanent loan commitments for as long as 30 to 36 months are not unusual. There are three basic things any developer must take into consideration: loan amount, annual constant (annual interest and principal payments), and "points." A "point" is defined as 1 percent of the gross amount of the loan. It is a fact that most developers use a mortgage broker to obtain their financing for them. It is quite impossible for a developer to know who among all the lenders is in the market at a specific time for a specific type of loan, and who is also competitive as to interest rates, constants, pay-off terms, and points.

Not knowing any of the above facts can be very time consuming and might result in no loan at all. Most lenders look askance at a loan that has been shopped around. Since many principal loan officers attend mortgage banking industry functions on a relatively frequent basis, they get to know one another. Since they cannot help talking shop with one another, you can imagine the embarrassment that can be caused when one loan officer, working for Equitable Life Assurance Society, says to another, "I'm working on a great loan for an office building in Washington, D.C. It is located on the corner of 20th and K Streets, N.W." And the other loan officer who works for Prudential Life Insurance Company says, "Gee, that sounds great, who is the developer?" When the first loan officer says, "Swesnik and Blum," the same loan application better not be on the Prudential Loan officer's desk! The result is predictable: Swesnik and Blum won't be able to obtain the loan from **either** company.

An analogous story will help you understand. A television interviewer once asked an Arab sheik how could he have four wives. The sheik replied that we did the same thing in America. The only difference was that he did it simultaneously while we Americans did it serially, one at a time. The moral is that in America you had better not apply to more than **one** lender at a time for the same loan. It may be all right in Saudi Arabia (though I doubt it), but it just isn't done here. Here you do it one at a time. Your best bet is to find a mortgage loan broker who represents **you,** not the lender. The difference between a mortgage broker and a mortgage banker is quite evident. Traditionally, a mortgage broker represents the borrower, whereas the mortgage banker represents the lender. The mortgage banker represents one or more lenders on an exclusive geographic basis; he services the loan by collecting it monthly and frequently ensuring real estate taxes are paid and doing other chores for the lender. Thus to a large extent, he is the lender's alter ego in your specific geographic area. Another difference is that one or two clients of the mortgage banker are sometimes out of the market at a given time. A mortgage broker always has a handle on institutions that are in the market.

Another advantage of having a mortgage broker representing you is that he can give you a status report on the market conditions. You will need to know how much you can borrow and the approximate annual constant many months in advance of your actual negotiations with your lender. With this information, you will be able to prepare a tentative pro forma cash flow operating statement to aid you in your earlier decision making, especially in the proposed rental structure. Even though rents are properly a function of market demand, you are not alone and you are not functioning in a business vacuum. The rents you will necessarily have to collect are tied to costs—and there will be no larger cost than that of servicing your permanent loan. Your competition is also functioning in relatively the same market place, thus his costs are similar to yours. In order to show a decent cash flow on the equity dollars you and your associates are investing, you must obtain enough rents to justify **all** of your costs.

Your strategy in seeking the permanent loan is to employ a mortgage broker and borrow at the lowest possible rate with the lowest annual constant, insuring that you will not need more than 80 percent occupancy to break even.

why you are in the driver's seat in obtaining lower interest and lower annual constants

One of the most pleasant aspects of seeking a permanent loan commitment is the knowledge that you are about to become a "preferred" client. Of course, you will be romanced by your mortgage broker; his job is to perform as best he can so that he will have a steady client in the future. More importantly, you make his job easier for him for a variety of reasons. First, your location will be a good one and getting better. Second, you will have done your homework regarding the design and specifications. Your best asset, however, is that you are **not** seeking to borrow out. This one fact is the most important one you will have going for you.

You will recognize how important it is to never seek the top loan amount once you understand how most lenders are organized for loan purposes. When your mortgage broker seeks the loan for you, he will capsulize all of the important data: location, size, pro forma cash flow statement, a brief description of your background, and the date at which the permanent funding will be required. He will also indicate the amount of loan requested. He will then circulate this data among the few lenders he knows who are seeking loans to be funded at some future date (this may be less than a year for garden apartments, 18 to 24 months for high-rise apartments, and two years, up to three years, for office buildings).

As is usually the case, he will elicit interest from one or more lenders. After all, he is not shooting arrows into the sky hoping to hit a flying duck; he has previously zeroed in on only those lenders with the desire, experience, and capability to make such loans. The interest in your future project that he will receive will be from a loan officer, let's say, of a major insurance company. The loan officer may not be geographically located in the city where you are located, and he might request a market analysis to help him determine if you will have problems renting up, based on market absorption. Your mortgage broker may have this data readily available, or may ask you to hire a real estate economist to make such a study.

As indicated earlier such studies are hot air, but you will comply anyway. Merely understanding that a junior or middle management person (the loan officer) needs this information for his files, will help keep you from getting irritated. No loan officer in his right mind is anxious to recommend to his loan committee acceptance of a loan that could eventually become a problem loan: slow paying or ultimate foreclosure. He wants to save his neck, and thus he may request a market analysis. So, if requested, you let him protect himself by ordering such a study. Remember, you have a feeling for the market, he doesn't and needs assurance he is doing the right thing in eventually recommending your application for a loan to his committee. Be assured a request for a market study indicates serious interest on the part of a lender.

As soon as interest is shown in your proposed project from a specific lender, your mortgage broker will usually send a copy of the architect's general layout (but not the working drawings; they will have to be approved by the lender, but at this time it is much too early). Along with the general layouts, your architect may also furnish an artist's rendering of how the project will look when completed. This is usually done in color and we include at least one color rendering in our architect's contract. Naturally, my partnership pays for the rendering and any photos (copies) of the rendering. This cost is merely added in the price quoted by the architect. You will need these copies at a later date anyway. Your local newspaper(s) will want a photocopy of the rendering if they want to run a story about your project; your potential investors will also want to see it—they want to make sure they are investing in something that doesn't turn them off.

Again, one of the main reasons that a potential lender becomes interested is the amount of loan you are requesting. Most developers will be seeking a top loan. You won't be. This removes some of the "spots off the dice" as far as the loan officer is concerned. He knows that both now and at a later date, he cannot be accused of recommending a top or high loan. You make your loan officer emotionally comfortable by seeking only the amount of loan that you can service comfortably with only 80 percent occupancy. Because of this conservative approach, our loan record has been such that we feel we have a competitive marketing edge. We actually borrow at rates somewhat lower than our competitors, and we always seem to have a longer time to repay the loan. This makes our **annual constants** lower than our competition.

It is very important to your leasing program that you are not leasing under near panic conditions, where you **must** have the tenant. Some developers have managed to borrow out in the initial instance, but in fact needed 95 percent occupancy to break even. This is tremendous pressure to put on your leasing program, assuming you could obtain such a top loan. Because the risks to the lender increase when they make top loans, even in "hot" markets, be assured both the interest rate and the annual constant will be higher. Let your competitors obtain these top loans, let them sweat in the leasing market or lose their buildings through foreclosure. Isn't that a stupid strategy? Remember you will have partners and can obtain as much as 25 percent of the venture for acting as the developer. Earlier you were asked what was 25 percent of nothing. The answer is nothing, and add to that a couple of years of hard work at **no** pay. In no way can a certified loser help your track record.

At our offices we frequently are called by lenders or their representatives to find out if we have any projects "on the boards." The reason we receive such inquiries is that we are known to ask for under the maximum amounts—and consequently our loans are safer. It might come as a shock to you that there are lenders out there that are primarily interested in safety. Believe me, there are such lenders. All of them. How long do you think a senior vice-president in charge of real estate loans working for a major insurance company would last if he is supervising a loan portfolio that is loaded with "maximum" loans that are not being repaid? He cannot blame market conditions—his superiors need not tell him that well-capitalized projects can readily weather bad market conditions for a considerable period of time. His superiors need not tell him that if a project has $3.5 million in cash invested above a $16 million loan in a project, when it is finished it will be worth over $22 million and that, barring a national economic collapse, the loan is safe and will be repaid.

Make no mistake about this: safety is the lender's creed—speculation and chance can produce mistakes putting the lender and the company he works for out of business. Make it your creed too.

You want to last. Once your lender (loan officer) wants to make the permanent loan commitment, he will negotiate with your mortgage broker his very best rate of interest and the best annual constant. He can make your annual constant extremely low once he knows the loan is safe and in a good location that may become the **best** a decade hence. He can give you 35-year pay-out terms but require a balloon (a balance due at a due date on the loan that is sooner than the scheduled amortization will repay it). Such a balloon may be at the end of 20 years, or even earlier. My own strategy forbids balloons earlier than 20 years. At any rate, once your lender commences serious negotiations, remember you are in the driver's seat. Your loan will be a safe one—he'll reach to make the loan in terms of both interest rate and annual constant.

avoiding lender participation

I have always sought to avoid lender participation in my partnership's loans because we are not seeking the top loan amount. I also strongly believe that if a lender wishes to participate in the fruits of my efforts beyond interest for his money, then he (the lender) should **invest** right along with the other partners and accept the possible risk of loss. After all, there is no such thing as something for nothing; even lenders know this. They will try to get as much additional interest as they can obtain; if you do not resist this, you will have an extra partner who is not investing. You need not be reminded that a lender is seeking interest on funds he is lending whereas an investor is seeking profits on funds **invested.** Anytime a lender starts behaving as an investor he is merely getting himself screwed up. Don't help the lender foul up mentally! Help your lender realize the dichotomy between a lender seeking interest and an investor seeking profits. Explain to him that his loan to you is a monetary asset. It has all the characteristics of a monetary asset: it has a **fixed** return, it is interest the lender obtains, the lender has a date at which the loan matures, and most of all the loan is a promise to pay. Explain to him the difference between a lender and an investor. The investor owns a non-monetary asset with all of its characteristics: there is no fixed return to the investor, cash flow distributions are **not** interest, there is no maturity date on the investment, and most of all there is no promise to pay.

For some reason unknown to me, the lenders are not always aware of these differences. We developers can have an important effect on the lenders by educating them as to the difference between lenders and investors. Besides, since you are not seeking the top loan amount, you will have no trouble avoiding lender participation in the equity.

Occasionally, however, a lender may offer you a **below** market loan with a "kicker"—a percentage of gross income well above your projections. You may want the loan, so compute the percentage as additional interest and see if it makes economic sense. If it does, take it, and if it doesn't, remember you are not developing income-producing properties for the sole benefit of the lenders.

points

The paying of points is just another way of paying a lender for the time and trouble he takes in first analyzing and evaluating your loan request and finally in deciding to offer you the permanent loan commitment. Points are usually considered as interest for federal income tax purposes. They are considered as income to the lender and as an expense to you. Unfortunately, the points you pay to the permanent lender are not deductible when paid. The amount of money paid as points can only be deducted annually, amortized over the life of the loan. As an example, suppose you obtain a permanent loan commitment in the face amount of $5 million and are required to pay one point ($50,000) to the lender. If the loan is for 20 years, you may deduct $2,500 each year as an additional interest expense for obtaining the loan. Because of the equal annual deductions of the permanent loan fee, it makes sense to avoid points attributable to the permanent loan. Points paid to your mortgage broker are not interest, but an expense in acquiring mortgage financing and therefore are similarly to be capitalized and deducted ratably over the term of the loan.

Some institutions, especially savings banks, prefer to make the construction loan on any projects that they will eventually fund the permanent loan. In instances where one lender makes both the permanent loan commitment and also acts as the construction lender, the lender frequently does not charge any points for the permanent loan. These charges are specifically for making the construction loan and all the extra work (inspections, draws,[2] etc.) that this entails. Under these circumstances, the points may be deducted as expenses during the construction period. Consult your tax attorney on the timing of the deductibility of points for construction loans.

Most lenders charge at least one point for making the permanent loan commitment. You may also have to pay your mortgage broker one point. On larger loans, in excess of $10 million, some mortgage brokers charge one point for the first $5 million and smaller amounts for the rest of the loan amount.

Most modern loans are "closed" usually for a period of 10 years from the date the permanent loan is recorded. From that time, the lenders have various terms, but they all relate to the payment of points. A typical situation wherein you cannot, indeed are forbidden, to pay off the loan during the first ten years is as follows. You pay off the loan by paying five points during the eleventh year and four points during the twelfth year, declining one point each year until the fifteenth year when the loan may be repaid in full by paying one point. Some lenders may attempt to close the loan for longer periods or charge a minimum of three points even after the loan is 15 years old.

I don't know how or when the lenders and the borrowers seem to have established an **adversary** relationship wherein they and the borrowers are constantly at odds and indeed may be scrapping with one another. Be assured that this need not be the case with you. Your mortgage broker should know who are the lenders with the worst reputations in the field and steer you away from them. You should always research this yourself by finding out from other developers whom not to borrow from. Some major lenders have such a horrible track record when it comes to making adjustments after the permanent loan is on record that you would do well to avoid them altogether. You may be required to go back to your lender for an extension of time if you find it slow going during the rent-up period. How tenderly will your lender treat you? Will he charge you more points for such an extension?

If things are really slow, will your lender tear off your arms by charging you a huge amount for deferring interest and principal? How about refinancing, say after five good years of steadily increasing cash flow? Will they make you a new loan at favorable terms, or, because you are locked in, will they stick it to you? Unfortunately, there is no published list of lenders with loving and tender decision-making personnel with whom you can deal. People who will not jump all over you in an attempt to win points from their supervisors by showing how tough they are, are not too difficult to find. There are however, a lot of toughies who like to arm twist, especially if you are in the slightest bit of trouble. Now is

---

[2]Monthly progress payments to you by your construction lender to cover some of your costs at that particular time during the construction period. Draws usually require your architect's certification that the work is in place.

not too early for you to research the major lenders and make a firm determination as from whom you will **not** seek loans.

Because I failed to do my homework in this area, quite early in my career, I acquired and syndicated an apartment project whose lender was represented by a loan officer who was an unadulterated schmuck. We were locked into a bad loan and he would not accept any amount of points we offered to get us out of the bad situation. I finally went above his head to the senior vice-president in charge of real estate of this insurance company (among the top 15) and appealed to his sense of fairness and decency only to find out he was worse than the loan officer! Now one does not hang up the phone, nor tell a senior vice-president of real estate of a major insurance company to stick the loan up his "ear," but I did.

At this writing, that senior vice-president not only is no longer employed by the insurance company, but is heading a real estate investment trust that is about to go belly-up. Leo Durocher once said, "Nice guys finish last." This may be true in sports. But in business, I don't believe it. Indeed, I have had occasion to observe some top executives in this country, and I find them all (with rare exceptions) to be fine fellows. They couldn't have made it to the top if they were not, because their superiors would not have recommended them for promotions. You do not have to be an able bastard to get ahead; you have to be able and well liked to get to the top of any large organization.

I resent it, and I'm sure you may resent the fact that when top executives are portrayed in the movies, on T.V., and in books, they are shown as scowling money-grubbing finks. In fact, the reverse is true. But if we must generalize, I have observed that most successful men (whatever your definition of success) are also possessed with relatively high libidos; this sexual drive being concomitant with their success. In other words, there are very few successful men with tiny libidos. Because they are successful, I presume they are thus sensuous men. I've met only one or two out of hundreds that weren't decent, understanding gentlemen. After all, men with such good libidos have learned that to satisfy their sex needs, they can't be imperious, callous, greedy, or unloving as they are so often portrayed. I am not making the point here that some truck drivers don't have good libidos. It is that I never met a successful man who didn't have a good libido. I'm sure they are out there, I just haven't met them yet. What does this have to do with obtaining permanent loans? Well, institutions don't make loans, people do.

When I was about 35 years old, I was negotiating a loan with an elderly senior vice-president of a major savings bank. He was shrewd and tough and didn't seem to be into anything except his work. We were at an impasse on the loan amount. He seemed intractable. I don't know why but I suddenly remembered that a friend had given me a patently offensive pornographic booklet earlier in the day. I reached for the booklet in my briefcase, opened it and pretended to read, "Right here, on page 33, it says that you will split the difference with me." He reached over and plucked the booklet from my hands. When he discovered that I had been faking what I read on page 33, he read the page silently to himself (I nearly died) and when he finished he started roaring with laughter, smiled at me and said, "OK, we'll split the difference." I have never forgotten this incident. Remember the folks that are on top in the business world have decent libidos. A little levity about sex may help you break the ice.

nonrecourse mortgages

In classes which I teach at the various real estate institutes, the students often are amazed when they are told that there is **no personal liability** on the permanent loans we obtain. Most students seem to have experience only with residential loans. Since virtually all residential loans for houses and duplexes involve the signing of a note, deed of trust, or mortgage, which involves personal liability on the part of the borrowers, most students have no real familiarity with commercial loan transactions. It is a fact that there is no personal liability involved in obtaining large commercial loans. The lenders recognize that persons with moderate net worths couldn't come up with the monies during bad times, and persons with serious net worths wouldn't risk anything beyond their equity investment. These being the facts, the loan commitment bears a legend that says something like this, "The sole security for the repayment of this loan is the property itself, and the lender will not look to the borrowers or their assigns in the event of foreclosure." The legend may also read, "In the event of foreclosure and the obtaining of a deficiency judgment, the lender is prohibited from enforcing such judgment against the makers of this note or their assigns." Please have your own attorney ensure that there is either a sole security clause or a nonenforcement clause of a deficiency judgment, or both, in the mortgage, deed of trust, and the note itself. Laws relating to foreclosure are not precisely the same in every state, thus you or your attorney must consult local counsel.

obtaining the construction loan

It seems odd on its face that a **different** lender other than the permanent lender makes the construction loan. But this comes about because commercial banks, rather than insurance companies or pension funds, are uniquely qualified to make short-term loans, usually for 30 months or less. They not only have such short-term funds available but commercial banks generally **seek** to make construction loans. Their security is so great that their risks are all but nonexistent. This is so because they rarely make construction loans without an explicit agreement with the permanent lender to buy, at face, the construction loan upon completion of the building.

When the Equitable Life Assurance Society of the United States (or any top insurance company) makes a commitment to make the permanent loan upon completion of the building, the bank need only concern itself with the integrity of the developer and his general contractor. There is no risk to the ultimate funding by, let's say, Equitable. The only risk for the bank is seeing to it that the building is completed in accordance with the plans and specifications. Not only does the developer's architect certify as to the work in place during construction, but so does the general contractor. Banks have been "had" before though, so they hire an independent inspector, usually a civil engineer or an architect, to make monthly inspections prior to the disbursement of monthly progress payments, universally called "draws." Your bank will solicit this kind of business from you and all you have to do to keep your bank competitive is to inquire among your local banks what their rates would be for construction loans.

gap loans or take-out commitments

It is unclear when the word "gap" was first used in connection with a real estate loan, but the word describes the kind of financing that is usually necessary in the development of office buildings and shopping centers. It has been used in connection with the development of high-rise (luxury) residential buildings, but it is virtually always used in connection with the proposed development of office buildings and shopping centers that are not preleased to the break-even point. If you were a lender and wanted to be as certain as possible that you would not have to foreclose, you would try to make your loan commitment as safe as possible. You could insist that you would not make any loans on any project unless and until the developer had leased up enough space to pay all operating costs and still have enough cash flow to service your loan. That policy would be just fine except that no developer would borrow from you. Because you know how important the permanent commitment is in order to borrow monies from your construction loan lender, what construction lender would lend you the monies to complete your project if one of the requirements of the permanent commitment is that you must be at least 80 percent leased in order to receive the entire permanent loan proceeds? None, of course, and that is why the gap loan was created.

This is how a gap loan works. Let's say you have received a permanent loan commitment from a major insurance company in the amount of $10 million for an office building to be developed in your city. One of the requirements of the loan is that the building be 80 percent leased before the insurance company will "close" on the loan, i.e., fund the loan. Because this commitment is impossible to borrow against until 80 percent of the building has been leased, no commercial bank would make the construction loan. Your major insurance company knows this, however, so the insurance company takes a slight risk by stating flatly that when the project is completed in accordance with approved plans and specifications, the permanent loan may be funded up to $8 million. The permanent loan commitment further states that at closing, if the building is

80 percent (or 75 percent or 85 percent) leased, the entire $10 million will be funded. Stated another way, the insurance company will settle and fund the $8 million at any time (within the time constraints of the commitment), but will only fund the entire $10 million based upon approved leases totalling at least 80 percent of the rentable area. The commercial bank making the construction loan is thus guaranteed $8 million of funding when the building is completed and if 80 percent or more leased, it is guaranteed $10 million.

The developer is in the position of having his permanent lender, and thus his construction lender, "hold back" 20 percent of the funds needed to complete the project. Because of the hold back feature of the loan commitment, the developer is required to obtain a gap loan. This can be done in several ways. He can visit a lender in his area who is familiar with the leasing market and who has confidence in the developer and project, say a local insurance company, savings bank, or savings and loan association, and apply for his $2 million gap loan commitment. The lender making the gap loan has some risk, but assuming good knowledge of the market and the developer, it is a rewarding risk. The worst that can happen to the gap lender (after funding) is that he becomes the second trust lender (a holder of a second mortgage). The gap lender comes ahead of everyone, excepting the first trust lender, so the project's equity will have to be lost before he, the gap lender, is at risk. Generally, all the gap lender does is issue a commitment to the developer, with no intention of ever having to fund the loan. The developer takes his permanent commitment to the construction lender, usually a bank and along with his gap commitment is now able to borrow the entire $10 million loan.

A gap lender will usually charge a couple of points for his commitment and will make the interest rate of his gap loan quite high, normally several interest points higher than the first mortgage commitment. Additionally, his payoff rate (the annual constant) is high, perhaps 15 percent or more, so that the loan is rarely funded. Inasmuch as the project can't stand such a high cash outflow, either the developer and his partners, if any, will make other arrangements to borrow the $2 million from another lender if it becomes necessary when the project doesn't have an 80 percent rent up. The developer and his partners may wish to provide the project with additional capital instead of either seeking another loan or, heaven forbid, have to service an onerous second mortgage.

Major developers with substantial net worths are not plagued with having to obtain gap or take-out financing. They merely furnish the construction lender with either a letter of credit or give a personal guarantee covering the $2 million gap to the original permanent commitment lender. This is done to induce the construction lender to fund the construction loan, through progress payments as the work commences, to the full amount of the permanent commitment. In most cases, when the project is 80 percent leased, the permanent lender will release the developer from any financial commitment, feeling the substitution of several credit-worthy tenants on relatively long-term (5 to 10 year) leases is better security than the developer's net worth. Major insurance company real estate lenders are aware that net worths of developers ebbs and flows, the nature of the development business being speculative.

advantages and disadvantages of using leverage

My partner, Herb Blum, and I used to call some of the real estateniks that hung around what then was called real estate row in Washington, D.C., by the respectful term of the "smart money boys." This was before we entered the real estate field, when we were young and impressionable. These real estateniks were characterized in a general way by their clothing, which looked quite expensive. Almost all these gentlemen seemed to smoke massive cigars, similar to those smoked by Winston Churchill. We were in awe of these men, some of whom deigned to talk with us. How impressed we were when we learned of deals in which they had "made a fortune" by borrowing out! Now, some three decades later, we still kid about the smart money boys. Incidentally, whenever Herb and I walk together, we get a kick out of pointing out derelicts, winos, and other assorted bums. One of us usually says to the other, "Look, a former real estate developer," or, "Look, there goes one of the former smart money boys."

What we are really doing is reemphasizing our strong belief that excessive leveraging is the path to economic failure. By definition, the act of leveraging a real estate project intensifies the economic result. Because the economic result is influenced intensely by leveraging the property, the question always pops up as to how much to borrow. If you are showing an 11 percent cash-on-cash return on a project which you own, any borrowings that require an annual constant to service the debt that is less than 11 percent will produce "instant leverage." As an example, if a community shopping center is producing $11,000 on an original down payment of $100,000, and you are servicing a $350,000 mortgage with an annual constant of 9.86 percent, you could theoretically borrow out by obtaining a new loan of $450,000. The new loan would carry an annual constant of 10 percent and the debt service would be increased by approximately $10,500 annually. The original $350,000 mortgage with a 9.86 percent annual constant required payments of $34,510 annually. The new mortgage at $450,000 with an annual constant of 10 percent requires payments of $45,000. Instead of receiving an annual cash flow of $100,000, the cash flow is reduced by approximately $10,500 now to $89,500, but you could have put your original $100,000 cash investment back in the bank.

Using this example of "instant leverage" helps make me understand that borrowing out is possible, but only after achieving 100 percent occupancy, with the majority of tenants having excellent credit ratings. This advantage of using leverage is just fine and you need not concern yourself with our 80 percent rule of occupancy. But before a project is built is not the time for excessive optimism. You **must** be at least at break-even if you are 80 percent occupied or you may have leveraged yourself into a failing project! Our industry abounds with many good shopping centers that were slow in getting started—think of the original developers who went belly-up because they had no staying power because they had borrowed too much! The time for a little cupidity is after the project is 100 percent leased.

negotiating the contract with the general contractor

The sum total of several decades of developing income-producing properties has brought me to the inexorable conclusion that the best way to proceed with your general contractor is on a negotiated price with an incentive for cost savings and a penalty for cost overruns. Let me explain.

When the plans are in the preliminary stages, the general contractor reviews them so that an estimate can be given to you. This will enable you to help determine the project's costs. The preliminary estimate will be rough, but it is the best you will be able to obtain at this stage. When the final plans and specifications are available, your general contractor will be able to give you a precise cost. He will do this after he has obtained estimates from his subcontractors and materials suppliers.

Generally, he will seek to build into his estimate a fee approximately 5 percent of his actual cost. To be on the safe side, he often will inflate the costs a little, and this is quite understandable. Chances are you will do better in your negotiations with the contractor if you resist the temptation of haggling over price. A more pleasant way of negotiating is to propose a cost-saving plan after you finish the basic negotiations.

During the negotiations, your contractor may make cost-saving suggestions that may either change the layout slightly or call for the substitution of less costly materials than those you originally selected. In order to save you money on the final negotiated price, he will necessarily need to "buy" the labor and materials at a price below his final estimate. Should he be very efficient or just plain lucky, either will result in a cost saving because the job will be finished more quickly. In order to keep your contractor's enthusiasm going, he should participate in any savings below the final negotiated price. Our organization has concluded it is best to build in a cost savings incentive on the following basis: 25 cents to the contractor for each dollar saved and 75 cents to the developer; 25 cents cost to the contractor for each dollar expended over the negotiated price (excluding change orders) and 75 cents cost to the developer.

On all tenant finishes over standard and charged to the tenant, two-thirds of the 21 percent (see Chapter 4) goes to the general contractor, $\frac{1}{3}$ to the developer. As developers, we represent the owners, thus these dollars flow to the owning partnership.

Let's look at an example of over-standard tenant finishes. An attorney wishes to have his private office walls finished with a vinyl wallpaper. The building standard calls for two coats of flat paint in an egg-shell white. Since his request is for an over-standard item (vinyl wallpaper) we obtain a price from the general contractors' painting subcontractor. He will credit the tenant for the saving of paint and quote him a price for the vinyl wallpaper. To this price the general contractor adds 10 percent for overhead and 10 percent for profit. Of this 21 percent, 7 percent is credited to the owning partnership. In other words, the partnership shares in the profits from any over-standard tenant work requested and paid for by the tenant.

After you have developed your first project and feel you have been treated fairly by the general contractor, by all means don't flit around. You need to build a relationship with your contractor based on mutual trust and confidence. Don't ever allow yourself to get in an adversary position with your contractor. You will lose every time—the worst of it is that there are so many ways he can "rip you off" without your being aware that he is doing it. And don't ever get angry and threaten or endeavor to intimidate him. You may be faced with a job that has been totally halted. It may take as much as three years to go through the courts, meanwhile interest on your construction loan continues. Remember another Swesnikism: "It is not important to win an argument unless winning will **save** you money." There is no joy in being right if it becomes costly. Surely you agree with me that there is no joy in beating up a cripple. Pick on people brighter than you to poke fun at or argue with.

You must insist on approving all subcontractors to be employed by your general contractor. There are many reasons for this. Among them are:

1. You may want to avoid nepotism (his tile and marble subcontractor may be his brother-in-law). Nothing wrong on the face of this, but the brother-in-law may have a history of screwing up and your contractor is helpless to employ a different contractor because he is the brother of your contractor's wife. The general contractor may love you for seeking and obtaining the right to veto the use of his brother-in-law.

2. You may be helping your general contractor avoid cronyism by weeding out a subcontractor who has a terrible reputation for "sticking it to" the owners every and any time there is a change order.

3. You may have seen a competitive building where there was an exquisite mosaic tile mural in the lobby and want to employ the same tile subcontractor.

Finally, do what you say you will do financially. Your contractor has weekly payrolls to meet "up front." Remember, you are "holding back" 10 percent of his request for monthly draws at the beginning and usually 5 percent starting in the middle of the job. Don't expect your contractor to carry you financially. It is much cheaper for you and will make for a much cleaner relationship if you pay your general contractor promptly. Don't go for a "cost plus" contract. There is no real incentive for your general contractor to save money.

talk with the real estate assessor

Once you have projected all of your costs, it will be rewarding if you talk with your local real estate assessor prior to beginning construction. You will need his estimate of the assessment in order to realistically project your future operating costs. The time to parley with the assessor is before construction commences. This is an absolute imperative to insure you are giving your investors an honest projection of your owning costs. You will also be educated in how assessments are actually computed. Once you learn this, you will be able to prepare your own estimate in advance of your next project. You may be able to help correct an incorrect assessment in advance by ensuring each assessment is correctly computed.

Recently, some urban areas have adopted real estate tax moratoriums as an incentive for new construction. If these are available in your area, you must determine what the terms and conditions are **before** you structure yourself into a program that will fail to qualify for such benefits. Something as nominal as a change in timing or a failure to obtain a municipal certification before beginning construction may be all that stands between your development and a substantial cost saving.

By now you should have a basic plan or strategy should you decide to develop a project. Make certain you have given careful attention to the costs and most especially to the equity requirements. Don't "force" your numbers to make you look like a hero only to find you've knocked yourself out of the development business.

Be aware of your selection of all the real estate specialists and do your investigations of their respective qualifications in the manner suggested. Don't get "conned" or allow your ego to be massaged by your architect. The moment you hear the phrase: "form follows function," run like hell. This is your project, your reputation or track record will be assessed by the success or failure of the project. Do your own research. If it hasn't been done before, don't let them use you as the guinea pig. From the building's exterior through the lobbies, elevators, bathrooms, and the building's guts, the specifications must ultimately be decided upon by you.

Look for the good guys when you are considering permanent financing. The bad guys always seem to want a higher rate of interest and will murder you if you get into the slightest bit of difficulty. Avoid lender participation and watch out for "points" in connection with the permanent financing. Consider using a mortgage broker. **Never** sign a loan with any personal liability. We're all optimists or we couldn't be in this business, yet personal liability should never be required.

Set up a good banking relationship and stick with your bank by giving your banker the first opportunity to make your construction loan. Gap loans may be necessary if your long-term loan commitment has a "hold back." Understand how they operate and search for your lowest "gap cost." Consider all the advantages and disadvantages of using leverage. Remember the 80 percent occupancy rule.

You now understand the guaranteed maximum upset price and a way to penalize the contractor for costs over the contract price as well as a reward for cost savings. By all means contact and make an appointment to chat with your local real estate assessor before starting construction.

reception area of the lounge of the national lawyer's club, washington, d.c.

7

who and
where are they?

chapter 7 outline

lining up the investment offering

As soon as you have done all of the things necessary to develop a mortgage package fully, you are on the way to lining up your investment offering. By this time you will have done the following:

1. You will have developed a pro forma cash flow statement based on income and expenses with an estimate as to the amount of the loan, the interest on the loan, and the annual constant. The bottom line of the cash flow projections will give you real insight as to the amount of equity dollars you will be able to raise based on varying assumptions of the cash-on-cash return. If your market will respond to, let's say, a cash-on-cash return of 6 percent annually, you will be able to raise $100,000 for every $6,000 of "bottom line," that is, cash flow. Remember that if you are developing, 75 percent of the cash flow will flow to 100 percent of the capital. Stated another way, the equity partners do not receive all the cash flow and are subject to the developers or syndicators' proportion of the cash flow as distributions of the cash flow are made.

2. You will have a pretty fair idea as to total costs after having several discussions with the general contractor of your choice. Be certain to be generous in your estimate of rent-up time. You will find it easier raising capital before you start than trying to plug up the monetary hole if things drag during the rent-up process. Don't forget to include as part of your costs all professional fees: attorneys, accountants, engineers, architects, economists, and appraisers. Be sure also to include real estate taxes in process as well as tax amounts you may have to post in advance. Include liability insurance during construction. Be generous in estimating your interest costs during construction. Remember, you are not trying to impress investors with your acumen and sagacity in doing the job at a lesser cost than they might expect, you are trying to be ultra conservative and hopefully when the job is completed, you will be able to return to the equity investors some of their capital. Returning capital is a delicious feeling both to you and them.

3. You will now be in a position to start writing the "offering," private or public, that you will soon be making.

Nothing could be more fatal to you and your project than to try to raise money at this stage in the development process. Many things could happen and none of them are good. For one thing, your lawyer can't protect you if you get anxious and jump the gun. At worst, you probably will have to offer recision. At best, you will become depressed. Even though the temptation is great, you must do everything in your power not to discuss the offering with anyone except the professionals who will be doing your legal work and accounting.

In your enthusiasm for the project, you may be tempted to forget that you do not as yet have the permanent financing, the construction financing, and you do not have a guaranteed maximum upset price with your general contractor. You will find it impossible to raise equity dollars at this point because you will be unable to answer questions about the partnership agreement, the absolute costs, and details of the financing. Everything is too chancy at this point. Years ago in the flush of enthusiasm, I started an equity search quite early because investors were calling me regularly. Each one was pleading with me that he be allowed to go into a venture we were forming. I discovered at that time that it is not possible to raise money until the construction is ready to start. I couldn't really answer questions about costs, financing, or any other question for that matter, because there was no permanent loan commitment, no gap loan, no construction financing, and no guaranteed maximum upset price with the general contractor. No doubt about it, there was plenty of interest, but (looking back) only an idiot would part with his money on the basis of the little information I had then available. I have since discovered that this is one of the most serious errors of most neophyte developers and syndicators. They really knock off part of the investing community by making an offering before they should. **There is no doubt about it, a serious investor is willing to take the rental risk—and that is about all.** All other aspects of your venture must be firm, and if not quite firm (such as rent-up time) then your estimates must be generous.

how much to charge

We have previously discussed the fees that generally will be acceptable to the investing community: 25 percent if you are developing and 15 percent if you are acquiring. These fees are not immutable. This is because no two projects are identical. It follows that there may be less room for your piece of the action in one project than there is in another. I have a general rule that helps me determine the amount of the action my partner and I can receive. If the potential cash flow, without my piece of the action, is less than 10 percent, it is unlikely that I could receive more than 25 percent if it is a development, nor more than 15 percent if it is an acquisition. This means that a potential investor in a development will receive approximately $7\frac{1}{2}$ percent cash-on-cash return on his investment and on an acquisition he would receive approximately $8\frac{1}{2}$ percent cash-on-cash return. If the potential return appears to be as high as 12 percent to 14 percent on a development, there is a potential for a somewhat higher fee. This would also be true for an acquisition. Under our current tax laws affecting new projects, there are greater write-offs, mainly because of points and interest during construction. As a result, sophisticated investors are willing to accept a smaller cash-on-cash return on new projects. This is so because not only are the write-offs greater, but also the investor feels there is a better chance for greater cash flow on a new project than there is on a project that is not new. His opinion is a correct one.

OK, what do you do, charge a greater fee if the figures show a greater return? I think not, although the temptation to do so is great. What you should do is restudy the income and expenses and make sure you are not kidding yourself and the potential investor. Most ventures, if conservatively structured, rarely show a greater return than 10 percent to 12 percent during the first year or two of full operation. Because this is true, avoid the temptation to force figures or to get a higher piece of the action. If you are going to do something funny with the figures—increase costs and reduce the potential income. Sound dishonest? Not at all. What is dishonest is to inflate the return by increasing income and kidding yourself by reducing probable expenses. Here is another point to remember: if your project produces less cash flow than the amount of cash flow originally projected, you might be accused of being dishonest. No one will accuse you of being dishonest if the return you project turns out to be higher. Another important point to ponder is that the sophisticated investor is frightened off if the return sounds too juicy. He may think you are inflating the return artificially in order to attract him to your project. I know you will probably wonder about this statement. Take it from me, a projected return over 12 percent will **lose you some investors.** If your project does better than your projections, how sweet it is!

There are times when you can obtain a greater fee than a 25 percent participation in a new development and over 15 percent in an acquisition. But the cash-on-cash return should not be the sole determining factor. The factors that determine the greater fee are those relating to greater risks that you as the developer or syndicator are taking. There are times when, as the developer, you may have to guarantee a portion of the loan to the project on behalf of the partnership. Obtaining the gap monies and perhaps the construction loan may call for putting some or all of your credit on the line. There is also much to be said for having a building 60 percent rented prior to inviting in investor partners. This certainly reduces their risks and allows you to consider a higher participation for yourself.

recording the "certificate of limited partnership"

When syndication was relatively new to me, I was constantly on the defensive. This is no posture to be in if you are organizing an investment group either to acquire an existing project or to develop a new property. What had me on the defensive was the fact that sooner or later I would either meet an investor's attorney or talk with him over the phone. Since you know what exquisite detail I go through every time I am involved in a venture, especially regarding the drafting of the partnership agreement, it's no wonder that I found myself in an adversary position. I would either be arguing about the size of the piece of the action all the way through to my choice of the general contractor and even the bank I chose to deal with. Amazingly, the solution appeared before me because of the enactment in the District of Columbia of the Uniform Limited Partnership Act, which has been adopted in most states. What was required under the act was a recordation of the more important facets of the partnership and which included the recording of the limited partners' interests in the partnership.

The recording of the Certificate of Limited Partnership actually helped tremendously in my marketing program. This is how it happened. I was ready to put together a partnership to develop a fairly large (over 400 units) apartment complex. As it happened, I had plenty of time because together with my partner and another chap we had owned the land for several years prior to development. Our office went about the usual procedures for us, and it was my job to develop the partnership agreement. My attorney casually suggested that we record the partnership agreement (actually, the Certificate) prior to making any overtures to other participants. This came about because we had to please the other owner of the ground by protecting his interests in the newly formed partnership simultaneously with his conveyance to the new partnership of all his right, title, and interest in the land for a capital interest of 30 percent. In order to fill out the certificate correctly prior to recordation, the unsold portion of the limited partners' interests was recorded in my name. Because this was done for the land partner's convenience, I merely executed a non-recourse note, interest bearing, for the entire amount of the unsold partnership interests. Later on the interest on the note was "forgiven." This meant that as each new limited partner was admitted, I would admit him to the partnership as a **substitute** limited partner for whatever of my portion he had purchased. This worked just fine, and turned out to be the format that our office now meticulously follows. After the recordation of the Certificate of Limited Partnership with the Recorder of Deeds in the District of Columbia, the partnership could not be easily amended or changed. It can be amended, but all partners, general and limited, must agree in writing to such an amendment. This became apparent when one of our investors forwarded a copy of the agreement, along with the Certificate of Limited Partnership to his attorney. The three of us (the investor, his attorney, and I) had lunch together about a week later and during the luncheon, the attorney turned to his client and said, "This is a very clear agreement and it sets forth all of the rights of Messrs. Swesnik and Blum and limits your rights to decision making to two areas: you may vote on a sale or on refinancing. If you agree that you are unwilling to be "active" in the partnership, put up your money and hope the venture is a winner. Besides, I can't get anything changed for you as the essence of the partnership agreement has already been recorded with the Recorder of Deeds showing the general partners' interests along with the 30 percent land contributor as a limited partner."

I could have kissed the attorney right then and there because he had stated something so obvious, and yet to me the recording of the Certificate of Limited Partnership prior to the offering on my part was done merely as an accommodation to the contributing land owner. What was before obtuse was now obvious: I couldn't change the partnership agreement because the Certificate of Limited Partnership had already been recorded. From that time on, whenever any person suggested changes, I pointed out that what was on the public record **was and is** the only agreement by and among all the partners. How good it felt to say that. While you may think this is a cavalier or imperious way of treating the investor (and it may be), it avoids bringing into the partnership any contumacious or litigious investors.

marketing the equity participations

There are those developers among us who will have nothing to do with raising equity capital for a real estate venture. I have reasoned that it is mainly because of fear of failure to raise such funds that a developer would not market his own equity participations. He may feel that someone else, perhaps even a Merrill, Lynch, Pierce, Fenner & Smith, could sell the participations more easily. They not only have the investors practically in hand, but everyone knows it is easier to have another person sell you than it is for you to sell yourself. For whatever other reasons, including the status of having a fine stockbroker raise the money for them, some developers have chosen this method of obtaining equity capital.

Is there a catch to all this? You bet there is. The fees to sell equity real estate participations are quite variable but they are rarely less than 8 percent of the capital raised, and usually are not higher than 12 percent. These rates are negotiable, but plan to pay at least 10 percent to someone else for raising your equity dollars. This will either have the net effect of lowering your piece of the action, or ultimately showing the investor a lesser return. We all know there is no such thing as something for nothing, yet some developers try to obtain a large piece of the action and allow a third party to raise the equity. This does not and realistically cannot happen. No developer can expect a large piece of the action and let some outside third party keep as much as 10 percent of the partnership's cash. Part of the rationale of a developer obtaining a 25 percent piece of the action includes his ability to raise the necessary equity capital without charge to the partnership. Part of his ability to raise the capital certainly rests on the anticipated cash flow return; having to pay out 10 percent of an investor's capital in a real estate transaction can mean the difference to an investor of an ordinary cash-on-cash return instead of an exciting return on his investment. Yet there are organizations devoted to raising equity capital for real estate ventures, either to be developed or acquired. Peculiarly, these organizations for the most part are either stockbrokers or affiliates.

Perhaps the developers who use other offices to raise capital are really not at all certain that the project will be a winner. They might reason that they do not wish to raise the equity in the community in which they live and work because the project might do poorly, and they do not wish to injure their reputation by raising capital locally among friends and business acquaintances. This seems to be the reason one of the developers I know prefers not to raise his own equity capital.

Another reason focuses on what I call the "I don't need money syndrome." Those of us who were raised during the Depression in the 1930s remember that to not dress well meant one was poor. To talk about lack of money except among the immediate family was also taboo. You must remember that prior to unemployment compensation, workmen's compensation, social security, welfare, and free day care centers, as well as all the other social programs designed to help the less fortunate, a person had no alternative if he wanted to live except to obtain gainful employment. Although the city of Chicago had soup lines and "relief," no one with pride would consider either of these as a alternative to full-time work. I was in high school in the mid-1930s when the family was absolutely broke; I delivered both the morning and afternoon papers and after dinner, I solicited subscriptions door-to-door for the **Saturday Evening Post** and **Collier's** magazines. This brief description of my early life isn't meant to elicit sympathy, but to emphasize that the alternative to not working was **not eating.** I learned quite early that to be shy and diffident was a prescription for starvation.

I don't know what others did or thought, I was so busy obtaining money, but I suspect that the developer who is reticent about asking for equity capital from individuals may be so because of the "I don't need money syndrome." He may be ashamed, frightened, or may feel that the task of raising money is beneath his dignity. Is he or are they kidding? My formula for raising equity capital for real estate ventures is an absolutely proven method. It is foolproof in every respect. It is not time consuming and most importantly it will keep you listening to the investors' wants and needs. Besides, it's really fun!

difference between tax loss and tax shelter oriented investors

When you are ready to raise equity capital and you and your attorneys have finally produced an honest, forthright, and extremely informative private placement memorandum, you will have in your possession all the necessary tools to raise the equity capital. Your private placement memorandum will contain all the goodies that you as the developer could possibly obtain and will contain, word-for-word, the partnership agreement. It will also include your cash flow projections as well as all construction and related costs. The projected taxes and tax treatment will also be available, prepared in principal by your tax attorney but implemented fully by your accountant. It may show projections for as long as ten years. It must **not** show any potential profit at sale, although you may crank in a projection based upon a portion of the cost-of-living increase from inception. You will discover there are investors who will skip over almost everything except the tax projections.

Some professionals (such as doctors, dentists, and lawyers) who have half their income over certain levels taken by taxes are really articulate and angry with the Internal Revenue Service, the Treasury, and everyone else because of what they call "confiscatory" practices of the government. What they don't seem to understand is that the Treasury and the Internal Revenue Service merely administer the laws and do not make them. Although some of the IRS rulings seem to make new laws where none seemed to exist before, the tax courts as well as the federal district courts do a pretty good job in ensuring that the IRS does not go beyond its statutory authority.

If these same professionals would merely take time out of their busy schedules to write their congressman or senator, explaining how they feel or helping their representatives understand when a particular law is hurting them, changes could be made. Generally all tax law changes originate in the House Ways and Means Committee. The Senate Finance Committee hears voluminous testimony too, and if there is some disagreement between the two bodies, they form a committee to settle their differences. This is how tax laws are made or changed.

At any rate, many professionals in the past have made real estate investments in income-producing properties to be built, mainly FHA sponsored or insured apartment houses, and have been clobbered with taxes when the project was either abandoned or foreclosed. I note that this always seems to happen when there is a terrific amount of losses, usually during the first year or two. It seems there are "investors" for every scheme wherein the losses for federal income tax purposes are enormous during the first year or two. "Zu viel ist ungesund" "Too much is not healthy," my maternal grandma told me when I was a boy. Too much of anything, including fun, good food, fine wine, love, sex, and all the other of life's goodies in excess is no good. The other side of the coin, too much work and too little of life's goodies is no good either. Most folks would agree that, ideally, one should strive to keep all things in balance.

There has been too much emphasis on tax losses and not enough emphasis on quality real estate with a bright future. Most investors are familiar with tax shelter, and what I hear most is the need for income, preferably tax sheltered. When someone calls me and pleads for tax losses especially during the last quarter of the year, he usually explains that for some reason, evidently not planned by him, he has an enormous federal income tax liability and wants losses to offset the liability. Obviously, neither I nor any other developer can accommodate this type of investor. Under our current tax laws there are not the up-front write-offs that existed prior to 1976. When we are in the first or second year of development, the equity interests have already been sold. The best we can do for an investor is to try to place his capital in a venture wherein some or even most of the projected cash flow is not subject to immediate taxes. So enamored is the potential investor seeking "losses" that I liken him to an accident about to happen. There is no question that if he continues his search he will find losses to offset his gain. The only real problem he will face is that his so-called "investment" may produce nothing but "losses" and not just the income tax kind, but a real economic loss. Nothing much can be done with this type of person. Some con man will find him and press his greed button, and this kind of investor will have all the losses he can handle.

The kind of investor who realizes his choices are narrowed because of inflation, who knows the kinds of risks he is willing to take, and who understands how tax shelter comes about, fits a pattern. I call it the investor profile. It is interesting how this profile emerged. All intelligent policies seem to promulgate themselves as a reaction to some negative situation. I was syndicating a venture when suddenly I seemed unable to raise equity funds for the project for which only one-half the equity participations were sold. This was in 1954, quite early in my career, and the lessons I learned have stayed with me to this day. I asked myself questions such as: "Why have I run out of prospects?", "Have I lost my ability to close sales?", and "Why aren't these prospects asking the right questions?"

Because I was having considerable difficulty with these doubts, I started out to prepare a game plan that would be fail-safe. This is what I did.

locating the investor

Studying the entire investor as a person after first determining every possible thing I could find out about him was the key not only to locating the next group of potential investors, but also to avoiding running out of investors. I knew that all the investors must have had certain common elements either in their occupation, education, prior investing experiences, or saving habits that appeared to be the reason they were investors in income-producing properties. Which elements were the key? Was where they were born a key? How about their ethnic background? Were they religious people and was any religion predominate? I did my own research in this area and while it was the kind of research that was not professional (I'm no statistician), the results were remarkable. In a moment I will give them to you. First let me explain that my inquiries were almost all by phone, usually by calls made directly by me starting about mid-morning and continuing until lunch. I knew all the persons I called because they were people who had invested with me previously.

The questions I asked were related to their education, type of occupation, prior investing experiences, and their investment strategy (was it a strategy or was it a case of just reacting to circumstances?). I asked their ages (they were all men), if they regularly attended religious services, what they thought about charitable contributions, and a whole lot of other nonsense, because I really didn't know what I was looking for. What I ultimately discovered by questioning over 160 individual investors was the correct method of locating the investor. It was by accident that among the questions I asked was where had the capital come from for their last real estate investment. As I skimmed through the answers first, I thought how great it would be if I were able to code the answers, weighing the more important ones on a scale of one to ten and then if I could only have pressed a button that would have given me the investor profile I was looking for, how fortunate I would have been. Alas, computers were just being developed in the early 1950s so I had to study each card for obvious similarities. Incidentally, I received virtually no opposition to most of my questions because I really was not doing the survey to sell anything to the respondents. I informed them I was doing the survey of investors for a book I was about to write about how necessary the equity investors were in keeping the construction business and thus the economy in solid shape.

The result of all this was L.E.E.P., my acronym for the four **essential** characteristics of investors, which must be met to be invited to invest in one of our ventures. L.E.E.P. is simply: living at a profit, education, experience, and profession. Here is how I got to it and what it all means.

following the l.e.e.p. acronym

The acronym L.E.E.P. is a creation of mine that has helped me to market equity acquisitions in a fail-safe manner and virtually guarantees that **every time** I make an actual equity participation offer, the chances are 14 out of 15 that the person will enter the venture. Sounds fantastic or unbelievable? It probably does, yet to me and my partner (we have no salesmen) it is just a great deal of fun. The secret, of course, is L.E.E.P. It is a method of qualifying potential investors that is so perfect it has become the easiest facet of the development business. Make no mistake about it, my partner and I are perhaps a little better than most salesmen when it comes to closing the investor, but the L.E.E.P. acronym is a **qualifying method.** When you use the L.E.E.P. system for qualifying, your ratio of presentations to closes should be at least seven out of eight. Why would you let someone else do this for you and give away either part of your goodies or cause your investors to receive a lesser return? You won't after you have memorized L.E.E.P. and have used it just a few times.

l. stands for living at a profit

It means that the person you may wish to invite to participate with you has a greater net worth at the end of the year than when the year started. It also means that the person living at a profit has saved some cash and has it in some monetary asset as a temporary resting place. This part of the L.E.E.P. acronym is as important as the other three, yet it is the "sine qua non" (without which there is nothing) of investing.

It is such an obvious thing to know about before you invite any person into one of your ventures, that you may ask, "If I were to offer you a compellingly attractive income-producing investing opportunity, where would your funds come from?" Asking this question sorts out the phonies from the real investors. What's more, the respondent can't really lie to you unless he has gone through considerable research in order to make up the lie. Don't worry, liars never do—that's why they lie. The only correct answer acceptable to you is that the money is on deposit at a savings bank, a savings and loan association, or that it has been temporarily invested in a certificate of deposit. Treasury notes about to come due as well as short-term savings and loan certificates are OK too, but no other answer will do. In this area we have absolute unanimity of opinion: no one **sells** stocks or bonds to enter your real estate venture.

Your job is to do a little research yourself to insure you are not about to be lied to. Call your local bank and obtain their savings rates, both passbook and certificates of deposit. Do the same with a savings bank or a savings and loan association. Call your stockbroker and he will tell you where to find the market rates in **The Wall Street Journal** that major banks will pay for certificates of deposit for 90 days in amounts of $100,000 or more. The entire research project for just this information should not take over a half of a day. From the moment you have the rates in your hand (I have these typed on a card I keep in my wallet), no potential investor can con you.

Why is this so important? First, anyone can have the appearance of money. The indicia of wealth in this country have been blurred, because most people have different life styles. Some people live as conspicuous consumers in a magnificent house. You and I both know people who can't afford this mark of wealth, but some of the people living in high-priced houses would sacrifice **anything** to continue to live this way. Others drive Rolls Royces, wear designer clothes, and/or wear jewelry that could be worth over half a million dollars. All of this is pure window dressing. The important thing you must remember is where is the cash? Don't be afraid to ask the question, "If I were to offer you a compellingly attractive income-producing property opportunity, where do you have the cash so that you could consider the investment?" Any similar question that suits your personality will do. **I beg of you, do not, repeat, do not,** discuss **any** facet of the venture you are about to syndicate unless and until you are convinced the person has sufficient cash on hand to invest with you. In order to convince you he will say for example, "I have the money at Perpetual Building Association." The next question you **must** ask is, "What kind of account and what rate do you earn?" You will know if you are hearing the truth from your research into monetary, short-term rates. Every potential investor knows how much interest he is earning.

When I first entered the real estate field in 1951, one of my first jobs was to sit on an "open house." This was a large subdivision sample house and another salesman, Peter Margelos, was there to help me in my training. At first we took turns in showing the house to couples, but in a moment of greed, I jumped up to greet a lovely looking young couple who had just entered the house. As I did this I couldn't help noticing the sardonic grin on Pete's face as he showed the house to the next couple. What made me approach the first couple with such enthusiasm was that they had driven up in a brand new Cadillac while Pete's clients had driven up in a slightly battered older Ford. You have probably guessed the end of the story, he sold the client and I didn't sell mine. He later said, "Swes, the reason I sold the house to my people is that my people had moeny, yours had already spent theirs!" I have never forgotten that incident, which happened on my second day in the real estate industry. The lesson is obvious. People whom you observe leading "the good life" may just be living part of the good life, mainly because they don't have enough money left over for savings, vacations, or anything else, much less a decent home.

You must qualify any potential investor that may wish to enter one of your syndicates by first discovering, in the manner already discussed, **where is the money?** That is what L. stands for: Living at a profit. These people have money in a temporary resting place. Because this is so, they have an investment problem. They know the interest they earn is taxed while inflation is lessening the value of their savings. Find out where it is and if they are telling you the truth. If you are satisfied with their answer, you are ready to further qualify your potential investor with the next question.

e. stands for education

You need to know if the potential investor is capable of understanding how tax shelter occurs in a real estate transaction. The question I like to ask is, "Do you know how tax shelter occurs during the ownership of income-producing property?" Hardly anybody says, "To the extent that depreciation is greater than amortization, then some, all, or more than all, of the cash flow is not subject to federal income tax." But I expect them to understand that depreciation and construction interest write-offs reduce the **taxable income** while there may be plentiful distributions of cash flow.

Obviously if the potential investor is a professional of some sorts, he is educated. Surprisingly, most educated people by the time they're fifty seem to have given up reading. This I cannot understand. Every waking hour I can save from other pursuits, I read. This has to do with the knowledge of the prospective investor, who if he reads, may know how tax shelter comes about. Does he remember the difference between monetary assets and non-monetary assets that we all learned in Economics I, or was he a late bloomer? No matter, I strongly believe it is not possible to "sell" a limited partnership interest to someone who doesn't understand how tax shelter comes into being, in other terms, (C.F. + A − D = T.I.)

To prove how dumb one can get, I remember in 1953 giving an actual sales presentation to a grocer whose back was turned to me while he was putting cans on the shelves during the entire presentation. You can readily understand that there was no way he could have the slightest idea about cash flow or tax shelter. I later learned he had a sixth grade education. I am an "up person" but you should have seen me after my sales encounter with the grocer! At least I learned several things from this single encounter. The first thing I learned is it makes no sense to talk Arabic to an Australian; second, what decent salesperson ever gave a pitch without first qualifying the potential buyer; third, because I felt so annoyed with my lack of common sense by even being at the grocer's, I really felt "depressed" or at least "down." At least I learned how to empathize with someone who is depressed.

The potential investor must be educated, not necessarily formally, but educated. "Street smarts" won't do—but common sense to **understand** the investing formula is a must.

the second e. in l.e.e.p. means experience

We already know that if the potential investor has no ready cash or cash equivalents, he isn't granted the courtesy of further qualifying. If he has the money and understands tax shelter, what kind of experience must he have had?

Without question, he must already have demonstrated his willingness to subordinate his judgment to that of another "pro." He must have previously been a part of a group of other investors headed by an expert and have had made an investment with such a pro. My question to an investor prospect is, "In what have you previously invested?" This question works well for me and I know that this question that sounds so innocuous can easily be asked by you. And you will know by the response if indeed you have your investor. Let me give you some representative **answers** that you will recognize as being unacceptable:

1. "I have always invested in the market." You then ask, "Specifically what are you in?" "Oh, I've got GM, Exxon, a few other blue chips, and a few flyers." Is this acceptable to you? No, this person is the captain of an investment ship, he'll never be a passenger. Where has he demonstrated his willingness to subordinate his judgment to that of a pro?

2. "I've bought and sold a few properties by myself, but I'm getting too old to be running my own properties." This response is no good either. He has not demonstrated his willingness to subordinate his judgment to that of an expert, he just appears willing to do so now. But he won't. Probably because he is already in real estate, he merely wants to know what he could expect in a new venture. It's none of **his** business, so don't tell him.

3. "I've invested with several other doctors in a group we have formed to acquire some land." You then ask, "How did you get involved?" If he says another doctor interested him in it and there is no expert running the joint venture, this answer is no good either.

What do you do when these people give you negative answers while you're qualifying them? Merely say, "I have concluded that the real estate investment I was about to offer you is really not for you." This will drive most potential investors crazy, but no matter how sincerely they beg you for more information, do **not** give them any. I usually find that by telling him he does not "fit" the investment pattern of previous investors, he graciously fades away and stops wasting my time. If he presses you for more data—**you** fade away. Just stand up, extend your hand, and thank him for coming to your office. It is absolute nonsense to waste your time with this type of unqualified investor. I have in the past and I'm sure you have also given a sales presentation when there was an absolute certainty the person could not or would not buy. Remember how foolish you felt afterward? Don't allow yourself to fall into this trap again. Unless he gives you an acceptable answer, terminate your conversation with him. I know that you are not a rude or unrefined person, and thus the temptation to continue your conversation in a polite vein is almost irresistible, but resist you must. **You cannot do business with a virgin investor.**

Any of the following answers are acceptable because they all demonstrate that the investor has admitted to himself he lacks the knowledge and sophistication to develop or acquire income-producing real estate on his own.

1. "I have invested in a mutual fund." Great, just great. He has made a statement, "I don't have any stock market expertise so I've left the decision making to someone who has."

2. "I'm in a tax free money fund." This translates to: "I don't know how to intelligently evaluate and analyze city, county, and state bonds; I've left all of that to other experts. Besides, the federal government doesn't tax me on the interest I'm earning." This person is **qualified** through **experience.**

3. "I've invested in oil and gas well programs before, and I've done well." This translates into—"Hell, I don't know anything about oil and gas wells, but I have confidence in the promoters and I like the tax effects of such transactions and I like the tax-sheltered cash distributions." This person has the kind of investing experience you're looking for.

4. "I've invested in a race horse 'stud' syndicate." "Are you an expert in horse breeding?" you may ask. "No, but the fellow who organizes and manages the syndicate is an expert." Translation: "I'm not an expert and I know it. I need an expert for such kinds of transactions." You can be sure he is qualified by virtue of his investment experience.

5. "I've invested in a real estate syndicate before." You may ask, "With whom?" He may give you a name of another developer or syndicator in your area. Or perhaps the person he names may be an expert in real estate but lives and works in another city. For gosh sakes, resist the temptation to "knock" another developer even if you know the venture he invested in was a loser. This is, of course, a perfectly qualified investor by virtue of experience. He did it once, he'll do it again.

In all of the above examples of responses to your questions, note that it is not necessary that the previous investments were **winners.** It is only necessary that a judgment was made to "let the expert do it." The fact that the potential investor felt he was not qualified to go it alone is implicit.

Assuming an investor is qualified in the first three ways: he has the money, he understands tax shelter because he is educated, and he has previously joined a group who relied on an expert, you are now ready for the last qualifying facet of L.E.E.P.

p. stands for profession

I discovered that virtually all of my investors were professionals of one kind or another. Just as important, with only two exceptions, **none were in the retail or wholesale business.** A retailer or wholesaler is in a cash-intensive business. He needs rental money for a store or showroom or warehouse. He needs money for his inventory. He needs money to carry his receivables. He also can't relate to real estate tax-sheltered investments for several reasons:

1. He buys something for $.60 at wholesale and sells it for $1.00 at retail. His gross profit is 40 percent. How can he be economically titillated by a 10 percent cash-on-cash return, even fully tax-sheltered?
2. He truly can make more money by turning over his capital several times a year or more than he can by investing through you. Note that most major retail chains rent real estate, they do not own their stores.
3. His income is generally too unsteady to commit cash reserves to an illiquid real estate venture. Retailers tell me their business frequently seems to be "feast or famine."

Now you know the last investing requirement of the investor profile. **He must be in a profession in which there is not a continuing demand for capital.**

1. Attorneys. As a group, the largest number of my investors are attorneys. As a rule you can qualify an attorney in thirty seconds or less because you already know he qualifies in two of the four criteria: education and profession. All you need to know is his previous investment experience and where he keeps his cash.
2. Medical doctors. This is my second largest group. A bit of thought and you will see why they would be qualified. You know they fit the same two criteria the attorneys do.
3. Dentists.
4. Engineers of every kind: electrical, mechanical, structural, and mechanical.

5. Architects.

6. Accountants.

7. Journalists and writers of every kind: newspaper, magazines, radio, television, novelists, and non-fiction writers.

8. Senators and representatives, both state and national.

9. Any member of the judiciary.

10. Top members of the bureaucracy.

11. Land planners.

12. Economists and statisticians.

13. Contractors, both general and those who specialize: road builders, mechanical contractors, electrical contractors, paint contractors. Note that this group tends to earn their excess money in the general field of real estate, so taht they like to put their investments in something with which they are familiar.

14. Real estate professionals such as appraisers, mortgage bankers, brokers, real estate economists, and (don't forget) the top producers in residential sales.

15. Officers and directors of medium-to-large manufacturing companies, preferably **publicly owned.** These folks don't like to fool around in the market and especially do not tend to be excessively invested in their own companies. The act of selling some of their shares exposes them to possible problems because of "insider" knowledge.

Is this list of probable prospects long enough? I didn't deliberately omit entertainers and sport stars, I just have never met one who fit all four criteria, hence there are none in my ventures.

old-money investors

I don't remember when I first heard the term "old-money investor," but I do recall it was early in my real estate career, probably in the mid-50s. Since that time I have heard the term often and have used it myself, especially in lectures. Because it is not in my dictionary, and unless someone tells me differently, I define it as wealth that has been inherited. An old-money investor would be someone who has not earned the money, but rather has inherited it. I don't mean someone who is working at a profession and inherits the money when he is 40 years old or older. I mean someone who was born into wealth.

This would be someone who was raised in a fashion befitting his parents' wealth. There are scads of these people around. They seem to congregate in or near the large northern cities during the spring and fall. During the summer, they tend to be at the "shore." During the winter months, they can be found in their other homes in Florida or California or the islands of the Caribbean. From the moment I started in real estate investments, other well-intentioned persons would introduce me to a wealthy old-money person. In a career of real estate investments spanning nearly three decades, I only have three old-money investors in my ventures, and I have never met one of these three. I know his tax attorney and investment counselor, but I've never met the chap himself. The other two old-money investors were represented by attorneys who were in one or more of my ventures. At my last count, my partner and I have had about four hundred investors in various income-producing ventures. Most of the larger investors have been of more recent vintage, during the past fifteen years or so.

We have also sold most of our earlier ventures so the number of investors currently in our ventures is now approximately 150 persons. Currently there remains only **one** old-money investor. Because of this fact, my recommendation is to **forget about them entirely.** With so many genuine prospects among all the professionals, why would you fool around with investors where your chances are only one in a hundred of developing such a person into an investment client? Perhaps neither my partner nor I know how to qualify such persons as they do not readily fit into our L.E.E.P. category. Or is it perhaps that old money is frightened money? Is an old-money person paralyzed with fear of losing some or all of his wealth?

Generally, I have found that it is quite difficult to make an appointment and sit down with such people. They want to see everything in writing and I don't want to give them anything in writing until I know that they are qualified. Besides, those that have received all of the written data before I have had a chance to qualify them, merely turn the data over to their attorney, banker, or accountant. With all due respect to the attorneys, who collectively are my largest group of investors, they do not have the knowledge or background to evaluate, except from a legal standpoint, the merits of the venture. Additionally, they are under pressure to say something that won't get their clients into financial trouble. They are thrust into a position to say "no," because if they say "yes" and anything goes wrong with the venture, they are liable to be blamed. They reason and rightly so, that if they say "no," their client will never know in the last analysis if the property was a winner or loser. Furthermore, it takes an extremely well-disciplined attorney to avoid giving business advice. The same rationale holds true for bankers and accountants. They just say "no." It really isn't their fault because the typical old-money investor doesn't know anything about real estate investments either and the tendency is to lean on an attorney by asking such a question as, "Is this a good deal?" Unless the attorney were wealthy and sophisticated with plenty of personal investing experience, his correct answer should be, "How in the hell do I know?" The point of all this is to demonstrate that the old money investor is a hundred to one shot at best, so why bother?

proven methods of closing the investor

Let me give you the scenario of what actually takes place with an investor, or a potential investor. The time is 10:00 a.m. I am in my office and I am about to start a private offering. Everything is done and ready and we will shortly start construction. All the financing is done. The architectural drawings are now "working drawings," and the general contractor with whom we have a contract is going through the process of obtaining a building permit. Everything is completed except the raising of the equity money.

I scan our investment lists and locate an attorney who has joined us in our last two ventures. I dial my own local investor calls and so should you. Now is not the time to irritate anyone. Quite a few persons resent it when they answer the phone and hear, "Mr. Smith, Mr. Swesnik calling, one moment please." There may be a silence of anywhere from three to thirty seconds (God forbid it should take longer!) before I get on the phone. To eliminate this annoyance, make the call yourself. After dialing Mr. Smith, I announce to his secretary that I am calling and more often than not the next voice is Mr. Smith's.

"Jack, this is Dick Swesnik. I've an investment that I feel you should hear about. Can you see me tomorrow morning at 10:30?" If he can't make it, I ask him to visit me any morning he is free and I'm not booked with someone else. There is no urgency in my voice, in fact, I'm most casual. **In no event will I accept the appointment at any other time of day. Neither will I go to his office.**

After "doing" investments of the syndicated variety these past umpteen years, these are two things you should never do. In the first instance you are at a psychological disadvantage and put in the category of a "salesman," if you do not have the meeting with your potential investor at your office. You really need to do the qualifying on your home grounds where phones and other disturbing influences can be controlled by **you.** Second, I've found that mid-morning, when I'm fresh and the potential investor is fresh, may be the best time to qualify and close. Sometimes we may run into lunch and that's fine, too. Hardly ever do you want to qualify and close after lunch. He may get sleepy or tired or have slumped mentally after his luncheon cocktail wears off. Because I need to "sharply qualify," (I don't have the time for the usual amenities) this type of activity should not be done in the evenings when hardly anyone is mentally sharp. Another disadvantage of doing this in the evening is that he may be very tired, hungry, and may have had a really trying (or miserable) day. **Therefore, only mid-morning will do.**

Students frequently ask me, "If you only do this in mid-morning you can only talk to one potential investor a day, isn't that correct?" "Yes, that is correct," I reply. Nothing in my rule book dictates that I must be "busy" on a full-time basis. What else do I have to do when I'm ready for the investors and construction may start at any moment? Strange as it may seem to the novice, during this phase of my activity I rarely see more than one investor a day. You must remember that I **start** with a previous investor.

When I first started it was very difficult **not** to "give a pitch" over the phone, so you must guard against saying anything more than, "You may have some serious interest in hearing about my latest venture." Believe me, any qualified investor will conform to your wishes in making himself available at **your** office during a mid-morning workday. Forget weekends if you're dealing in commercial properties. Weekends are for relaxation. Five days a week will do just fine. I know people that work from dawn until unconscious but don't seem to make any serious amounts of money and I'm convinced that developing and acquiring income-producing properties requires no more than a forty-hour week. If it requires more time, you're just doing something terribly wrong or you're pretending that you are working.

One of my favorite investors (he's very intelligent, and I love to talk with him) is a surgeon. Before he invested with me, he kept insisting I come to his home at night. I told him I didn't make "night" calls. He then suggested late afternoon. Knowing he was up at dawn, I refused that time, too. He kept at it until he could see there was no way he would get any information from me unless he came to my office, by appointment, during a regular weekday. This visibly irritated him, and he came in to my office firing questions at me before he had sat down. I just smiled and told him I'd answer any question he could ask but first, I'd need some answers from him. Then I qualified him. As a result of our meeting, he and I have been business friends ever since. The point is that the investor **must** come to you. This is not practicing intimidation but merely being practical. I don't put in a lot of hours so my time is just as valuable to me as the surgeon's is to him. Besides, experience has made a believer of me, "Remember, mid-morning at your office." Don't deviate, you'll come up empty-handed. You will also waste a lot of time.

Another example: My lawyer investor has just come into the office and I go through the social amenities as his host. I show him to his chair, offer him refreshments (coffee or tea), and ask him how much cash he has, where he keeps it, and how much it is earning. That fast, and that direct. Try as he may to obtain information from me **prior** to my knowing about his cash position, he will not succeed. You will note that because the lawyer is a previous investor, this is the only question I need ask. If he were not a previous investor I would have to lead him through the L.E.E.P. system of qualifying.

If he were or were not a previous investor and after I knew he had the cash, I would hand him a covering letter along with a private placement memorandum. The covering letter should never be longer than one and one-half pages and should be a synopsis of the venture. I urge him to read it and ask any question he would like to know about the new project. All along I am employing a technique that I call the "assumptive approach." I'm assuming that he will come into the venture as a limited partner and will do so not only because he is qualified but because he **must** so, so sickening are his investment alternatives. In the final analysis, I will "close" him because he **needs** my help in bringing him to the precise moment where he will write a check. Needing my help is a requirement because no matter how sophisticated an investor is, I have yet to hear one say, "OK, count me in." It just doesn't happen that way. As most salesmen are aware, you need an "objection" to close and I frequently push my client to an "objection" so that I can close using the subordinated question technique. After a few, or as many questions as the situation may dictate, I'll ask, "Mr. Smith (or Jack, if he is a previous investor) do you want to take title in your name solely or as joint tenants with your wife with the right of survivorship?" With that I ask for his check made out to the limited partnership. That's all there is to it for me, and it should not be any more complicated than that for you. Remember, you have nothing to **sell,** he must **want** to be a partner in your new venture.

Here follow some typical investor questions and here are the answers I frequently use.

Q. Dick, is this an investment you can recommend to me?

A. I can't make the investment decision for you, it's your decision.

Q. Can I get my money out at some later date, if I should need it?

A. No. You are very illiquid in this kind of venture. If there is the slightest question in your mind that you will need your money prior to our refinancing and ultimate sale of the real property, you should definitely not come in at this time.

Q. I don't have the expertise to make this kind of a decision, to whom should I go for objective advice?

A. Here is a copy of all the real estate counselors in our area who are members of the American Society of Real Estate Counselors. I've circled the names of those counselors who could give you sound investment advice. Those I have circled have indicated this is an area of their expertise.

Q. Who else is in the deal?

A. A call girl and the pope. Your question surely must be a joke. What does the investment strategy of other persons have to do with yours? Would you feel better about all of this if my mother and brother were investors? Do you think their being in the venture will help us rent or hold down expenses?

Q. Do you have any of your own money in the venture?

A. Refer to the beginning of Chapter 4 to read my typical answer, "I feel like a composer . . ."

Q. Can I lose my investment entirely?

A. If it doesn't rent up beyond 80 percent occupancy, you surely can.

Q. Is that likely?

A. Nothing is guaranteed, except death and taxes.

Q. What are the tax consequences?

A. I have it capsulized in the covering letter, and it is explained in detail in the private placement memorandum (PPM). (Open the PPM and hand the PPM to the investor with it opened to the section on "Federal Tax Consequences.")

Q. Do you honestly think the project will rent up quickly? There seems to be a lot of space on the market.

A. I cannot make an honest judgment as to the speed with which we will rent. We won't have the building ready for occupancy for another 18 months. Since neither of us has a crystal ball, your guess is as good as mine.

Q. When do you think we will sell the finished project?

A. From past experience, I could make a reasonable guess. We only have the past to go on so the best I could do is summarize what has happened before. Generally, we may sell the project between 8 and 12 years from the date of initial occupancy. This assumes there will be no serious changes in the federal income tax laws.

Q. What change could hurt us?

A. Any change that raises the taxes on capital gain. If the change is severe enough, we could be "locked in." That means we'll all probably die prior to the sale of the property and liquidation of the partnership.

Q. How reliable is your cash flow projection?

A. Very unreliable. I have **never** made a cash flow projection that has been precisely the same as the actual cash flow.

Q. Has the project developed more or less cash flow than you have projected?

A. I'd say the error has been down the middle. Some projects do worse, some better.

You will note there is not the slightest attempt at "puffing," pressure selling, or the like. The typical limited partner is likely to be quite sophisticated. Any exaggeration, however slight, will cause you to lose him. Here you have an opportunity to tell the truth as you know it. Nothing will turn on your tentative investor more than the funereal-type answers just listed. **They want to hear everything negative you can say about the project!** Peculiarly, the investor starts defending the investment because he feels you seem to be deliberately denigrating the investment.

letters of disclaimer

In order to protect yourself against future lawsuits and possible future actions from governmental authorities, it is imperative that you closely follow all the steps outlined heretofore regarding your offering. Additionally, your securities lawyer may recommend that concomitantly with the signing of the limited partnership agreement, your new investor limited partner execute a "letter of disclaimer."

Our office insists on this action. Who knows or can remember what an investor thinks he understood at the time he was furnished with a private placement memorandum? While the likelihood is slim that anyone can prove you deliberately misled them a few years back, the investor perceives he remembers something different from the facts. Though the odds against you are very slight, the penalties of giving misinformation are severe. The penalties for misleading an investor are very great. Therefore you should consider a letter of disclaimer an absolute "must," and it must be an integral part of your private placement memorandum.

Here follows an example of a letter of disclaimer I actually used in one of my private placement memoranda. You will note our attorney calls it an "Investment Letter." You are cautioned **not** to use this unless your securities attorney thinks it is necessary and relevant to what you will be doing. I have deliberately changed the name of the partnership and made some minor and unimportant other changes.

FORM OF INVESTMENT LETTER:
Mr. Richard H. Swesnik, General Partner
Hilarious Associates
1990 K Street, N.W.
Suite 400
Washington, D.C. 20006

Re: Hilarious Associates
District of Columbia
Limited Partnership

Dear Mr. Swesnik:

In consideration of my being permitted to purchase from Hilarious Associates (the "Partnership"), a District of Columbia limited partnership, limited partnership interests in the partnership (the "Interests") at $100,000.00 per $\frac{1}{30}$th of the total Interests as more fully described in the Partnership's Private Placement Memorandum dated August 1, 19———, I hereby represent that:

1. I had an annual gross income for the previous year (or estimated annual gross income for the current year) of at least $100,000. My net worth is $350,000 exclusive of home, furnishings, jewelry, furs, and automobiles.

2. ——————— has acted as my official representative under Rule 146 under the Securities Act of 1933 in connection with evaluating the risks and merits of this investment. [If no official representative, this paragraph should be deleted.]

3. I (together with my official representative, if any) have such knowledge and experience in financial and business matters so as to be capable of evaluating the risks and merits of this investment. I am aware that this investment is speculative and represents a substantial risk of loss; and I am able to bear the economic risk of this investment, even if it involves a complete loss.

4. I have been furnished (a) a copy of the Partnership's Private Placement Memorandum, which I have carefully reviewed and understand; (b) any additional information which I have requested; and (c) the opportunity to communicate directly with you and others to verify the accuracy of and amplify the information in the Private Placement Memorandum.

5. I am aware that the Interests are not and will not be registered under the Securities Act of 1933 and applicable state securities laws, and that I may have to continue to bear the economic risk of this investment indefinitely.

6. I understand that the Interests (a) are subject to substantial restrictions on transferability and (b) cannot be sold, assigned, transferred, pledged, or otherwise disposed of—and I agree that I will not sell, assign, transfer, pledge, or otherwise dispose of the Interests—without registration under the Securities Act of 1933 and applicable state securities laws, or exemptions therefrom. I understand that any proposed sale, assignment, transfer, pledge, or other disposition pursuant to an exemption must be supported by an opinion of counsel for the seller, assignor, transferor, pledgor, or disposor, which is acceptable to counsel for the Partnership, and that such restrictions are set forth in the Partnership Agreement. I also understand that the Partnership will be under no obligation to register the Interests, or to comply with any applicable exemption from registration, or to supply me with any information necessary to enable me to sell, assign, transfer, pledge, or otherwise dispose of the Interests pursuant to Rule 144 under the Securities Act of 1933 (assuming such Rule becomes applicable and is otherwise available with respect to transfer of the Interests) or pursuant to state securities laws.

7. I am subscribing for investment purposes only, and exclusively for my own account. I have no agreement, understanding, arrangement, or intention to divide or share ownership of my Interest with anyone else or to resell, assign, transfer, pledge, or otherwise dispose of all or any portion of my Interest to any other person.

8. I further understand that the Partnership is relying in part on my representations in this letter and, as provided in the Partnership Agreement I will hold the Partnership harmless from all liability, loss, or damage arising out of any breach of the foregoing representations.

Date: ——————, 19———

—————————
(Investor)

As harsh as this investment letter may appear to be it is merely an accurate epresentation to you of what the investor understands his risks to be. If your prospective investor will not sign such a letter he **cannot be allowed** to acquire one of your limited partnership interests.

The problems that could occur later **require** you to obtain the letter. Let me give you an example. An unmarried attorney bequeathed his interest in one of limited partnerships to a home for the elderly, where one of his parents or aunt or uncle (I never did know) apparently resided. A few years later the attorney died. His capital account was a negative $30,000. This meant if he were alive and sold the interest for $1.00, he would be subject to a long-term capital gains of $30,001! What had occurred during his ownership was a loss for federal income tax purposes of $60,000. He originally purchased his limited partnership interest for $30,000. His losses, which consisted of construction interest, taxes, and depreciation totaled $60,000, not only wiping out his positive $30,000 capital account, but reducing it to a negative $30,000. Realizing the tremendous gain he would realize if he sold the partnership interest, he cleverly gave his unit to the home for the aged while he was living. He probably deducted (I wasn't privy to the federal income tax form he filed) the $30,000 figure from his taxable income as a charitable contribution. He probably should have reported $30,000 taxable income. Fortunately, he had executed an investment letter when he first acquired his interest. While the home for the aged could not become a limited partner, they nonetheless received the quarterly cash flow distribution.

The home for the aged was preparing to enlarge its facilities and needed to "cash out" the partnership unit that it had received as a charitable contribution and they wrote me asking its "market" value. Inasmuch as there were no prior sales because the original offering was closed there was no "market" value. The partnership unit was not registered under the Securities Act of 1933, and the lawyer for the home for the aged was unwilling to give any outside potential investor a guarantee that the unit need not be registered.

He then had two options open: he could "canvass" the other limited partners in the partnership from the list of limited partners, which I would have furnished him, or he could offer the unit to me. The attorney, obviously well-informed about securities, did not wish to make an offering in which he might have to prepare a private placement memorandum in order to conform with the appropriate securities laws. The preparation of such a lengthy document is so expensive it might cost the home for the aged more in legal fees than they could realize from the sale. My partner and I personally bought the unit from the home for the aged at its original cost, which was at a price we deemed fair. Everyone in the transaction was happy. Probably the deceased lawyer would have been happy, too. The investment letter executed by the original investing partner would have forced the attorney for the home for the aged to obtain an opinion (or prepare one himself) stating that the limited partnership unit was exempt from registration under the Securities Act of 1933 **unless** he had arranged for or prepared a new private placement memorandum.

The partnership was thus protected from a total stranger obtaining the unit without such an investor being fully informed as to the risks and merits of such an investment. The absence of the investment letter could have forced us to accept the new stranger as a limited partner, and later we could have been sued on the basis that the new partner did not have all the information required in order to make a reasonable judgment.

"slow" sales back-up

Suppose you have marketed your limited partner interests and have "sold" about 60 percent of such units. Time may be running out as you certainly need to sell all of the participations to meet your financial commitments, having just approved the final building contract with your general contractor.

There are several things you may do—all of which I have thought about through the years in case of a need to back myself up. I wanted to be sure I could always meet my financial commitments on time.

First, you may want to talk with a family member who has some cash available, not necessarily to invest for the life of the venture because he is not or may not be qualified under L.E.E.P. However, he may be interested in purchasing as much as 40 percent of the venture under a predetermined buy-back arrangement. You will want this arrangement to be an integral part of your "full disclosure doctrine" so your securities lawyer will advise you on the nature of the documentations and he will want you to include the data in the private placement memorandum. The way this could work is as follows: He (the family member) will have a "put," which means that he could sell back to you one-fourth of the 40 percent each December for four consecutive years under a prearranged written agreement that could call for increasing buy-back prices. For example, supposing you agree to repurchase 10 percent each year (if he so desires) for an increase in price of 10 percent at the end of the first year; 20 percent at the end of the second year; 30 percent at the end of the third year; and 40 percent at the end of the fourth year. On the other hand, you would have a "call" (an option) on **all** the units he owns, at any time based on the same terms and conditions. If the unit prices were $50,000 for each of eight units, you could repurchase all eight units or any number of them at any time but he would have the right to force you to repurchase two units each year with a 10 percent profit, increasing by 10 percent each year. This would be $110,000 for two units the first year; $120,000 for two units the second year; $130,000 for two units the third year; and finally, the last two units for $140,000 the fourth (and last) year. This kind of business arrangement can contribute a great deal toward allaying your fears of being "sold out" especially with your first offering.

Years ago, thinking I would need it, I worked up a similar arrangement on paper with the help of my attorney. My family member was to be my brother but the arrangement was never finalized because my first two or three investors recommended my venture to their family and friends. The partnership was sold out completely so soon I never really had the chance to discuss it, in depth, with my brother.

After the partnership units were completely sold out, my banker took me to lunch. We chatted about the tentative arrangement I had worked out with my attorney. He said "Swez, as long as you stay with **quality** developments, you should never have to pay more than the prime rate plus one." The prime rate at that time was 6 percent so that meant I could borrow at 7 percent per annum, simple interest, should I need funds to back myself up in case of slow sales.

The greater the length of time you have before actual settlement, the smaller the possibility you will need to use the "put" and "call" technique described here. It is legal of course, but it must be disclosed.

resale of partnership interests

At the beginning of your syndicating career, either for developments or acquisitions, you must make a yes or no choice as to your involvement in the resale of limited partnership interests. Some of the factors that will influence your decision are the profitability of your office acting as a sales agent for the resale of units; whether you choose to become a licensed "securities" dealer; and finally to determine (well in advance of your first offering) if you are now, or think you will be later, in a financial position to acquire some of the partnership units you originally had offered in case of death or insolvency of a limited partner. Your securities lawyer can tell you all the things you will have to do should you decide to become active in the sales (for a commission) or in the purchase and resale (as a principal) of such units.

In my office we had originally decided to be "the market" for our own limited partnership units and had actually become licensed as securities dealers. We did this because virtually all of our original offerings were registered with the Securities and Exchange Commission. When we decided as a matter of business policy to concentrate on private offerings with higher units of participation (in one of our investments the **minimum** participation was $175,000), we also decided that we would no longer be active in the resale of partnership units. Because all the selling of the participations is done by me or my partner, be certain that all of the investors are well qualified and understand they are illiquid. As a result of informed selling, there are virtually no transactions of individual units during the lifetime of the original investor until the entire project is sold and all the cash is distributed.

You now know who and where the investors are. You should know how much to charge; how to market and close your participations; how to draft (with your attorney) an investment letter and a near perfect partnership agreement; how to provide back-up in case of slow sales; and whether you should consider handling the resale of partnership units. Construction is about to start so you soon will be busy on other important matters. You will consider such diverse things as signs, ground-breaking ceremonies and hiring your consulting engineer. There will be other things requiring your attention such as topping-out parties and the correct marketing tools. Will you need a brochure and if you do what will it say? Will you be doing different kinds of projects? If so, you will need to study the marketing problems among apartments, office buildings and shopping centers.

community shopping center, virginia square, arlington, virginia. prime success factor for shopping centers—location. this one is built in 1950's—value $2,500,000.

8

your development begins

chapter 8 outline

signs: starting the job

There is nothing that will produce better results without getting into much higher costs than to have a sign identifying your project. This is true for office buildings, shopping centers, and apartment houses. As a test, our leasing personnel are urged to ask a prospective tenant how they first became aware of the project. Approximately 60 percent respond that it was the sign that first alerted them to our project. Because three out of five persons respond favorably to a sign, this is an area where you must devote a fair amount of time. As you may be aware, the building of a sign that conforms to local codes and ordinances is a task for a signmaker. Unless the sign shop is enormous and tends to specialize in real estate signs, you will need to hire a graphic artist. A graphic artist will translate whatever you wish to convey to the public into "graphics," which is what a sign is—graphic art. By the clever use of color and light and after a study of the site for sign orientation, a good graphic artist can develop a sign that may increase the number of "leads," which you are seeking. A good sign can't sell your project, but it can increase the amount of interest in your building. Some persons, who otherwise seem knowledgeable, hire a sign man and the result is predictable: poor graphics. This is comparable to your developing a project by stealing plans from someone else's project and having the plans faithfully executed by a general contractor. Without proper site orientation and your input as to proper plans and specifications, the project will probably be a disaster.

Although you may feel you do not need to spend a lot of money on a sign because your project is so attractive, no one knows this during the planning and building phase but you—certainly not the public in the marketplace that you wish to attract. Also consider the length of time your sign will be in place. Sometimes it is in place for 18 to 24 months. Don't get stingy with your signs. The graphic artist you may wish to employ can be found in a large sign company (usually he or she is the owner) or at a good advertising agency. Whenever you notice an attractive sign, note who built it. Usually the sign company that built the sign is identified at the lower portion of the sign, in the middle or right-hand side. Remember, this is who built it, not necessarily who designed it. It is a good idea to have the preliminary sign drawings reviewed by your architect. Since most architects have considerable graphic skills, their input is frequently helpful. Make sure your completed sign is readily identifiable and readable from a moving automobile. This means the message must be brief. I've seen signs (and so have you) that only told who the developer was, not what the building was going to be.

Don't you think it is a good idea to restrict the number of signs that could crop up on your job (the architect, the contractor, his subcontractors, the lender, and others) to allow only those conforming to certain sizes and location on the job? I do—because I'm not going to hire a graphics artist who designs a fine sign, pay his fee and that of the sign maker, only to have my $5,000 to $10,000 (or more) sign be outnumbered and lost among all the other signs. Believe me, this is a hairy area because everyone on the job wants identity, but reasonable restrictions seem to be reasonably received.

ground-breaking ceremonies

In your cost budget, be certain to include the cost of ground-breaking ceremonies. The ceremonies are generally a good deal of fun and frequently bring together, sometimes for the first time, many of the important people without whom the job could not start. Here follows a list of such people you may wish to invite (not in any particular order):

1. The realtor who brought the site to you.
2. The former landowner(s).
3. The architect.
4. The construction lender.
5. The permanent lender.
6. The general contractor.
7. The mortgage broker.
8. The real estate editors of your local paper.
9. The pastor, priest, or rabbi of your choice (what harm can come from a blessing?).
10. The leasing personnel.
11. Any tenants you may have signed up prior to the start of construction.
12. Your tax and securities lawyer.
13. Your accountant.
14. Your company's main banker.
15. The highest local political official available.
16. Your limited partners.
17. A professional photographer.

These ceremonial affairs followed by a light, catered affair (buffet and bar) at a local hotel or club are always a "blast." I find the group is so heterogeneous, everybody seems to enjoy the ceremony and lunch. Here are some nonmandatory suggestions you may care to follow:

1. It seems to work out best to have the ceremony start promptly at the site at 11:30 a.m., mid-week if possible.
2. You personally should announce to all present (in your own words) how glad you are they took the time and showed enough interest to attend. Introduce as many persons in the group as you can, and finally the clergyman.
3. Insure your invitations are out at least two weeks before. Have your office check on those attending by following up with a phone call.
4. In case of inclement weather, provide for the ceremony to take place in the hotel or club, with the room clearly designated on your invitation. In the event of inclement weather, make sure someone from your office stays at the site to direct participants to the hotel or club. Indicate in your invitations that if the weather is bad the ceremony will be held at the designated room at the hotel or club.

5. Have a "gold" (polished brass) shovel on hand so that the photographer can shoot as many persons and groups as possible "breaking the ground."

6. Keep the entire ceremony to not longer than 10 minutes (you, the clergyman, you again, and the politician). People get bored or tired standing for any longer than ten minutes.

7. Have a souvenir for each person attending, passing it out as they arrive on the site. Look in the yellow pages under "advertising specialties." There are many items which can be "customized." Do this at least five weeks in advance.

8. If the group you anticipate attending is over 25 people, notify the local police because they may wish to control traffic at or near the site.

The entire ground-breaking ceremony with cocktails and the light luncheon buffet should end by 1 p.m. You have the best opportunity you will ever have to bring as many diverse persons together who have made or will make a substantial contribution to help your project. It doesn't cost a lot of money, and if it doesn't create goodwill, there is a notable absence of ill will. Just treat the expense as one of your soft costs. The partnership pays the bill, and it is always money well spent.

your consulting engineer

No matter how delightful your relationship is with your general contractor, his field superintendent is not an octopus and he has only one set of eyes. Consider that once your building is out of the ground, many trades are working simultaneously. Plumbers, electricians, carpenters, concrete finishers, tilemen, plasterers, painters, and many other persons are all over the building. Typically, these men are supervised by their own "straw bosses," usually journeymen, paid a higher daily wage for the job work and supervision. Assuming total honesty and a commitment to excellence, you will nonetheless need your own consulting engineer. The general contractor can only ensure timely arrival of materials on the job and do the scheduling of who does what and when. His field superintendent can only supervise his own personnel, generally carpenters, concrete finishers, and laborers. With so many people working simultaneously, you need a professional engineer to present you with a weekly job report. The engineer **must** inspect the job at least this often (weekly) to guarantee that the subcontractors are installing the designated equipment precisely according to the specifications. Nothing can cost you more than finding your mechanical system is fouled up because of substitute materials or sloppy workmanship. Occasionally subcontractors will get "cute," substituting either an inferior product or delivering a product from the same manufacturer with less desirable features. Let me be specific and give you two examples of how even the general contractor and the job superintendent can be fooled.

Our consulting engineer, who was furnished with a complete set of plans and specifications, has both a degree in mechanical engineering and one in electrical engineering, not as unusual a combination as you may think. He reported that the electrical subcontractor was substituting aluminum bus ducts for copper bus ducts (the bus ducts carry electricity to a transformer on each floor) in one of our office buildings under construction. We called our general contractor who quite naturally became upset and sent the owner of the electrical firm to see my partner, who is in charge of construction for our firm. My partner, Herb Blum, is not known for his gentility, but for his developmental and leasing skills. The saving apparently was so great by substituting aluminum for copper that the electrical contractor offered to pay our office $100,000 on the spot if we let him continue. Herb used four choice expletives and the aluminum was removed and copper installed in its place as the specifications required.

The difficulty with aluminum as a conductor of electricity is that it doesn't "give" (i.e., expand and contract) as copper will do because it is more rigid. All buildings move slightly. As a consequence in buildings where there are aluminum bus ducts **all** connections have to be manually tightened by licensed electricians, at least once annually. This becomes quite expensive as it **must** be done on a Sunday or legal holiday and because the main electrical service is disconnected by the power company, no one else can work in the building during the "tightening" process. You can hardly empty your building during a normal workday just because your electrical contractor can save you several thousand dollars in overtime pay.

Another time our consulting engineer examined the huge water tower, located on the roof, which is used to cool the water through evaporation prior to introducing it through the coils of the condenser, which removes heat from the refrigerant in the condenser. The heating unit in the cooling tower pan submerged in the water was not properly connected and therefore inoperative. Had the cooling tower burst because of freezing, you could guess the enormous cost of repair or possible replacement. One of our condensers is turned on during daytime hours regardless of the outdoor temperature because even in cold weather there is a demand for some air conditioning. This is especially true in restaurants or any other place that can attract many "heaters" (people).

You are responsible to your lender, your investors, and your conscience to produce the best building possible for the price you are paying. Unless you are technically trained to inspect, at least once weekly, the work being done on your building under construction, hire an independent consulting engineer. The cost is peanuts compared to the probable savings in preventing shoddy work and material substitutions.

Please do not have your architect act as your consulting engineer. He will probably not be qualified to perform this task. For that matter, unless you are the head of an institution with money no real object, don't have your architect "supervise" the job. He can't and neither can anyone else. No one person can be all over the job site watching everything going on all the time.

topping-out parties

Imagine my amazement when my general contractor called me to attend a topping-out party. It was 1958, I had been in the business since 1951, and although I am by nature very curious, I had never heard of such a party. Frankly, I thought I was being "put on" as I had been as a young man when I worked as a roughneck on a rotary drilling rig in the oil fields. On my first day on the rig I discovered I was to be the butt of all jokes and put-ons. My driller sent me to the tool shed to look for such diverse equipment as a "sky hook," and an "end rope" as well as sending me crawling up 110 feet to the top of the rig to change light bulbs. After getting the roof on the 18-story apartment he was constructing for one of my partnerships, the general contractor was doing what most builders do when they get to this point. He learned of topping-out parties from his father, who was also in the building business. At any rate, these parties have apparently been going on for generations. It was nothing to get excited about. It is essentially a drunken feast for all the men who happened to work on the job to the point of pouring concrete for the roof. We had booze, beer, several roast turkeys, roast beef, ham and fried chicken—all being consumed on the first floor starting when the afternoon bell had rung signaling the end of the workers' day. All the men played at "macho," swapping lies about their prowess with women. Yuck!

The main reason you should know this is that one day you will hear about a topping-out party to which you were not invited and may think you are being left out of something. If you dig headaches from excess alcohol, macho lies, and overeating, be sure to attend. In truth, it is just a more or less harmless party for the workers on the job who celebrate **their** feelings of accomplishment. You will therefore be an outsider, not one of them.

brochures and other marketing tools

The property speaks for itself. Or does it? Depending upon what type of space you are marketing, you will need more than just a sign in order to market the space. If you are doing an apartment house, for example, you will need something in writing to give to a prospective tenant. This literature acts as backup material for your rental clerks. You may wish to identify the types of apartments: one bedroom, one bedroom and den, and others. Showing approximate room measurements acts as an aid for future residents to plan their furniture layouts. Showing the location of grammar, junior high, and high schools and listing rules relating to student buses is very helpful. Locating churches and synagogues is usually helpful too. Identifying neighborhood retail shopping is a must.

Besides school buses, religious worship, and neighborhood shops, you or your staff should inquire about and include in your brochure all the data you can collect on transportation. Surely not everyone uses private transportation to and from work. How helpful it could be if your brochure contained bus routes to and from your project along with departure and arrival times. Ever see this in an apartment brochure?

The task of a residential developer is to try to relieve residents of life's minor frustrations. I defy you to telephone the public transportation office in the city in which you live and get an immediate **intelligent** response to inquiries regarding arrival and departure times of local buses and/or rapid elevated rail trains and subways. This task is yours, **not** the resident's.

But a word of caution relating to brochures—don't let some advertising agency talk you into spending a bundle of money for words. Costly brochures are mostly designed and printed to massage the ego of a developer. Words that describe the elegance of your apartment project are meaningless to anyone who can see. What can and should be described is data important to a prospective resident, without which he or she would necessarily have to conduct considerable research.

So, before you agree to produce an advertising brochure for your apartment development make sure that one is necessary. Assuming you think it is, be certain it doesn't contain such inane phrases as "a return to elegance," or "live as the glorious Romans did" (they didn't have inside plumbing, running water, electricity, or gas, not to mention heat and air conditioning—who in the world wants to live as the glorious Romans did?). **Facts** are what a brochure should contain, and these facts should be explicit and not conclusions of some far-out copywriter working at your advertising agency. You are selling space, visible space, not "fashions."

I have seriously questioned the need for brochures for office buildings. A typical floor plan is necessary, but of what possible use is it to a prospective tenant that a business card wouldn't suffice? Yet I have read dozens of office building brochures, some so fancy that they could have cost between three and six dollars each. Never have I read anything in these brochures that wasn't visible or already known to a prospective downtown tenant. The only brochure for an office building my partner and I authorized was for one in which we had a two-story shopping mall.

Shopping center brochures for prospective store owners or leasing specialists with major chains are a must because they show not only the layouts but usually provide space for the developer of the center to write in the name and type of store as each lease is executed. They also tend to outline the permanent market to which the center will cater frequently through demographics. Demographics are increasingly being used. They are a statistical study mainly of the size and distribution of the population. Recently it has also included average income, ethnic background, religious preferences, etc. Most of the data originates with our census data. It is very important to a store owner or leasing specialist to know if the size of the market the center is catering to is 30,000 persons, or 100,000 persons. These are facts and are absolutely necessary for a prospective tenant to have to evaluate the space he is being offered.

Advertising, whether newspaper, radio, or television, doesn't seem to do a darn thing except to advertise an "opening." When I first started, an ad man convinced me that advertising was absolutely essential to remain in business. I don't see a real need for anything other than a properly designed sign for office buildings and apartments, except perhaps a small blurb for the apartments in the classified section of a local newspaper.

the rent-up period

This time during the development period seems to be the most hectic and when uncertainty and apprehension abound. If you have done everything **without error,** which is a goal and rarely a reality, you still can't predict the speed with which your project will rent up. this is not a business for the timid or ulcer-prone because markets truly are not predictable. They behave exquisitely or there is no rental action at all. The project will rent up slowly, possibly taking years to achieve 100 percent occupancy or will rent so quickly you may think you may have set your rents too low.

apartments

If you are doing an apartment house project and find difficulty in renting up quickly there is something you can do. You can lower rents and positive results will occur. This is a proven fact: the lower the monthly rent, the greater the possibility of faster rent-up. To insure your apartment rental project will rent up quickly, it will be necessary for you to survey the competitive rental market just prior to your grand opening. This will be your second competitive survey and your task will be to verify what you had originally learned. Chances are that during a period as long as 12 to 18 months the apartment market may change, especially in a dynamic city. Once you have established the correct rental price, don't panic! Remember that you should have allowed for dismal rental conditions in your projected pro forma cash flow statements. You should be breaking even at 80 percent occupancy. If you either didn't allow for slow rent-up in your projections or can't break even at 80 percent occupancy, pray for divine intervention.

Nothing else works except lowering the rents further—and this may produce negative cash flow, which causes further problems. Still, don't panic. This won't help the project, and if you act without confidence in the project this attitude will pervade not only your central office organization, but will permeate down through to the rental clerk, who above all others needs to be "up."

A successful rental project has the "smell" of success. Fresh flowers in your model apartments twice weekly is money better spent than larger classified ads. Most folks are unaware of subtle odors, but nearly every adult seems to like the smell of a new automobile. It seems to smell "leathery." Your architect can help you choose a room deodorizer that has a "woodsy" fragrance. Most folks like to move in to a **new** apartment as opposed to one that has been formerly occupied.

All of these things help—but on the outside chance that nothing seems to help the rentals, there are rental specialists, independent contractors who for a fairly stiff fee will rent up troubled properties. Most of these firms are located in the Southwest and West but will travel—of course. Many major management firms have used these rental specialists at one time or another, so don't feel disgraced or crushed if you need them because you either borrowed too much, didn't raise enough capital to cover longer rent-up time, or can't break even at 80 percent occupancy.

office buildings

If you have an office building that is ready for occupancy and rentals are slow, you have to employ different tactics. For one thing, and this amazed me, **lowering** the rental price produces **no more possible tenants.** If you are in a $10.00 per square foot (yearly) market and you really cut the rent, say by 15 percent down to $8.50 per square foot, all that happens is that you attract a worse class of possible tenants. These may include collection agencies, "bucket shops" that either sell securities, or set up appointments for encyclopedia sales, aluminum siding, or worse. These assorted cheapies lend nothing to the building that will help you attract other quality tenants. Inasmuch as you don't want this kind of tenancy, the best strategy is to **raise** the rental price. This lets all prospects know that you will not sell your quality space for less, even in a soft market. Office building tenants will want to be in a well-located, expensive, and quality building.

If you have done all of your homework you will realize you have indeed produced a quality building. A "sharp" lobby, well-planned toilet facilities, and attention to your elevator planning will set apart your building from the competition, especially those with built-in design errors. Because this is so, you will have created an atmosphere that will especially attract the quality tenant. Don't give the space away, on the contrary, charge more. Cadillacs and Lincolns cost more than Chevrolets or Fords, not because they are approximately the same size and may give one status, but because everything about them is better—the motors, the comfort of the ride, the amenities. Only when you get into a Mercedes-Benz or Rolls Royce are you into snob appeal. A Mercedes or Rolls may be a better car than a Cadillac or Lincoln, but most folks agree that they are not worth approximately twice as much than a Cadillac or Lincoln in the case of a Mercedes, or four times as much in the case of a Rolls Royce.

You can command a higher rent if you have created a Cadillac or Lincoln building. I hope you have not created a Rolls Royce type of office building. Unlike autos, office tenants will pay only the going rents (plus or minus 5 percent). But yours should be priced among the top buildings and if it is renting slowly, the rates should be increased. Everytime my partner and I have been in a slow rental market we have done better with our buildings by increasing the rentals slightly. This helps the quality tenant in his decision making. He feels if we are asking for more rent than our competition, we are probably offering a better building. In Washington, D.C., our tenants are mainly legal and accounting firms and trade associations. They want to be in the same kind of location as their counterparts and frequently try to outdo one another. They are not attracted by cheaper rents. They reason that either the location is bad or the building does not have the amenities they are seeking if they are offered a bargain rent. The actual lease negotiations are conducted by leasing brokers working and living in your community or by your own personnel or yourself. To the extent you have quality negotiators representing **you,** that is the kind of lease you will obtain. In order to protect yourself, you need yet another attorney, one who specializes in leases and other forms of real estate practice.

In the first place, be aware that your lease must protect you against increases in operating expenses including real estate taxes and insurance as well as normal operating expenses. Normal operating expenses include but are not necessarily limited to management fees, utilities, repairs, on-site engineers, and porters as well as janitorial services.

Increases in both operating costs and taxes and insurance are payed by each tenant in accordance with the space the tenant occupies in relation to the entire rentable space. If all expenses escalate $50,000 over the base year (usually an estimate of expenses for the first full year or if lower, the actual expenses for the first full year), then a tenant occupying 2 percent of the total space would pay $1,000 in addition to his regular annual rental.

Since 1975, our office (Swesnik and Blum Companies) has been charging an escalator related to any increase of the Consumer Price Index (the CPI). Our reasoning for such an increase follows. We believe in large equities, and it is our equity we are trying to protect. If we are putting in $4 million equity above $16 million in financing, we are making a 20 percent down payment. Since all the other escalators **hold us even** in relation to escalating costs, we are going backwards (the dollar is losing value because of inflation) with our equity dollars. For example, a sale at cost would give us back our $4 million, but those dollars are worth less as each year goes by because they have lost some of the purchasing power those dollars had in 1975. We carefully explain this to each prospective tenant and ask for an increase tied to 20 percent (our cash equity) of the total annual increase in the CPI. We think we pioneered this type of increase in the greater metropolitan area of Washington, D.C., because now our fellow developers protect their equities in the same fashion. This makes asking for such protection commonplace in the marketplace.

The same tenant occupying 2 percent of the rentable space thus pays us an equity escalator tied to 20 percent of the CPI. Should the annual increase be 6 percent, then our 2 percent tenant has a rental increase of 20 percent of the 6 percent or 1.2 percent for the year just concluded.

We collect such escalators in the CPI and operating expenses including taxes and insurance at one time, payable 30 days after we present the tenant with the figures supplied by our accountants. At the same time, his basic monthly rental is increased based upon the past year's total escalations. This process continues each year. Protecting your equity is certainly not a new idea, but it may be that in your area you have not done it as yet. Try it. Reasonable and intelligent tenants understand the concept. It is helpful if you have your leases already **printed** in advance with care taken to insure that all possible escalations are spelled out in plain English. The only blanks in the lease aside from the basic rental and tenant's name should be for the percentage of space the tenant occupies in relation to the whole. Lawyers will use the terms "pro rata" or "ratable" or "ratably" all meaning the proportionate amount of space occupied by the tenant in relation to the whole, always expressed in a percentage.

shopping centers

Most developers generally can't obtain permanent financing for a shopping center without a fair amount of preleasing. Yet, occasionally a developer will believe in a site that he owns or has just agreed to purchase and will seek to develop it. He believes it will rent because of traffic counts in front of his area or because he has employed an economist who will statistically demonstrate that the site will support "X" square feet of retail space. That is why you occasionally see a failing shopping center. The developer used his own money so there was no external financial review of what he was doing.

There are two truisms many retail executives and store owners believe. First, no rent is too high if the store can do a high enough volume of business. Second, you can't **give** (charge no rent) a store to a retailer who has no faith in the location. Hence, a retailer has three rules about where to go into business: location, location, and location.

A personal acquaintance of mine specializes in community shopping centers, usually between 100,000 and 150,000 square feet of retail space. His pattern was to place a drugstore on one end of his shopping strip and a supermarket on the other. Nothing spectacular about this. Hundreds of centers follow this pattern. He told me the "AAA" tenants with national reputations and impeccable credit were difficult to deal with. In fact, he said, you couldn't really make any money leasing to such tenants. They helped pay the mortgage, and they were necessary to attract decent financing. The bottom line or cash flow he would earn was invariably from relatively "weak" (meaning local ownership without strong credit ratings) tenants. As examples, he cited the shoemaker, the beauty salon, the dry cleaner, and the barber shop—generally not retailers, but types of stores essentially selling service. Added to his list of service stores would invariably be a local bakery (usually a mom and pop operation) and a hardware store. My acquaintance is financially well off but his monthly income is essentially dependent on tenants with weak credit.

He told me that while attempting to rent up his first new center, he offered his cousin, who was a barber, a store for absolutely no rent for the first two years—free rent. He reasoned it was better to have a rented store than a vacant one, so he would give his cousin a break. He was flabbergasted when his cousin laid down the conditions under which he would open the barber shop. The center owner was shocked to learn he would have to advance the cash to equip the store and **pay the tenant** $300 monthly for the first year. This was the barber's financial assessment of the location. He felt he had to be subsidized in order to build a following at that particular location. The point is there are locations that seem so undesirable to a future tenant that free rent is not good enough to attract them.

Happily the center was doing well two years later and is performing superbly now. Shopping centers of the community type are risky because they do not follow a behavioral pattern that objective observers would like them to. For a variety of reasons some centers get off to a good start only to fade as the years go on. Others have a devil of a time attracting shoppers and limp along for a few years and then they take off like a jet with soaring overall sales figures.

The important money made in the shopping center development business is made by the large regional mall developers. All leases are negotiated on a per square foot price per year, which is the minimum. This rental amount is paid monthly. Gross sales are computed either semiannually or annually and, as additional rent, the tenant pays a fixed percentage of the gross sales. He gets credit for his regular monthly rent **against** the sales percentage. These percentages are more or less standard in the industry and are readily obtainable from books and other data that one can purchase through the International Council of Shopping Centers, the industry trade group.

Additionally, if real estate taxes are **increased** on the overall project, the leases require each tenant to pay his proportionate share. The lease usually will state that store #4, for example, occupies 1.7 percent of the total rental space. In the event real estate taxes are increased $10,000 in the year next following the base year, the tenant in store #4 will be assessed 1.7 percent of $10,000 or $170 per year. These increases for real estate taxes (and sometimes increases in the overall insurance to protect the basic exterior from fire, storm, and personal liability) are quite small in relation to total rent and are universally acceptable. If the developer does not protect himself by asking for them, some national tenants with plenty of sophistication will not offer to pay for them on their own volition. **Ask not, get not.**

The same conditions relating to escalations (operating expenses, taxes, insurance, and the equity percentage relating to the CPI) should apply to shopping center tenants except that because of possible gross sales increases, some tenants may resist the CPI escalation. They will argue that as the dollar decreases in value, their sales are increasingly based on "funny" dollars (inflated dollars) and thus you will be collecting percentage rents in excess of real value. They may have a point, but who knows if they will ever exceed their minimums and pay percentage rents? Printed leases are helpful here too. The psychology of printed leases is not lost even on the most sophisticated tenants. He feels that **all** tenants are agreeing on the same basic tenants of the lease and thus feels he may as well go along too.

Certain regional shopping malls have been enclosed and thus are weather proof. Tyson's Corner in northern Virginia (a D.C. suburb) is a good example of this kind of shopping mall. The Fashion Mall in Pompano Beach, Florida and the Galleria in Houston, Texas are also outstanding examples of enclosed malls.

I can't help think that we may be currently constructing enclosed shopping malls which are technologically obsolete. Here are some things to think about. Let's suppose it is raining or snowing. What good is it to enclose the mall while the customer drowns while walking or running to her car? This especially is frustrating when the customer is loaded with packages. Does it rain or snow where you live? If the weather statistics are correct, it must be a real damper on business when it rains in Seattle. Inasmuch as we started to enclose malls to foster better sales in extremely hot, cold or wet weather, why didn't we cover our customers' cars? And why don't we now? We ought to do everything possible to encourage shoppers. We ought to have day nurseries, enclosed parking, skateboard rinks and other recreational features which could include "family sports" of all kinds such as bowling centers, roller rinks, ice-skating rinks, swimming pools and diving facilities in our malls. Why can't we encourage Y.M.C.A.s or Y.M.H.A.s to locate in our malls? Everything in our malls do not have to be wild money-makers. We just don't want activities which are a real drain on our resources. The large developers of the future will include many features which the shopping public soon will be demanding. The great challenges in shopping malls lie ahead; the innovative and creative developers will be the new mall developers of the future.

At this point you will know all about signs, topping-out parties and groundbreaking ceremonies. You will have hired your consulting engineer and depending upon your judgment, will have decided upon the need for brochures.

You will have put into effect and will know how to use your marketing skills. You should know all of the reasons for reasonable equities and why you allocated so many dollars for the rent-up period. You know that speed of rent-up, even after doing everything correctly, is still a function of the market. Assuming full occupancy, you will now need to manage your property in the best manner so as to maximize the cash flow.

groundbreaking ceremony for the lafayette, washington, d.c. 1970. such ceremonies bring together investors, lenders, tenants, contractors and media editors to create goodwill and good publicity.

9

your property is leased

chapter 9 outline

managing the property

Some developers feel that the day-to-day management of the property is a bore. They feel their creative minds can best be spent in setting up ventures and they wish to be divorced from the management process. They love to whip up a gourmet meal, select the appropriate wine, and then relax, leaving the cleaning up to someone else. Happily I have never felt like this. When I first went into business for myself I personally managed the property we had acquired. What a surprise it was to me to learn of the myriad of problems involved in managing apartments, which I feel are the most difficult to manage of all income-producing properties.

In order to be certain our apartments were competitively priced, it was necessary to visit other apartments in the same area. I would talk with other resident managers and question them as to the problem areas they had encountered and how the problems were solved. I was amazed that intra-tenant problems could become so annoying that tenant A could become a bitter enemy of tenant B. Backbiting and squabbles were always going on between tenant A and B, each accusing the other of violating either the lease agreement or project regulations. Pool regulations were constantly being written and rewritten because of the use of pool furniture. Some tenants would apparently be up at dawn during the summer, wait for the pool to open, spread beach towels on the lounge, go in for breakfast, and then return to their "reserved" lounge. Other tenants would neatly fold up the beach towels of the early bird tenants, place them in a conspicuous place near the pool, and use the lounge originally selected by the first tenant.

This kind of in-fighting seemed to occur no matter how high the rent or the educational level or social background of the tenants. Some of the written complaints were so "pornographic" they could not be printed here. Other residents would complain about such private matters as "noisy lovemaking" by other tenants. This was the nasty end of the business, at least to me. Surprisingly, the Institute of Real Estate Management (I.R.E.M.) of the National Association of Realtors has some fine property managers who are very good at settling disputes and still can remain on good terms with all parties. The requirements are quite high for the designation of Certified Property Manager. When candidates complete certain designated courses and have met on-the-job requirements relating to properties managed and length of time the candidate has worked, the candidates may then be eligible for membership. Individuals meeting all of the requirements receive the C.P.M. designation. Organizations that are headed by at least one C.P.M. and that otherwise meet all the requirements, (financial, legal, etc.) are eligible to be accorded the Accredited Management Organization (A.M.O.) designation.

Our organization not only manages our own ventures but also those projects owned by others, so we are quite active in management. There is absolutely no substitute for the practical experience and knowledge of the Certified Property Manager. He is an important part of the review process of the plans and specifications of any new project we are contemplating. His knowledge of prior errors and "people" responses is absolutely necessary. His views on lighting, security, trash, utilities, loading docks, and other such data are necessary and very valuable. His remarks as to why one loading dock is not sufficient, size and location of air conditioners, elevator size and speed, signs and many other details are what make a building or project easier to manage. Certainly one of the most important aspects of the chief property manager's work is his responsibility for preparing operating budget estimates for each of the properties. Without manager comment, most of our buildings just wouldn't work well. You can be sure the tenants will let management know when something isn't right.

In reality, to be a successful developer you need managerial and tenant input. Don't give your projects to other companies to manage. As mentioned earlier in the book, giving management to others restricts your ability to learn.

managing the partnership

quarterly reports and disbursements

Under the uniform limited partnership act, general partners have a **fiduciary** responsibility. Explicit in your fiduciary responsibility as the general partner is the fact that you are managing the affairs of the partnership property of all the partners. Implicit in your role of general partner is the responsibility to inform your partners on a regular basis of what is happening with the gross income. It is incumbent on you to see that quarterly reports are sent to all the partners. These reports are essentially cash flow statements for the three-months operation immediately preceding the report. For example, our mid-April report covers the period from January 1 through March 31. The bottom line (distributable cash flow) is what is important to the limited partner. Along with each report is the limited partners pro rata share of the cash flow for the previous three months. A partnership check signed by one of more of the general partners is one of the developer's quarterly rewards. The act of signing a goodly number of checks may seem like boredom to most of you. But it seems to me to be a reaffirmation of what in the hell I'm supposed to be doing: developing a stream of income-producing projects that have a happy and rewarding future.

adequate reserves

In order to avoid wild swings in the amounts of each quarterly check, be certain to set up adequate reserves covering intermittant and seasonal reserves. As indicated in Chapter 4, these cash deductions set aside as reserves should be covered in the original partnership agreement. Naturally, any unused reserves above those no longer necessary should be distributed annually.

if no check, communicate

Early in my real estate business life, especially during the ownership of my first income-producing property, I was reluctant to communicate with the investor partners because there was no cash flow to send them. I hoped there would soon be cash flow and then I would communicate. What a mistake this was. I was bombarded with phone calls and personal visits from irate investors wondering whether I had skipped town! This early lesson convinced me of two important public relations truisms, especially as regards syndicates:

1. You must communicate factual and actual data at least once a quarter if you are unable to distribute checks because of little or no cash flow.

2. You must **not** forecast. If you send a delightful, optimistic letter indicating what will occur three months later, and there is no cash flow to distribute at the end of the next quarter, then what do you do? Therefore, merely send the factual data with a covering letter indicating what, if anything, you are doing to help improve the cash flow. But **don't** forecast! Your investors are not going to be happy if they do not receive a quarterly check, but sophisticated investors frequently believe you may have some really bad news if you fail to communicate with them at least quarterly.

Avoid chest thumping and patting yourself on the back when you do send checks. There is no good time to do either of these things; besides, the checks speak for themselves. After all, that is the nature of your discipline as a developer—to create a project with a good economic future all the while distributing cash flow.

why the investor must be inactive or dormant

Your tax attorney can only create a limited partnership agreement that will avoid double taxation. The Internal Revenue Service may determine that your limited partnership is really an "association" and has corporate characteristics. For practical purposes, this means it is the responsibility of the general partner(s) to administer the affairs of the partnership in such a way that its tax posture cannot be attacked. My securities attorney recently told me that the Securities and Exchange Commission is in favor of group and investor meetings for the purpose of having the general partners quizzed on any and all matters relating to the partnership business. This would especially be true if you were to invite "sophisticated and rich" investors to a group meeting (a sales meeting) relating to a private offering you were about to begin. This is commendable in that anyone could have access to any data in your possession that could help them make an intelligent investment decision. Because the principal Securities and Exchange Commission employees are, in the main, lawyers and accountants, it makes sense to them. They are not real estate practitioners however, and certainly are not sales oriented.

As pointed out in Chapter 4 relating to the drafting of the limited partnership agreement, in my book such meetings are taboo. In the first place, you can't (neither can I) sell anything to a group. In the next instance, when they are already investor limited partners, group meetings are virtually always a disaster with the investors taking cheap (or expensive) shots at the general partners. Besides, doesn't having group meetings sound very much to you like corporate stockholder meetings? Here is the real dilemma: the SEC says group meetings are just fine, maybe they should be encouraged; the IRS says "you are having stockholder meetings—your limited partnership may lose its status as a partnership and may become an association taxed as a corporation." Contradictions such as these abound in Washington, D.C. because each department or regulatory agency rarely coordinates its efforts with that of other agencies. And, frequently it makes good sense not to try to obtain opinions that are viewed from a different vantage point. Besides, the bureaucracy can only do what it is congressionally mandated to do. Thus the SEC seeks to help the investor from getting conned into deals and remaining in bad deals, because the investor is not being given access to all that is going on. The IRS seeks to administer the tax laws as legislated by the Congress.

Be certain of your limited partnership tax status by making sure the partners vote on only two issues: refinancing and sale. The vote should always be by written notice, never by a possible "shareholder's meeting."

termination is virtually up to you

As time goes on, you may receive inquiries from commercial real estate brokers as to whether your property is for sale. Such inquiries may also be initiated by principals seeking to acquire one or more of your developments. You certainly remember that you have the exclusive rights of resale of the property at a commission of 5 percent of the gross selling price, and if the sale is satisfactory to 51 percent of the partnership, the property may be sold and you can collect the commission in cash.

The commission is so large and fetching that it is very unlikely you will deal with any other broker on a split commission basis and, rest assured, if another broker has the purchaser in hand, you can and should negotiate a commission arrangement with that broker. You must make it plain to the other broker that part of the original impetus to acquire or develop the property was the commission at sale. Because of this, you cannot split a commission that, in a sense, is part of your original development fee. To make certain the other broker understands this, you can explain that the property is not for sale. This is true because in order to "offer" the property for sale you really must have the authorization of 51 percent of partners in order to make a presentation to a would-be purchaser. Further, you can explain to the broker that even if the property were to be marketed, he would necessarily look to the **purchaser** for a commission. In the last analysis, you as a fiduciary and a real estate broker must truly represent the sellers. If another broker has an investor "in his pocket," let the new purchaser pay a fee to his broker for negotiating a sale on his behalf.

If your noncooperation in your "private" commission arrangement upsets you because you are a Realtor in your community and wish to protect your reputation with the other brokers, remember that at sale is the **only** time you will not use another broker's services. You will need and want a broker to offer you land; you will need and want a broker to offer you quality income-producing properties; you will need and want a broker to assist you in obtaining commercial leases. In all these instances you have never tried to put your hand in the broker's pocket through some commission-sharing arrangement.

On the other hand, to ignore another broker's plea that he has a client in hand who is ready, willing, and able to purchase your syndicated project may bother you because you have a fiduciary responsibility as a general partner to all the limited partners. Don't let this bother you. Your fiduciary responsibility is to bring the purchase offer that is the highest possible price obtainable in the marketplace. To have some broker importune you for data on your development so as to offer it to his or client is not even legal in Washington, D.C. In order to legally present a commercial property in Washington, D.C., a Realtor must have a listing in **writing.** Because this is so, I have no conflict with other brokers in Washington, D.C.

When is the time to offer your property for sale? This occurs between the eighth and twelfth year because sometime during this period **all or more than all** of the cash flow is subject to federal income taxation. Going back to our formula: cash flow plus amortization minus depreciation equals taxable income, so you can understand there is a point when the amortization exceeds the depreciation allowance. When this occurs, your investors will be aware that the project has "run out of depreciation." This is not technically accurate because there is always some depreciation allowance left, however small. But the investor is in the position of having to pay federal taxes on **more** than the cash flow he is receiving. Be assured several investors will call or write as to your plans to either refinance or sell the property or do both. Because you will have as much as 25 percent as your piece of the action, you will need only 26 percent more (25 percent + 26 percent = 51 percent) of the limited partners votes to effectuate either the refinancing, sale, or both.

All investors love to refinance. The proceeds of refinancing that you will be distributing are borrowed monies and thus are not considered income. New financing proceeds distributed to your partners are not taxable so be assured this is the first action you should undertake. In all probability, you will need to deal with your first mortgage lender, who made the original loan. This is so because chances are you are "locked-in" and cannot pay off the original loan for the first ten loan-years; afterwards for each remaining year until the end of the fifteenth year you will probably have to pay points. The customary arrangement is to pay 5 points after 10 years, 4 points after 11 years, 3 points after 12 years, and so on, declining a point each year. You will remember the earlier discussion concerning mortgage lenders and their policies in regard to borrowers. Now you may realize how very important it is to choose a tractable lender in the first instance.

recasting the loan

When you are nearing the point of having to pay federal income taxes on more cash flow than you are receiving because loan amortization exceeds your depreciation allowance, you may wish to consider **recasting** the loan. This may be a very good alternative to refinancing, though you will not be making non-taxable distributions to yourself and your limited partners. The effects of recasting the loan is to slow the rate of principal curtailment of the loan so that amortization is (hopefully) less than the depreciation allowance and will continue so for a few more years. Recasting is also a wonderful financial tool when your project is a sensational winner and you know that your limited partners are not really interesting in selling the property.

While your original loan at $8\frac{3}{4}$ percent interest (for example) is payable at an annual constant of 9.19 percent in order to repay the loan fully in 35 years, and you originally borrowed $10 million, you will find the balance of the loan is approximately 9,320,000 after ten years. While your regular monthly payments total $919,000 annually, including interest and principal (9.19 percent constant), your **real** annual constant on the unpaid balance will be 9.86 percent because you are still paying $919,000 annually.

The recasting of the loan leaves the balance due the mortgage lender the same because the recasting process merely changes (lessens) the annual payments based on the original annual constant for the (then) remaining balance. This reduces the amortization by "flattening it out" as a result of lesser annual principal reduction. If the project is doing so well that it would seem inappropriate to sell, consider recasting. Most intelligent lenders like to do recasted loans because their financial risk is rarely increased. They have no new money at risk and probably are safer by recasting the loan than they were when the original loan was made.

Using the same sample, because the interest ($8\frac{3}{4}$ percent) would remain the same and the 35-year amortization schedule would remain the same but be **based** on the remaining loan balance, your annual payments would then be approximately $856,500 increasing the cash flow by $62,500 and reducing the onerous problem of amortization exceeding depreciation.

When the annual cash flow distributions received by the limited partners are fully taxable and then some (because amortization exceeds depreciation), you will necessarily have to refinance, recast, or sell. Let's assume you have either refinanced, or recast the loan and in three or four more years you are faced with the problem again. The second time this happens is the best time to sell. You will study the market at that time and because the sale of large income-producing property is time consuming and seemingly cumbersome, these disadvantages are very helpful to you. It is not critical the sale take place immediately, not even during the year, but within two and a half years. Surely this is enough time to expose a winner to the marketplace. Here are some tips on how to quietly market your project.

sale of the project

be sure to offer the property to your mortgage lender

Your mortgage lender knows how well the property is doing because you may have been required to furnish audited statements annually on the operation of your property. At least, you have had to furnish the lender unaudited annual (but accurate) statements. He knows the history of the project and may indeed have an acquisition policy that fits your project. Further, he may wish to have your company continue management and leasing because he reasons you can (and have done) a good job originally of developing or acquiring a winner. You will disclose this fact in your letter to your limited partners, and you will also disclose the proposed new management and leasing fees.

Some lenders are not permitted to purchase income-producing properties—for example, certain pension funds are disqualified from owning such projects by virtue of their investing policies. Retirement plans must be approved in their initial instance by the IRS in order to qualify for tax deferrals on earned income. On the other hand, most of the major insurance companies are not only lenders but have a separate funded department or subsidiary for the exclusive purpose of acquiring income-producing properties.

follow the "wall street journal"

This way, you can see what is happening to the U.S. dollar, especially as it compares to western democracies—notably Swiss francs and German marks. When the U.S. dollar loses value compared to the franc or mark, U.S. properties become especially attractive to West European purchasers. You will have your attorney check the laws of the state in which the property is located to determine if sales of income-producing properties to foreigners is legal. If such a sale is legal this may be your next best source, because in the conversion of francs or marks to dollars, the foreign investor will have more dollars to play with when the conversion is made at a time when our dollar is "weak." I recently have entered into a joint venture with a European group (mainly Swiss, French, and Belgians) because the dollar was especially weak when we were looking for investors. Peculiarly, these investors are **all** real estate developers in their own countries. What a pleasure to work with such knowledgeable people! The language barrier presents a slight communications problem but with a good technical interpreter, all soon becomes well.

advise your limited partners

Tell your limited partners that the time to sell is approaching rapidly. They will be aware of this because of the tax consequences of continued ownership. In advising your partners that you will be seeking the highest possible price in the marketplace, you should also indicate that if any of the limited partners wish to purchase the property they should immediately notify you. A few limited partners may get together and decide to purchase the property. As long as at least 51 percent of the limited partners are "different" or new "partners," the IRS will allow new depreciation starting from the new basis: the purchase price of the property (excluding that value attributable to the land).

phone canvass

Because good business practice dictates your maintaining a purchaser's file, you may now wish to start a phone canvass among all those principals who have indicated to you their interest in purchasing income-producing properties. Don't underestimate a principal who in 1973 indicated he can handle a down payment of $1 million. By 1980 this same person (along with a probable associate or two) may have as much as $5 million to use as a downpayment. You have heard of people who are all tied up in cash. Whoever told you this didn't really mean they had "cash," they mean people who have short-term monetary assets that are "resting" until an appropriate investment in income-producing real estate presents itself. Chances are the "cash" is in a treasury bill or note, a certificate of deposit, or short-term commercial paper.

The reason I'm cautioning you to avoid underestimating how much cash an investor may have to invest is that I'm guilty of consistently underestimating this myself. It took years for me to understand there are umpteen persons in every major city who can and often do make investments in income-producing properties requiring downpayments of from one-half million dollars to $3 million. I know this is a shocker to you and my mind had difficulty accepting this fact too, but it is nonetheless true—there is plenty of equity money seeking quality real estate investments. Everytime you have an inquiry directly from a principal you should put all relevant information known to you on a 3 × 5 card and keep it filed under "prospective buyers." These cards could be the perfect tool with which to initiate the sale of your property in the marketplace.

other prospects

You may be aware that there are real estate counselors and other organizations who are searching for fine income-producing properties, **who represent the buyer** and who therefore will respect your commission arrangements with the seller. As of this writing, there are several major organizations who are quite active on behalf of institutional investors. In order to compile a complete list of such organizations you should subscribe to the **National Real Estate Investor,** a monthly magazine in which such organizations regularly advertise (for the correct and most current address of the publisher, obtain the latest copy from your public library or ask a commercial real estate broker to lend you a copy).

taking back paper

Should you receive an offer that is **not** for all cash above the first mortgage and requires taking back a deferred purchase money second mortgage, you will not be able, as a practical matter, to terminate the partnership. This is because a termination and liquidation of the partnership requires you to liquidate the assets and distribute the cash proceeds. Alternately, (but I believe it to be impractical), you could provide for one second mortgage with as many second mortgage **notes** as you have limited partners. The difficulty with doing this will be evident in your selling negotiations. No buyer wants to make umpteen payments a month on his second mortgage. In event of default, in order to start the foreclosure procedures, you would have to provide for a trustee to act in behalf of all the noteholders. This may not be practical as deaths of several noteholders could have occurred prior to default, while others could have left the area. Besides who would pay the trustee—and what about filing the final partnership tax return?

Taking back paper undoubtedly requires the partnership to remain active until the second mortgage is fully paid, and all other possible assets of the partnership are distributed. When all of this has been accomplished, you may properly terminate the partnership.

consider selling the partnership

As a means of raising revenues, it seems local jurisdictions (cities, counties, and states) look to real estate owners as one of their major sources of income. Some cities, counties, and states are levying special transfer taxes when one owner deeds a property to another. Unless there is a specific law or regulation against it, consider selling the partnership interests themselves instead of the sole asset, the income-producing property owned by the partnership. There is language that can easily be provided by your attorney when you are drafting the original partnership agreements. While I have alluded to this in Chapter 4 when I have discussed in great detail what the partnership agreement should contain, I feel that the partnership agreement should provide language that will require that the will of the majority cannot be flouted by an obstinate minority. In order to sell the partnership interests, any investor will need **all** of the limited partners to join in such a plan. A provision that appoints the general partner an attorney-in-fact in order to transfer the unwilling or unable partner's interest in the event of a sale involving the sale of the partnership rather than the realty may work. This is something to discuss with your attorney, who may suggest another method that may allow you to act quickly in the interest of the majority partners.

Because there is no explicit listing procedure when the sale should be pursued, it is also a good idea to provide for an appropriate rebate of out-of-pocket cash you may spend in seeking an offer only to find your partners may reject the offer. The agreement should also cover amounts you could spend by having your attorney review a sales offer you might receive.

At the outset of your sales negotiations you should immediately inform a prospective buyer that you, acting in your fiduciary capacity, are not empowered to say yes or no to any facet of the negotiations. This fact may temporarily affect your ego but it is very helpful during delicate negotiations to indicate that "this is something to take up with my partners—I have the power to act but the decision must be theirs, acted upon only after a written vote."

You know about not only managing the properties you will develop or acquire, but just as important, you know how to manage the partnership. Termination is virtually up to you, as is financing and recasting of the loan. You cannot properly terminate the partnership until the property is ultimately sold and **all** the monies are paid in and distributed among the individual partners. For this reason you should definitely consider selling the partnership whose sole asset is the income-producing property.

Limited partnerships which you can form on a one at a time basis is not the only way to syndicate or develop income-producing properties. The next chapter suggests at least two other ways of approaching the acquisition and development of such properties.

the solar building, washington, d.c. acquired in 1972 at a cost of $6,000,000.

10

other ways
for you and them

chapter 10 outline

During the 1960s and 1970s, some realtor-investors and developers felt it was too much trouble to syndicate each individual property. Not only was it time consuming, but also, because of the nature of the business, a decision to buy land for development or to acquire an existing property could not be quickly followed through and title obtained. Intelligent developers and syndicators were frustrated at the long waiting times caused by public offerings, private placement memorandums, and the actual time related to individual "selling" of partnership interests. There was also the problem of inability to act and close quickly (say within 30 days) whenever a quality project was offered that seemed to require a quick settlement.

organizing a real estate investment trust

Because of the aforementioned problems, real estate people experienced with income-producing properties began looking at the possibilities of having equity dollars in a large money pool. Older, established trusts (which until 1960 were subject to double taxation, once on the taxable income and again to the investor when dividends were distributed) also helped lobby for the Real Estate Investment Trust Act, signed by President Eisenhower into law. I was among those who helped lobby for this needed change in the law to eliminate double taxation for real estate investors. Little did any of the men who originally headed the equity real estate investment trust then in existence dream that someone would organize a R.E.I.T. for the **sole** purpose of lending money. I was astonished that this new owning vehicle, a R.E.I.T., would go into the mortgage lending business. At the time (about 1961), short-term money was in terribly short supply because of the policies and actions of the Federal Reserve Board. I know of developers with permanent mortgages committed for an office building upon completion two years from the date of the commitment who were **unable** to borrow short-term funds from a commercial bank, so tight was short-term money. Money again was tight in 1963–64 as well as 1969–70. History repeated itself again in 1974 and mid-1978 as money once again became tight.

Mortgage brokers and bankers all over the country were also aware of the problem and thus a new industry was born. It has been estimated that over $1.5 billion in savings monies were withdrawn during the 1960s and exchanged for certificates of beneficial interests in mortgage trusts alone. Many of these trusts lent monies at rates **floating** four points above the prime rate, which ranged approximately from 7 to 10 percent during this decade. Sophisticated and experienced developers with previously good banking connections could obviously still borrow from their regular sources and usually did so at prime or perhaps one point over prime. These sophisticated and experienced developers had no need for the services of a mortgage R.E.I.T. whose main business was the making of construction loans at very high rates but who occasionally made permanent loans with 10- to 15-year balloons coupled with high interest rates.

The better, experienced developer could borrow money from banks at the same interest rate as R.E.I.T.s could borrow, and in **my** case at a **lower** rate. You see, among the things R.E.I.T.s usually had to do in order to establish credit lines at banks was to keep a deposit of 20 percent as a "compensating balance" for any monies the R.E.I.T.s borrowed. If the prime rate was 10 percent, the R.E.I.T.s were forced to leave 20 percent of all borrowed funds idle, interest free at the bank, as a compensating balance. This meant the bank was actually earning 12.5 percent on a prime rate loan. Stated another way, in order to borrow $100 and pay interest at 10 percent, the R.E.I.T.s had to leave $20 in a compensating non-interest-bearing checking account. The (borrowers) R.E.I.T.s thus had the use of $80 while paying the 10 percent (the prime rate) on $100. Thus the banks collected $10 interest on $80 ($100 less 20 percent compensating balance of $20), or **12.5 percent simple interest annually!**

In order to cover the relatively high cost of monies, the R.E.I.T.s lent money to whomever couldn't borrow it from a regular commercial bank. To understate the matter, the mortgage R.E.I.T.s lent money to peripheral location developers, developers whose net worths had to be suspect, and developers with little or no track records. The real estate doldrums of the early 1970s didn't knock out the mortgage R.E.I.T.s. The cost of money and the speed with which they had to repay it coupled with loans in peripheral (mostly bad) locations to questionable developers are the main factors that ended the mortgage R.E.I.T.s. Of course they **had** to lend money to questionable developers doing projects at questionable locations—who else would borrow from them? So much for the mortgage R.E.I.T.s. In my opinion, as currently constituted, they cannot survive.

Most of the new equity trusts are doing quite well, and some equity trusts whose shares of beneficial interest are traded on the American Stock Exchange have survived not only the crunch of the early 1970s but continue to show rising prices of their shares. Two Washington, D.C.-based equity trusts, Federal Real Estate Investment Trust and Washington Real Estate Investment Trust are both doing well. This is not to tout the shares of either trust to anyone, but merely to contrast the moribund mortgage trusts with the well-managed equity trusts. I believe one of the keys to the well-being of both trusts just mentioned is the fact that neither were offered (nor would then accept) enormous amounts of equity money at one time.

Suppose you were so highly regarded that Merrill, Lynch, Pierce, Fenner & Smith offered to raise $100 million in one lump sum for your equity trust and gave you the net after commissions, legal fees, and what not approximating $90 million. What kinds of properties would you invest the money in and how long would it take you? Let me answer first and then it's your turn. I probably couldn't find $360 million (assuming 25 percent down payments) of quality income-producing property at cash-on-cash returns of at least 9 percent annually. Let me change that statement: I know I couldn't find such properties unless I had at least 10 years in which to attempt to get all the monies invested. Chances are I couldn't do the task at all—unless I could **develop** the properties. Then I would need at least 15 years. The purpose of this discussion is to point out the darned near impossibility of investing substantial amounts of monies in equities of fine income-producing properties unless **time** is of no importance. Now you try.

Here are some other things to think about. Would you invest **only** in your jurisdiction or would you strive for geographical distribution among the fifty states so all your eggs wouldn't be in one basket? Would you invest in only one type of properties, for example, only office buildings, only apartments, or only shopping centers? Perhaps you would consider only commercial properties and no residential properties, including income-producing properties. Just taking a quick look at these problems will give you an understanding of why most successful equity R.E.I.T.s developed so **slowly.**

Some R.E.I.T.s have been in existence for over 75 years (Real Estate Investment Trust of America is one that comes to mind). It is an equity R.E.I.T. whose investment policies have been to acquire commercial properties exclusively. Prior to 1936 this R.E.I.T. had the same tax treatment as it has today. The Real Estate Investment Trust of America had to wait approximately 25 years to regain its single tax status. The fact that any trust has been in existence for so long indicates there is an investment need for an equity R.E.I.T. General Motors and American Telephone and Telegraph were not even a glint in someone's eye when the Real Estate Investment Trust of America was making its first dividend distribution. As far back as anyone can remember, real estate investments were popular.

The fact that a trust can exist solely from income from mortgate loans has been disproved. There are quite a few equity R.E.I.T.s that are continuing their conservative policies, limiting their debt to mortgages only, that have served the investment community in good fashion.

If you feel that the steady income from management and brokerage fees beats doing individual ventures, by all means investigate the possibilities of organizing an equity R.E.I.T. headquartered in your hometown. There are some attorneys with considerable experience in organizing R.E.I.T.s. Your securities attorney can advise you which attorney to see for advice on what it takes to form a trust.

One of the requirements for forming an equity trust is that there be at least **100** different owners of beneficial certificates of trust. Another requirement is that five or fewer individuals may not control more than 50 percent of the total beneficial certificates outstanding. Because of these two basic tests for allowing a trust the special tax treatment the law allows (one tax at the investor level), you will necessarily be required to "go public."

As a former chairman of the board of directors of a public company listed on the American Stock Exchange, I can assure you that being a public company requires the expenditure of a fair amount of dollars on a consistent basis. Just in round numbers, and purely an educated guess, it costs about one-half million dollars annually to be a relatively small public company. Legal and accounting fees are quite high because of the tremendous amount of reporting required. Besides quarterly reports to shareholders and the SEC, annual reports must also be prepared. Business strategy requires internal forecasts for as far into the future as three to five years. Printing and mailing costs to as many as 2,000 shareholders is an enormous expense too. The status of running a public company fades quickly when you consider that for all practical purposes you are living in a public fish bowl. You really can't invest in your own company to any considerable degree because if you make any money by buying low and selling high, it may appear that you, as an insider had inside information. Whether you did or didn't, a good argument can be made that you did. Thus, any profits made from such a transaction may have to be returned to the company treasury.

Still, the American economy needs the private sector, publicly owned by individual shareholders to keep the American industrial economy strong. Like it or not (and I love it) the American system of private enterprise has produced the most envied country in the world because our standard of living is higher than any other country. Surely we can improve, but who can knock the country of immigrants that has created a nation where the finest consumer goods ever produced are practically in every home?

blind pool limited partnership

In the early 1970s, a West Coast syndicator and entrepreneur didn't like doing individual syndicates and was unhappy with the idea of "doing" a public equity real estate investment trust because of its continuing nature. This brilliant young man felt his individual syndicates could have done better if he were free to go to a relatively large pool of money and buy existing quality properties. Cash-on-cash returns in the early 1970s could be obtained (on the average) at about 9 percent. He first formed one large pool of private limited partners, raised the dollars through stockbrokers, and proved so successful in raising money that two other public limited partnerships were formed. In cash equities, over $35 million was raised and allocated among three funds, each a public limited partnership.

I was in on these funds from the beginning as an outside director. The amount of deliberation by the board of directors was tremendous. First, a policy or strategy of what kinds of property had to be adopted. Actually, this policy never was refined to writing and as time went on there were deviations. Second, we also had to determine if there was to be a geographical distribution and this was more or less settled by confining purchases to the western and southwestern states. Third, we had to determine minimum and maximum equities. Lastly and obviously the most important, we had to approve or disapprove purchases.

These decisions, especially those related to the actual purchases, were extremely difficult. Even though there were appraisals submitted, or appraisal letters to be followed by written reports from members of the Appraisal Institute (an affiliate of the National Association of Realtors) something was lacking that may or may not have had a bearing on our collective votes. Just like most equity R.E.I.T.s, real estate commissions were paid to the broker representing the funds. Most equity R.E.I.T.s pay their organizer (or manager or promoter) real estate commissions on their acquisitions too. This is obviously a built-in conflict of interest but one which obviously cannot be avoided. The broker-syndicator had to search for properties. Only the **worst** offerings come in unsolicited. The real missing factor was a totally objective report from someone with no financial interest in such an acquisition. After all, the **best** appraiser (M.A.I.) can't predict with perfection a ten-year trend that can be relied upon. Probably no one can. But that was one missing ingredient—the "feel" for the property.

The funds were to be self-liquidating at the end of five years: there were to be no more purchases five years after each fund's initial organization.

I resigned in 1977 after liquidation commenced mainly because another outside director H. P. Skoglund of Minneapolis passed away. Most meetings were held in either San Diego or Honolulu and it took about three days out of my life to attend a quarterly meeting. With "Skog" as an outside director, the meetings were fun. Also, director's fees are **never** high enough to compensate quality directors. Because this is so, most outside directors do their work because of friendship with other directors or management and the intellectual challenges such meetings usually present.

The **pressure** to "place" the entire $35 million in income-producing properties was immense. Until about 1976, I was never quite satisfied with the actual property management. Prior to 1976, the directors changed management companies at least three times. At best it is extremely difficult to manage a portfolio valued in excess of $130 million when the properties are scattered over 15 or 16 states. Since 1976 the funds have been well managed by experienced professionals. I hope the funds succeed as planned and that the investors will have an excellent investment result.

A blind pool limited partnership could function in a similar fashion as an equity R.E.I.T. with two exceptions: if publicly traded there is obviously more liquidity with the shares of an equity R.E.I.T.; and a blind pool partnership is self-liquidating, while the R.E.I.T.s could go on indefinitely.

The realities of investing in real estate are such that the smaller investor needs to pool his money by investing in an equity R.E.I.T. or a blind pool limited partnership. This is so because $5,000 to $10,000 in cash can't buy the **safety** that is a concommitant of a larger project. The "economies of scale" bring down the per unit cost (per square foot) of not only acquiring but managing larger properties. On the other hand, smaller properties cost more per square foot to acquire and also cost more per square foot to manage.

Knowing there are alternative forms of organizing capital other than for one project, and as a consequence, one limited partnership may be helpful to a realtor-developer or syndicator who is seeking more permanence (and security) than single projects offer. Forms of ownership such as blind pool limited partnerships and equity real estate investment trusts may one day become the accepted form of investment for the small investor. If you are seeking what appears to be a form of ownership that will give you more permanence than a series of individual syndicates, consider organizing either a blind pool limited partnership or an equity R.E.I.T.

original federal bar building east, washington, d.c. 1950, cost $3,250,000. home of the bar association and the national lawyers' club.

11

will they come back?

chapter 11 outline

investor repeats

I am almost always asked at lectures, speeches, and seminars if the same investors join each and every venture. How nice that would be if it were true. I'm not so sure I'd have as much fun because raising equities is a fun type of challenge that I thoroughly enjoy. I do know several investors who will join each venture I am forming regardless of the type of property and size of the investment "unit," be it $50,000 or $175,000. These few investors are not only sophisticated and rich but have planned real estate investments as a strategy for financial security. Between ventures, if they have accumulated a lot of cash, they invariably put it into certificates of deposit or some other short-term resting place until I organize another real estate venture. Inasmuch as they are illiquid in real estate, their other assets are "all tied up in cash." By this I mean cash equivalents such as C.D.s, treasury bills, or commercial paper. These few investors are among a small coterie of investor friends and they do not behave in the same way as other investors. Let me explain.

Let's assume investor A likes an income-producing venture such as an office building I'm getting ready to develop, and he invests $100,000. Three years pass by and the investment is a wonderful winner. Instead of cash flow in the 10 percent range (cash-on-cash), it is in the 16 percent range and the major tenant (86 percent of the building) is a large multinational banking group. The lease is for a period of ten years and the tenants have moved in only one year ago so we are enjoying 100 percent occupancy. It also appears that the return will increase, not only because of escalators including a CPI clause, but because our parking garage tenant is doing extremely well and after the full year of operation informs us we will be getting average rent payments sufficient to lift our cash-on-cash return to just under 18 percent.

Let us further suppose we have another project, also an office building we wish to develop, which is located near by. We have acquired the land, agonized over the plans, obtained permanent and construction loans, and additionally have just executed a guaranteed upset price with our general contractor. Our projections, which are our cash flow pro forma statements, show a cash-on-cash return of 10 percent, just as our other project did three years ago.

The same investor A is in my office having made the usual mid-morning appointment to discuss entering the new venture. The first task I **must** do is to **disabuse** him of the assumption that the new venture will produce as splendid a result as the last project. I can't dare let him assume we can obtain as much cash-on-cash return as in our previous venture. This is extremely necessary as galloping winners in real estate investments occur less frequently than abysmal losers. When an investor is on a winning "high," he is very difficult to bring back to reality. What makes matters worse is that he thinks I'm personally responsible for the splendid investment result he is currently experiencing. If I tell him we were all just lucky with the previous investment, he thinks I'm attempting to be modest. (Me, modest?) He doesn't want to hear that we may not rent up as quickly, or that we will have less strong tenants than in this other investment. But I must tell him the risks are just as great and perhaps even greater than the first venture.

One out of three investors, coming off a winner, cannot be dissuaded. The other two investors, who seemed to understand thoroughly the risks and rewards inherent in this type of real estate investment, may suddenly demand that I **guarantee** or represent to them that the new venture will produce as good a result as the three-year-old venture they are already in. At this point, I have to sort of lecture them, perhaps actually threaten to not invite them as participants if they keep comparing the new venture with the old. I explain that the **timing** alone is so different only an idiot could make comparisons because even though both investments are in office buildings no two office buildings behave financially in the same manner. If they are too eager, I'm very nervous. Having had eager investors before, I know from experience they can badly misbehave as partners. Because of this reason, and because the time between ventures may have not allowed them to accumulate enough surplus cash, only about one-third of investors in the just previous venture will join the new venture.

The other reasons they may not be interested in a new investment with me is that the prior investment hasn't proven itself to be a winner, at least not yet. The project may have taken 24 months to rent after the shell was already completed. We may have borrowed money from the limited partners to cover the negative cash flow. We may have gone to a commercial bank for the shortfall of cash and they may have been in the venture for four years and received only taxable losses. Such has been the case in one of our office building ventures (which now is a lovely cash flow producer) but didn't look like it could make it just two years earlier.

Therefore, if your last project was a serious winner or a "limper" because it did not rent up quickly enough, investor repeats are only possible, on the average, with about one-third of the previous investors. I have been seriously asked by an investor in a runaway winner, what do I do for an encore? I have also been asked where did I get the nerve to dare call an investor about an investment in a new project when the previous investment he was in was still limping along. I do know this: a quality building in a good location that is getting better, properly financed with sufficient equity capital, can hardly ever be a loser. I have never had a loser in an office building in a good location getting better, properly financed with sufficient equity capital (remember the 80 percent rule), but I have some that took quite a while to rent fully.

You will therefore, of necessity, follow the guidelines indicated with regard to new investors: the L.E.E.P. acronym and proven methods of closing the investor. This has been fully explained in Chapter 7.

federal bar building entrance, washington, d.c., attractive modern interior architecture features spiral staircase leading to national lawyers' club.

12

you and them and special risks

chapter 12 outline

unusual risks to the developer and investor in raw land

Assuming you are titillated by real estate investments, should you put together a land-owning venture? Only if you like punishment. This facet of real estate investments is strictly for masochists, and here is the main reason why. A business friend of mine (Peyton Klopfenstein) has charted a ten-year investment program covering land investments and he maintains that in order to break even, after adjustments for inflation and income taxes, you **must** triple your money in ten years.

You must consider that owning raw land is a classic example of producing negative cash flow. Generally, after the down payment, there are three other major payments for which an investor is obligated: principal, interest, and real estate taxes. Liability insurance, while not expensive, is a must. Vacant land is considered an "attractive nuisance" in many legal jurisdictions and if children play on this land and get hurt, the general partner (you) may be liable. Because all of these activities occur **after** the purchase and produce negative cash flow, how does one ever expect to please an investor? After months and years of paying and paying, an investor gets terribly edgy. It is not uncommon for them to call and ask, "What's doing with our land?" And there it sits; what do they think you are doing with the land? Of course the investor is initially pleased with the tax losses, but what if he thinks these tax losses are **real** losses and may not even be recovered? He can only look at you as the big, bad boy who "put him in this stinking land deal." Take it from grandaddy, I've talked with many land promoters and land syndicators, and they **all** wish they could go someplace and hide. Leave land investments to the professional civil engineers who know what they are doing. Leave land investments to the land speculators who have the pragmatic experiences to sort winners from losers. Don't be responsible for organizing land joint ventures. It doesn't always triple in value within ten years and if it did, everybody would break even and there would be no room for **your piece of the action.**

hotels and motels

What about organizing investors for the development or acquisition of hotels and motels? There is nothing wrong with this particular investment strategy except that unlike apartments, office buildings, and shopping centers, hotels and motels have a much higher risk and reward ratio. An acquaintance of mine owns seven motels (he is a franchisee of a well-known national motel chain). He knows the hotel and motel business for what it is—the hospitality business. He understands food and beverage operations, room services, housekeeping, and convention services. If his actual figures do not match his projections, he can pinpoint the problem instantly. He knows the ratio of food and beverage costs to sales and has told me he is aware of every possible way his employees can steal from him. Contrast this kind of operation to a fully occupied office building with relatively long-term leases and you can readily see the tremendous risks involved in the ownership and operation of hotels and motels.

The hotel and motel business owner theoretically begins each day with 100 percent vacancies. The fully leased office building owner starts each day with 100 percent occupancy. Many forces, totally uncontrollable by a motel owner can and do occur. When the Arab oil embargo was in force, the occupancy of my friend's seven motels dropped from an average occupancy of 80 percent down to 30 percent and stayed that way until the embargo was lifted. People just didn't travel as much by car during the embargo. Had the embargo continued, he could have lost **every single motel he owned!** He needed an average 67 percent daily occupancy to break even because of conservative borrowing practices. Other hotel and motel owners need better than 80 percent occupancy to break even because they either borrowed too much money or do not know the hotel and motel business well enough to discover that their other operating costs may be too high.

Another difficulty the informed developer would have is the day-to-day management of one or two motels. If a key person doesn't come to work in one of my friend's motels he can shift an employee from another motel (they are all in a 50-mile radius from his main office). Still another difficulty occurs in the food and beverage area if personnel fail to appear for work. Suffice it to say that if you have the special skills required to develop and manage motels and hotels and the conservative policies of organizing the partnership and obtaining equity and permanent financing are followed, chances are you could do very well. On the other hand, remember that hotels and motels have more business characteristics than investment characteristics. Because the risks are so much greater in the development and operation of hotels and motels, the rewards are correspondingly higher when you have a winner. Cash-on-cash returns of $33\frac{1}{3}$ percent or higher are not uncommon in the hospitality business. Failures also abound in this field. Most of the failures are caused by factors that might have been controlled by the developer. Therefore, they are largely internal. These failures can be traced to too much debt, poor design, inexperienced management, poor locations, etc. The main external causes of failure, however, are severe competition (after one has a successful motel another will be built nearby by a competitor), poor occupancy, and inconsistent demand for food and beverages. All of this makes sound planning virtually impossible.

industrial buildings

In our metropolitan area of Washington, D.C., there are very few "industrial parks" where warehouse buildings are developed. This is so because there is very little industry in the area with the exception of research and development firms. Most of the industrial Realtors I have talked with who live in other areas feel the big money to be made in industrial and warehouse buildings came about because of the development of industrial parks.

This development requires the advance purchase of large tracts of land zoned for this use. Railroad sidings to service the buildings plus superlative road access are important, and sometimes critical. Inasmuch as loans for **unleased** warehouses or industrial buildings are virtually non-existent, the **tenant** must come first. Therefore a thorough knowledge of industrial markets are required by the developer who controls a large, prime, industrial tract. As facilities are planned for each tenant, financing can be obtained, usually based on the **credit of the tenant.** This requires extensive promotion and advertising, which in turn requires a heavy "up front" cash investment. This is a development area that you would do well to avoid. There are exceptions, of course. One exception I know involved a young man who inherited a large industrial tract, with only one tenant in occupancy. There was no debt on the property and with proper promotion and **on tract** field personnel (an industrial leasing specialist and a secretary), he was able to fully develop this 100-acre tract into sixteen different buildings. Each building was built to the specifications of the tenant and happily each tenant was a worthy credit risk, AAA, or AA at worst. Each building was leased on a "net, net, net" basis. Industrial Realtors love these kinds of leases in which the tenant is obligated to pay all operating expenses (the first "net"), all interior and exterior repairs (the second "net"), and all real property taxes and insurance (the third "net").

Occasionally a developer may acquire several tracts and have such a grand net worth, he can develop a single building himself. This is a terrific gamble because without a tenant in hand he doesn't know how much "load" per square foot to build. The load is determined by the type of activity and would vary greatly from tenant to tenant. A manufacturer of lead fishing sinkers and other lead products would obviously need a heavier floor (greater thickness and larger reinforcing rods) than let's say a producer of pharmaceuticals. Clear floor to ceiling height would vary also as would the air conditioning and heating requirements. Therefore, building an industrial building for an unknown tenant is real estate risk taking of a very high degree.

other special purpose buildings

What would you do if an undertaker, a bowling lanes operator, an auto dealer, or a restauraunt operator called you and wanted you to develop and own the buildings that would house their businesses? I know what I would do— I'd say thanks, but no thanks. The problem is one of risk. Your sole income from the building rests on the ability of the tenant to pay. The real problem occurs if he doesn't pay and can't pay. You then have an empty "special purpose" building. Don't misunderstand, there have been owners with exceptionally fine imaginations who have converted special purpose buildings to other uses. One fast-food operation went broke and the owner converted this free-standing building (with plenty of outside parking spaces) to a "farmer's market." He says he is making more money from the current group of tenants than the former "chicken" operation that was there before. His building is located in south Florida on a major state road. What could he have converted the fried chicken store to if he lived in Denver? Any northern, upper eastern, or upper western location in the United States has a short growing season. He could hardly run a profitable farmer's market during a three-month season. Most Realtors would ask what's wrong with a single purpose building if it were occupied by a business with impeccable credit? Nothing, at least at the outset. But businesses ebb and flow as do their credit ratings, and it makes no sense to obtain an extra 1 or 2 percent cash-on-cash return if you have to concern yourself with the validity of the credit rating assigned to your tenant.

A stockbroker friend recently took me to lunch and explained all of the advantages of municipal bonds. I noticed the difference in return between the best and the worst was only about 2 percent. I know that it sounds as if I'm comparing apples with oranges but darned if the same 2 percent (cash-on-cash) return can be found in real estate income-producing properties between the best and the worst. This 2 percent spread just isn't enough to justify the extraordinary risks of owning a fried chicken fast-food store returning 12 percent cash-on-cash as compared to a major shopping center or multi-story office building returning 10 percent cash-on-cash. And yet the two percentage points is all that separates the two different real estate investments. Which would you rather own?

emphasize multi-tenanted properties

If you are going to have a lasting career in real estate development, you must have a crystal clear understanding between risks and rewards. What makes income-producing properties of comparable size and costs different are the **quality** and number of **tenants.** This is a function of risk. If you have 80 percent major (AAA) tenants occupying 80 percent of the space in one office building with the rest of the tenants occupying 20 percent of the remaining space, they will probably be local tenants such as lawyers and insurance agents and if the total number of tenants is 20, only 20 percent is "at risk." This is the kind of risk you probably would be willing to take.

If you have multi-tenanted properties, you have the best of both worlds: the least amount of risk consistent with a very acceptable cash-on-cash return. An apartment complex of over two hundred units in a good location getting better is a classic example of multi-tenanted properties. If a couple of tenants move out, you have a 1 percent vacancy factor. If you have a special purpose building with one tenant and he moves out, you have a **100 percent vacancy factor** and you have a very narrow choice among prospective tenants. If you have a 12-story office building and each floor has 20,000 square feet of rental space with the average amount of space for each tenant at about 10,000, you would have 24 tenants. If one moved out, you only have an approximate 4 percent rental vacancy. You can't be clobbered financially by a few vacancies in either decent-sized apartment developments or good sized office buildings.

If you have a 150,000 square foot community shopping center with 15,000 square feet each rented to a major food chain at one end (AAA-1 rated) and the other end rented to an AAA-1 drug chain, you would have about 120,000 square feet left to be rented either to major shoe or dress chains plus all the service stores needed in such a center. Probably of the 120,000 square feet not used by the food chain and the drug chain, there would be between 18 and 25 other tenants. If one of the smaller tenants couldn't survive, you really couldn't be hurt. Inasmuch as these smaller tenants would each average about 5,000 square feet (50 × 100), the vacancy factor if one were to close would only be about 3 percent.

No doubt about it, your development strategy should emphasize multi-tenanted buildings. I received this good bit of advice when I had been in the real estate business for a very short time.

Take the time to interview at least three major lenders who make loans in your area. Try the Equitable Life Assurance Society, the Prudential Life Insurance Company, and Metropolitan Life Insurance Company for starters. These big three of commercial lenders generally have their own loan offices in virtually every major city. Discuss with them the kinds of loans they will make and also the kinds of loans they won't make. You'll soon discover that a multi-tenanted approach to income-producing properties is a correct strategy.

crazy "quirks" to guard against

let the buyer pay the commission?

A long time ago, we sold a project, and as luck would have it, we successfully negotiated the sale so that the buyer paid the commission. The commission was significant as the event took place in the mid-50s, and the commission was $75,000. Along with our attorney, we carefully drew up the contract so that we could qualify the sale as an installment sale. The rule then in effect is still in effect and relates to the down payment. If not more than 30 percent is received in the year of sale, you may report your gain on the installment basis. We were careful to collect only 29 percent down so as to avoid having a taxable transaction at other than capital gains rates, and, therefore, were sure we were going to be taxed on a long-term **installment** basis. We were only going to pay capital gains taxes each year as we received the installment payments.

Instead of qualifying as an installment sale, the Internal Revenue Service, on audit four years later, held that we had to pay taxes at capital gains rates on 100 percent of the taxable profit in the year of sale even though we had only received 29 percent down. We were mortified to learn that the $75,000 commission paid by the buyer to the broker was "constructively received" by us, the sellers, as an additional payment in the year of sale, thereby putting us over the 30 percent limit. To make matters worse, the Internal Revenue Service was **absolutely correct!** We paid the tax!

Needless to say, the fine attorney representing us was mortified along with us. Unfortunately, he was not a tax attorney who would surely have known better. You'd better believe we now have our contracts (both to buy and sell) drawn by or reviewed by a tax attorney.

why, of course, it is less than 29 percent down, so, therefore, it is an installment sale?

Here's another situation in which we were about to do something stupid but which we happily corrected in time. We were set to sell a building for a $4.75 million down payment against a sales price of $17.55 million. If one computes 29 percent of the sales price, the result is $5,089,500. What was overlooked, at least initially, was the fact that our mortgage was at $10.6 million while our book value (cost less depreciation) was at $9.6 million.

So what? Just this—if the book value is **less** than the mortgage the difference (in this case, $1 million) is deemed to be "constructively received" as of the date of sale. That was the case in this instance, so, we could not qualify for an installment sale. We solved the problem by reducing the down payment by $1 million, having the $1 million portion of the deferred purchase money second mortgage become due in the year next following the settlement date. Whew!

the lafayette, washington, d.c. the facade is pre-cast concrete. modern, good-looking building material at reasonable cost. home of the inter-american development bank—cost $14,500,000.

13

sharpening your negotiating skills

chapter 13 outline

we are all different

I have always marveled that with the few variants nature has to work with and with the billions of persons on earth, no two persons are identical. Consider that nature only tinkers with skin color, stature, hair, eyes, nose, mouth and general facial contours. There are only seven of these variants. Yet there are no two persons identical, not even identical twins. When you analyze people's personalities and try to understand their natures you may conclude that the real mystery of life is the **differences** among us all. People not only don't look alike, they don't sound alike, smell alike, feel alike, taste alike, laugh alike, and are emotionally different in their responses.

Inasmuch as such differences abound and in order to negotiate anything with anyone, we have no real options open except to focus on our similarities. In order to do this we need to understand basic emotions, and stimulate those basic emotions in others in order to help us to accomplish our goals of profitably buying or selling.

examining our similarities

It is difficult for two persons, one buying and the other selling, to come to an agreement involving large sums of money, $50,000 or more, without each person having a **compelling emotional reason** to come to an agreement. Because this is so, you must understand the other person's emotional needs and it would be helpful if you let the other person understand your needs too. In lectures before realtor groups, I give the following example of how easy it is to negotiate a deal if there is a compelling need on both sides to consummate the transaction. A good looking submariner with an unusually active libido arrives at shore after six weeks at sea. He meets an attractive prostitute who is also a nymphomaniac at a nearby bar. Query: How long do you think it will take before a transaction is consummated? The audience usually laughs because the answer is so obvious. The reason for the transaction **is** simple: there is a compelling need on both sides and they both have the knowledge and ability to satisfy these needs.

Simple as this example seems, remember that we all are born with only two basic emotions: to stay alive and to propagate. In the example given, the compelling emotional reasons are obvious, the only negotiations relevant were those involving money. In our capitalistic society, money is the "sine qua non" of survival.

We need to examine only a few emotions out of hundreds which we all experience in order to help us understand other people. Consider that every emotion we will ever experience, however, subtle, stems from either the will to survive or the will to propagate. The most common emotions are love, sex, fear, greed, guilt and status. We should "tap" these emotions in people with whom we negotiate in order to learn what emotions are contributing to that essential compelling reason for them to buy or sell.

In our culture the male is aware (although not always in a precise fashion) that in order to cater to his basic instinctive drives of survival and the desire to propagate he needs money. Women also realize that surviving and propagating require money. And more and more single women, widows and divorcees realize they need money to play the game of life. It is no longer a shock to me to see women in fields, where a few years ago they were hardly in evidence. In 1951, I worked in a real estate office and there were no women among 51 real estate salespeople. Today male residential salespersons are probably in the minority in the larger metropolitan areas.

love

This emotion is closely related to sexuality, our desire to propagate. It's important to discover the family status of the person with whom you will be negotiating. He may negotiate with you because he loves his wife and family and wants to protect them from financial problems should he die. On the positive side, his tax advisor may suggest gifts, such as real estate equities or common stock so his wife may have some economic security of her own. Together, the husband and wife may arrange their financial affairs in such a manner that his death will not result in a financial windfall to the U.S. Government. He may not want to invest, but because of advancing age he may wish to sell a property or vacant land (or anything of value) so that he may negotiate the best possible price. He may not fully trust the executors of his estate to handle his business affairs as well as he can.

sex

I frequently ask both men and women to rate their respective libidos. Aside from all other emotions, I ask them to assign a rating of their libidos on a scale of one to ten.

The reasons for my rating system are two-fold. First, I can fairly accurately predict social behavior if I know the other person's rating and you can too. Second, an aggressive libido and power drive often go together and power drive means successful business dealing.

guilt

Without this emotion, the entire life insurance industry could not exist. Guilt arises when a man with small children, without life insurance, is asked "what are you doing to provide an income stream for your wife and children if you die?" Ugh! But it is a reassuring emotion to tap lightly when, you are making an assembly for an office building and someone owns a 20 by 100 foot plot of land at the **end** of your large assembly. Showing photographs of a small non-economic building sandwiched between two large office buildings can load guilt on an owner who is holding out for a higher price. What has he done to obtain the maximum price for his parcel, and by extension, for his wife, children and grandchildren? If he persists in holding out for a higher price, he could be by-passed, leaving him with an uneconomic parcel of land which nobody will want for possibly at least 40 years. A Jewish comedian announced on TV he had married an Italian girl. He said he was teaching her 'guilt' while she was teaching him "shame." I thought it was a funny line but doesn't guilt produce shame?

fear

Fear produces either of two results: fight or flight. Many investors are fearful at the precise moment they are about to enter a syndicated venture. A significant number of people seem to be very fearful when they are about to part with a lot of money. Unless you are cool and calm when dealing with someone who has had this emotion he (or she) will back away from the deal. The antidote is a calm and reassuring approach . . . tell them **you've** done **it** many times, i.e., made that particular form of transaction.

greed

This emotion explains why communism cannot work in the long run. Greed is an exquisite combination of the will to survive and the will to propagate. A person with no **greed** finds it hard to survive, in our capitalistic culture.

So remember to point out the financial benefits flowing to the purchaser, investor or to the seller. My brother frequently says "luck is for the needy, not the greedy." In turn, a little cupidity is necessary in acquiring and developing income-producing properties. On the other hand, if you exhibit too much greed, no one will sell to you, buy from you, or invest with you.

status

In early times status belonged to the man with the most women, cattle or houses. In today's culture it is evidenced by lots of chips (money). Who your ancestors are is really helpful only if they left you with a bundle of chips. What you do for a living is important from a status viewpoint, only if it gives you power **and** money. As an example, every investor is seeking to accumulate more money and by his association with other investors he feels he reinforces his status in the eyes of others.

These six emotions, motivations and drives are found in everyone. It is these emotional similarities you need to know about and use to your advantage. You cannot be a successful negotiator without lightly "hitting" or "tapping" these emotions. Used correctly, they will help you tremendously in all of your future negotiations.

winning and losing

It is important you do not enter negotiations with an "adversary" point of view. This is not a sports contest. If you are acquiring land or a project or if you are seeking investors, your attitude should be one of cool confidence. **There are no losers in negotiations. All parties** to an agreement **must feel that they have won.** If they do not feel fairly treated they simply will not do business with you either now or later. You may get only one chance in closing a negotiation, so for goodness' sake, don't play 'I gotcha!' A **good deal is good for all parties.**

a strategy for improving your luck

Sooner or later you must make a decision—his place or yours. Earlier in the book I talked about mornings around 10 o'clock as being the best time, and your office as the best place, to make a sales presentation or a lease negotiation. This remains true even if you are buying. Going to the other fellow's place of business can cause many interruptions which you could control if the meeting takes place in your own office. Your task is to satisfy the other person's needs. You need to help solve his problems. Thus, you need all of your tools at hand **in your office.**

Make sure there are no interruptions when your negotiations have started. Inform your secretary and staff to tell all callers you are in an important meeting and you will return the call when the meeting ends.

making yourself likable

Try to be as natural as you can. Maintain your sense of humor and be sincere. Any phoniness or puffing is distracting, often offensive. Chances are the person with whom you are negotiating knows a good deal about you already: don't lose him by announcing your net worth, your valuable holdings, or any such puffing. It's unlikely you are humble if you are a developer or syndicator, or are already a success in another field. Nor should you try to be, but there is never a need to push. Just be yourself and by all means **listen.**

Of necessity you will have to make concessions and compromises. Deliberately adopt a malleable and tractable stance in all your negotiations. I once was given the opportunity to become the developer of one of the choicest tracts of land in downtown Washington, D.C. I was selected because I was so busy trying to work out the estate problems administered by a trust officer of a bank, I never had the time nor the inclination to tell everyone involved how wonderful I was. On the site is a $20 million office building in which neither my partner nor I invested a penny! I was told later the other possible developers were very busy telling the trust officer how much **they** would charge for the development job and how important **they** were in the community. I received my fee from my investors. That's why the bank appointed me as the developer.

never be intimidated and never intimidate

I read the book "Winning Through Intimidation," by Robert J. Ringer. I think it was a fun book but his approach seems to be "rear-end-first" or backwards. The point here is that you can't be in control of any negotiating situation if **you** are intimidated. But you certainly don't want to intimidate **anyone.** No investor will invest, no seller will sell, no buyer will buy and because this is so, winning through intimidation is nonsense. Make a promise to yourself, I will not nor cannot be intimidated. What is there to be afraid of? In nine cases out of ten, you will obviously be in the driver's seat because of your prior experience. But remember, putting someone on the defensive cannot result in a sale either to you or from you. Remember also every man, no matter how forceful or knowl-edgeable he appears, shares with you the identical six emotions of love, sex, guilt, fear, greed and desire for status. If this doesn't allay your fears, imagine him in some situation where he has lost his dignity. For example, imagine him naked in the doctor's office preparing to undergo a proctoscopic examination. See how vulnerable he now appears?

easy does it, but not always

If you are negotiating with a highly charged emotional person, and he is driving you crazy you may have to **tell him to cool it** in as pleasant a manner as possible. I've done this a time or two and have shocked people into taking a calmer approach. You have nothing to lose, because you can't negotiate with a maniac. But the important facet of any negotiation is: **Never close the door.** I learned this when I blew a negotiation because I allowed myself to become angry. You must always be in control of your emotions. If you become agitated or angry you will say something which forever forecloses your option to reopen negotiations. No matter how unreasonable the other person becomes, stay confident and keep the negotiating door open.

I have discovered that many people have a proclivity for seeking informa-tion by making a negative statement (usually about you, but attributed to some-one else) and putting you on the defensive. The motive is rarely nasty, it is just their irritating way of seeking information. As an example, such a person may open a conversation with a remark like "I hear you've had quite a few losers." What they should have asked was "How many ventures have you organized and what percentage are winners?" Understanding the thrust of this type of question, i.e., a negative statement which you are required to defend, can help you quickly identify the information desired. Part of such a negative approach is the **fear** of the questioner to reveal his ignorance. He is afraid to ask a question because he fears you will think he is ignorant. Poor baby, he is really asking you to educate him. Whenever you are asked to respond to a **negative** statement, quickly clear the air by asking yourself the question out loud in the **positive.** Find a friend with whom you can practice changing this type of negative question to a positive one. You both will become exhilarated by the speed with which you can convert the negative to the positive. Here are a few real estate nasties to practice with, but you can imagine many more, especially involving interpersonal relationships. Any negative question directed at you usually means the questioner wants to learn.

Q. So you're the rich, fat cat I've heard is such a genius and never makes a mistake!

A. I'm not going to tell you my net worth, but I'm 5 feet 11 inches and I weigh 175. The last genius who never made a mistake was crucified, wasn't He?

Q. You're getting too much in this development!

A. I'm getting 25 percent in profits along with the management and leasing. I'm good, but if I were perfect I'd get 50 percent and higher management and leasing fees. All kidding aside, you're really asking if our fees are competitive—of course they are. A little investigation on your part will confirm this.

Q. I read in your private placement memorandum that the limited partners can never all meet with you and decide on the correct course of action. You're afraid of us aren't you?

A. I think you are confusing common stock holdings with a limited partnership interest in a real estate development. You can be active as you want with your common stock holdings, and can raise all the hell you want with the management at the annual meetings. Additionally, you can write letters to the President every time you are in the mood. You pay a rather high price for that privilege . . . your corporation pays taxes and you pay taxes on your dividends. You give up this kind of activity and remain inactive (except for voting on refinancing and sale) and your partnership pays no federal income taxes. Which way do you want it?

Q. I want to discuss with you a proposition which has just been made to me. You are supposed to be an expert. I want to know if you think it's a good deal.

A. How badly do you want to know? My fees for counseling are $1,000 for a 6-hour day.

implicit or explicit

Years ago and perhaps even today, parents asked teenagers: "Where are you going?" They replied "Out!" "When will you be back?" "Later." This kind of question and answer drives intelligent people insane. What we have examined here is not only a classic case of non-communication but also a classic breach of manners. The purpose of manners is to create an atmosphere among people which imposes a requirement on all to do nothing offensive or unpleasant. Hence, it is a code of behavior designed to make everyone as comfortable as possible. Implicit conversations are therefore not only examples of poor communication, but of bad manners. Even if willfully practiced to avoid being specific, such communications are not only impossible to understand, they are implicitly rude. Unfortunately, implicit conversations abound. So never be guilty of implicit speech. The easiest way to understand why others are guilty is to listen for 'conclusion' statements. Salesmen and advertisers are also guilty when it comes to implicit statements. Here are some examples:

1. "This product has an extra ingredient that the leading aspirin tablet doesn't have" We all know that a plain aspirin tablet, e.g., Bayer, contains 5 grains of aspirin (acetylsalicylic acid). The advertiser **implies** an additional and supposedly beneficial extra ingredient. The reason he is not explicit is because the other ingredient is caffeine. Might as well drink a cup of coffee and take two aspirin tablets.

2. "This parcel of land is bound to go up in value." Why? Some land is worth **less** today. There are no **guarantees** anything is "bound to go up in value."

3. "I'm working late tonight. Don't bother with dinner, I'll get something at a fast food joint on the way home." What intelligent woman would buy this? With whom is he working? When did he know it? When will he be home? What does he mean: don't bother with dinner, it's probably already in the making.

4. "I'm going shopping today." For what: clothing, groceries, another guy?

5. "I don't want to talk about it." Among married people this could be **anything.** How can two people possibly get along when one 'pulls down' the curtain on any conversation?

6. "I don't like Phyllis." What does this mean? Does Phyllis have bad breath, is she a poor dancer, a poor dresser, or a bore?

7. "We'll see." Does "we'll see" mean "yes," or "no," or "possibly," and if any of the three, why not say exactly what is meant.

What's lacking in all implicit conversations is saying specifically, precisely, and clearly what is meant. How can you enter into a negotiation when either you or the person with whom you will negotiate are talking implicitly or in conclusions? You can't and the sooner your conversation becomes specific, clear and precise the better negotiator you will become. It will also make your life run more smoothly.

what are you seeking in your negotiations?

You should have your goals fixed before any meeting. Write down the specifics. If you can't memorize them, carry your written specifics with you and when you excuse yourself to go to the john, read them carefully again. I don't recommend you have **any papers** in front of you while negotiating. Someone could see your specifics and you may not wish to disclose how much you could offer or accept as the case may be.

be on time!

The worst thing you could do in a negotiation is to be late. Carelessness in this area can murder your chances. There are **no** excuses for causing other people to waste their time. Unless you are stricken and taken to a hospital, **be there on time.** Also you can make it clear in advance of the meeting that you want all the participants to be prompt. Indicate you have other pressing obligations following the meeting so others won't be late.

My partner allows local appointments he makes to be 15 minutes late. If they are later he deliberately walks out of his office and 'goofs off' somewhere else. His reasoning is sound: "If you're not here when you said you would be, you're a liar . . . and I don't do business with liars." He doesn't say this out loud but he expresses extreme discomfort with anyone who is not prompt when he reschedules the appointment for another time. Because everyone with whom you may negotiate is not in your city, late plane arrivals and delays are sometimes unavoidable. If you have a morning appointment in another city, fly in the night before and leave after the appointment. Top executives everywhere appreciate promptness. If others from out of the city are visiting you, suggest they arrive the evening before so that all can get an early start.

always do it one-on-one

How do you feel when you have a serious negotiating appointment and the person with whom you have the appointment has his attorney, accountant, and another associate or two awaiting your arrival? If you are alone, you must have a massive ego if you don't feel outnumbered. I always try to meet one-on-one. If the other side has more than one person, I insist on knowing this in advance. I don't wish to be outnumbered or surprised. If this is our first appointment, I actually plead to have only two of us there, me and him. Later on is time enough to bring in the legal, accounting and other professionals. Another good reason: I don't want to 'start the meter running' (start accruing unnecessary costs) until I have a precise understanding of our business agreements. I have been on many long, seemingly endless negotiations. The principal reason for these marathon sessions is that someone wishes to "put on a performance" for the benefit of someone on his side. I have also noted this occurs when there are business points still undecided and there are four or more persons attending the meeting. Get all the business matters fully negotiated and clearly understood and agreed upon prior to entry of legal, accounting, and counseling professionals. Avoid like the plague using a 'between' figure, e.g. a figure between $100,000 and $150,000. If he's buying he assumes $100,000 and if he is selling he assumes $150,000. This is another area when precision counts. If you're thinking $125,000, say so. **Rarely does a negotiation fail solely because of price.** There are many trade-offs (down payment, interest, speed of payment, etc.) and you will learn if you give up something specific early in a negotiation, the other fellow will give up something later on. You don't have to remind him he owes you one. He knows we live in a **quid pro quo** business world.

Frequently your negotiations will require another appointment and another time. When you realize it is not possible to accomplish everything you have previously reduced to writing, leave with a good taste in everyone's mouth. Go over the items which have been agreed upon, make a date for the next meeting and then **leave.** Don't hang around, you'll be risking being thought of as a bore. If you are an intelligent negotiator you will immediately avoid the most controversial items or those which the other side seems to oppose the most. Leaving in a friendly atmosphere will also give you some time to reevaluate the item or items which seem to be of most concern to the other side. Assign a value to each item between one and ten. You can give in on the lower valued items and make yourself seem more than willing to 'make the deal.' Naturally, you may have to scrap like mad for the higher rated items, but this can be done at another session.

in the matter of dress

Everybody wears a uniform. The investment bankers all seem to dress alike: Brooks Brothers suits (or the equivalent) unpadded shoulders, skinny pants with cuffs (the trousers always seem too short), cordovan shoes with laces, button-down oxford cloth shirts and 'rep ties'. Developers wear Oxford, Hicky-Freeman, Ambassador clothes, or the equivalent, or have them made to order. All of this dress conformity among persons doing similar work seems to be some kind of 'signal' to each other. I don't know, nor really care, how it all got started, but I do know that **not** to observe some of the ordinary elements of conformance which may be a form of courtesy, can get you 'written off' quickly.

In the mid-1970's I spoke to a five-state 'Western States Conference of REALTORS® in Spokane, Washington. One of the younger realtors was walking with me from the theater in which I spoke back to our headquarters hotel. He talked about his work, but among the accomplishments of which he was most proud was the fact that he "never wore a tie." I haven't seen this man since nor have I heard from him. I hope he is wearing a tie. If you do not wish to comply with dress standards, that is your option. You can do anything that's legal and there is no punishment. While there appears to be no punishment for not wearing a tie, the establishment may choose to **not** invite such a person to their homes or private clubs, because of the dress codes. He may **not** be invited to serve as a director of a board as he **appears** to be a maverick. Finally, he may **not** be as welcome at his bank as he would like to be, because a certain chemistry between business men may not occur because of his 'different' look which could be viewed as 'sloppy.'

Early in my career I began to taste success. I erroneously decided to encase myself with what I thought were the appropriate trappings: a diamond-studded platinum hand-made wrist watch, diamond cuff-links and even a diamond-studded belt buckle. After a few years wearing these items on a daily basis, I began to be aware that I was treated as either a rich nut, a member of the mafia, or an inveterate gambler. I am none of these, but I became aware I was 'giving off or sending out wrong signals' to everyone I met. Needless to say, these jewelry items are now relegated to my safety deposit box. When I am going formal, I'll wear them (along with diamond studs) just to hear the teasing or amusing comments they invariably invoke.

There is a time and place when you can dress as casually or flamboyantly as you want, but surely **not** when you are working with the establishment on a daily basis.

the end result is what counts

Before you enter any negotiation, you must introspectively determine what you hope to achieve. It will also help if you can reduce the main points to a few words and put them on a 3-by-5 card. Keep the writing without detail and determine a value to each point by assigning a number between one to ten. The least valued items can be as low as one, two or three; the more valued items could be in the six, seven or eight range. The most important item could be assigned a value of ten. Putting your goals in order of importance helps clear your mind and keeps you from getting bogged down on the items that are less important. It can also help you concentrate on the most important goals. Interesting to note, you will soon find yourself quantifying most of your goals in interpersonal relationships as well as in business. Focusing on important items and working on them while being fairly casual about the unimportant items can be the difference between success and an ordinary result not only in business but in your personal life as well.

closing the transaction

After all of the major items in any transaction have been negotiated, there will be a time when it is necessary to terminate all discussion and close the transaction. Top salespersons are aware they need an objection to close a transaction, thus they seek and welcome an objection so that they may close. Conversely, qualified salespersons are also aware that without an objection, the other person will not buy nor sell. They know that any time a person agrees with **everything** you say, they will not buy nor sell. Generally, this happens only when the salesperson fails to initially qualify a client. Do not allow your enthusiasm to diminish because you failed to understand the other person's motives and thus failed to properly qualify that person, simply **get out** and chalk up your failure to lack of proper qualifying. But never, never, leave on an objection. This is what you need. You need to answer objections with candor or by acquiescence to a minor item and then close. You will find that if you assume your negotiations will end with your attainment of your important goals, they will. This positive attitude has been called by top negotiators and salespersons "the assumptive technique." Why would you enter any negotiation with anybody if you could not positively assume you could accomplish your goals? Is it not natural for anyone, even those persons who are relatively shy, to assume their goals will be attained? Of course it is natural—so adopt an attitude that allows you to assume you will attain your goals. You have probably heard or at least are aware that many negotiated transactions have not closed because the negotiators or salespersons kept talking **after** the appropriate moment to close. If this is so, you need to identify the proper moment for the closing of the deal. Invariably, it will be the last major objection to the transaction brought up by the other party. You will overcome the objection with candor, good reasons why the objection should be withdrawn or by gracious acquiescence of a minor item. Then close! How? By using a method I call the 'subordinate question technique.' This is the simplest and easiest of all closing techniques and it is so effective it is fool-proof. Here is how it works. You have just answered an objection and since there appears to be no other objections, you can ask a question which does not require much thought on the other person's part, but avoids having to have the other party say "yes." Yet it is a commitment to say "yes" derived from a minor question. As an example, a salesperson could close an auto sale by asking a couple if they want the car titled in both names. Any answer except "drop dead" automatically closes the sale. Note that the auto salesperson didn't say to the couple, "Do you want to buy this car?" But didn't he say the same thing when he asked how the title was to be taken? Doesn't this same question hold true in a real estate transaction? Isn't it also true for a man who wishes to marry a woman, but because of shyness or fear of refusal, asks her to fix a marital date that would most suit everyone? He didn't precisely ask for her hand in marriage, he just said, "Honey, set a marriage date and time that will foul up the least amount of our relatives and friends." He could close by asking any number of questions subordinate to the main question of "will you marry me?" In fact, **the question,** itself, was probably not asked, nine times out of ten.

Likewise, doesn't "your place or mine?" imply a sexual commitment? Isn't this merely a subordinate question technique? I have a theory, which came about listening to women converse, that the word "yes" is not frequently used by them. I suspect most men don't use the word too often either. Because the word "yes" constitutes almost final agreement, it is best to avoid hearing anything but the most simple unimportant question answered by a possible "yes." This seems to run contrary to sophisticated negotiating techniques recommended by others who believe the idea of "training" the other person to say yes by asking questions such as "It's a lovely day, isn't it?" prepares them to say yes to the major question. My technique is to avoid the major question . . . "Then we have a deal?" or "Does that mean an unequivocal yes?" Don't risk getting shot down. Merely ask a seemingly unimportant question which is subordinate to the main question. The worst thing that can happen is another objection. This merely means you were closing a little too soon. Answer the objection and close again. When you have used this technique to close a transaction, you'll use it forever. Here follows some subordinate questions which may help you to get started.

1. (A stockbroker or syndicator of real estate) "Do you want to take title as joint tenants (with your spouse) with the rights of survivorship?"

2. (In mergers and acquisitions) "A year from now, does my salary increase depend on inflation or by negotiations with a compensation committee?"

3. (By a woman or man asking marriage) "Do you think your father (or mother or both) would accept me as a member of the family?"

4. (By a woman to a man asking for clean-up help) "When I cook for the both of us, can I count on your help with the heavier pots?"

5. (Wife or husband in regard to dining out) "Darling, we're having your favorite dish tonight (rack of lamb) at the Prime Rib." (This is how I discover we're eating out again. My wife makes a subordinate closing statement).

6. (In regard to a wife about to vacation for a long weekend) "Darling, this is **my** vacation too. Even though we've rented a furnished efficiency, do I have to be the maid?"

The important thing to remember about the subordinate question technique is once you have asked the question, you **must** close. I like to do something physical such as writing on a prepared form. This requires the person with whom I am negotiating to physically 'stop' me, or the negotiations are over and he has bought the deal. I have only been 'stopped' once or twice. This is because it requires a peculiar kind of courage for someone to interrupt a physical act even though by not interrupting, the deal is closed.

I cannot repeat often enough to get out immediately after the close. Everyone has second thoughts about every agreement and this is natural enough. The second thoughts seem strongest immediately after a close. Because this is true, let the other person cool down naturally, away from you. It is not necessary to make yourself unavailable, just physically remove yourself from the other person's presence.

Finally, you need to practice subordinated questions and closes with a bright friend, especially a friend who has a good deal of imagination and some creativity. While we negotiate more or less continually in our personal lives, unless we are solely in sales, we don't get enough practice when negotiating in business situations. Give up reading or TV one night a week and get together with a friend. You won't believe how stimulating and how much fun you can have in developing subordinate questions techniques and practicing closes. Practice will help you the rest of your life.

Here are some typical general questions and situations, with responses you may need to practice with your negotiating friends so that you can respond quickly.

"I need time to think it over." The other person is stalling, find out why. Something is still bothering him or her. Find out and close. I like to respond, with my favorite question: "What will you know tomorrow that you don't know to-day?"

Sometimes a 'mayvin' is brought into the picture by the other side. A "mayvin" is a self-styled expert who has very little knowledge of what your situation is about, yet obviously has the complete confidence of the other person. What do you do? Do you go to work on the mayvin and seek to discredit him? Tempting as this may be, don't. You'll only get the other side angry. You have just attacked one of **them.** I like to see a mayvin around occasionally just to take him aside. This is done by asking him, "Sir, can I talk with you alone for just a moment?" Usually he is surprised in your asking to speak with him privately and nearly always is flattered by the fact you think he is important. When you get him aside, tell him in a quiet but firm voice something like this: "The Wilburs have put you in a tough spot. You are charged with the responsibility of making a decision on their behalf. You see the spot they have put you in? If you say "yes" and later they become dissatisfied, the blame is yours. If you say "no" and they find out you've prevented them from making money (or whatever) you will again take the blame. For gosh sakes, get out of this situation . . . give them advice if you care to, but make certain the **responsibility** for the decision making is theirs."

It has never failed me. The mayvin either pleads ignorance, fades away by clamming up or keeps insisting "The decision is yours." How nice. I've used this technique since I encountered a mother-in-law mayvin in 1951 while I was showing a young couple a house. I took her to one side and told her that her daughter had put her between a hard place and a rock. I also asked if the son-in-law was going to pay the mortgage or she was. When she replied, "Of course, he will," I knew she would soon be out of the picture. At that precise moment I advised her confidentially: "This may be one of the biggest financial decisions your son-in-law will ever make, so let him make it. This way they can't blame you for interfering if anything goes wrong. On the other hand, and I can see they both love the house, he'll never enjoy it if you advise him to buy it . . . give him that opportunity. She nodded her head in agreement, kept still for the next few minutes, and when her son-in-law asked "Mom, how do you feel about the house," she said "Oh, I love it son, but I respect your decision, whatever it may be." The young man stuck out his chest, triumphantly turned to his wife and said, "Honey, it's ours if you want it." Inasmuch as I had just learned the "mayvin" technique from my Uncle George, I nearly fainted.

You will be in negotiating sessions whereby the other side wants to seek advice from his attorney or accountant. There is nothing wrong with this attitude. Your task is to find out if he is seeking strictly legal or accounting advice. If he is seeking business advice, don't discuss it any further in too much depth. Ask a question similar to this: "Who does your legal (or accounting) work?" Do you recall how to handle the mayvin? Use the same technique. Ensure that their accountant gives only accounting information and their attorney gives only legal advice. You do this by calling their attorney or accountant and advising them to avoid making the business decision for the client. This is easier than you think. Wise attorneys and accountants always try to avoid making business decisions for their clients because there is no reward for them in giving such advice. If everything goes well, their client assumes he made the decision. If the deal (or whatever) is a loser, what attorney or accountant wants to be blamed for bad business advice? My experience has taught me that only very stupid or very inexperienced attorneys and accountants will give business advice.

the winner's checklist

Inasmuch as negotiations will always be a part of your life, take them with some degree of seriousness. You can joke and have fun while you are negotiating, in fact this sometimes is a big help, but take the negotiations seriously. This means practice and a lot of understanding of the other side. Remember the winner's checklist.

1. In negotiations there are only winners, no losers.
2. You can't be intimidated, you can't intimidate.
3. The best way to make yourself likable, is to understand the other person's problems and needs.
4. Never close the door.
5. Always be on time.
6. Be explicit in all conversations. Say clearly and precisely exactly what you mean.
7. Insist on one-to-one negotiation. Avoid group negotiation.
8. Dress to insure success. Conforming gracefully in your appearance is a kind of courtesy which leads to success.
9. Close the transaction, and then get out.

national bank of washington, d.c., trust operations center—1977. cost $9,000,000.

14

don't just sit there

chapter 14 outline

I have often asked fellow realtors in classroom situations to think about the **worst** income-producing property they remember. They told me some real estate horror stories. When we discussed "finishes" in office buildings, apartment developments, and shopping centers, the student realtors had many suggestions for improving the quality of the properties. Most of the suggestions don't really require any more money to be spent, indeed, some suggestions seemed to require less cash expenditure than the developer had spent. All of the feedback and positive suggestions I received, especially from students in post graduate studies, convinced me there are no **better** observers of what is quality and what isn't than persons earning their full-time living in one phase of real estate or another. The fact that home builders often become developers instead of realtors is, I believe, an accident. The tract of land fronting on a busy highway owned by a home builder is what pushes him into becoming a developer. He is building single family housing at the rear of the tract fronting a quiet residential street and when he finishes his homes and sells out, he frequently will develop a small shopping center, an apartment project, or perhaps a suburban office building.

mentally gearing up

Ask yourself honestly, "Can I cause a project to be built that works better, has better quality, is easy to look at?" Of course you can. Any structure, anywhere, built by **anyone** can be improved upon. Take the time to study the project and you will find build-in obsolescence, even in a brand new development. It is easy to be critical, but the realtor who is mentally gearing up to do a development needs to spend a good deal of time looking at competitive buildings. I would like to make you a private wager that you will be so "turned on" after your first critical look at your competition, you may make being a developer into a full-time career. The worst that will happen is that your competitive juices will start to flow—and that's good. The best that will happen is that you could make a ton of money and leave your "work" behind you as a kind of legacy to what you have thoughtfully developed.

Ask yourself another question: "Can I show my completed developments to my grandchildren without causing them either to regurgitate or laugh with derision?" You could probably guess that many developers wouldn't dare show their finished developments to **their** grandchildren. What I am talking about is that good old-fashioned feeling of **pride.** The dollars generated from developments that flow to you are so substantial you need not dwell on these splendid financial results. Your job is to think, plan, and execute. In order to start thinking along the correct path you will need a positive plan.

a positive plan

You must commit to writing every negative development thought along with all of your positive development thoughts. An ordinary sheet of paper with positive facts on the left side and negative thoughts on the right side will help you tremendously in assessing the risks and rewards of development or acquisition. You will benefit by having three sheets, one each for apartments, office buildings, and shopping centers. After you have spent as much time researching your market and competitive projects as to make you feel more comfortable about what you are about to do, then is the moment to invite submissions to you (as a principal) from your fellow realtors. Without the proper research on your part you will only have a vague notion of which direction to follow.

do not react to individual presentations

As just mentioned, you will have to react by feel to individual submissions if you do not have in front of you your research documentation. Reacting by feel is about the same as trying to fly a Boeing 747 without the instrumentation available to you. You will be flying by "the seat of your pants." Pilots have a saying of unknown origin: "There are old pilots and bold pilots, however there are no old bold pilots." Developments are too costly and last a long time, often 40 years or so, for you to react to individual submissions without having completely memorized your do's and don'ts of acquisitions and developments. I can't do anything more to help you than to point out **some** of the things already mentioned for you to consider. I wouldn't have helped you or your community if you abdicate the **responsibility** of development that a person in real estate should feel. For taking on the responsibility of development, you will be amply rewarded financially. You also will be rewarded mentally to the extent you feel you have completed a worthwhile development.

remember the emoluments

Being a developer of income-producing properties is probably one of the highest paid positions in the business world. You may or may not be aware of the fact that most developers of income-producing properties are multi-millionaires. The **average** annual incomes to successful large city real estate developers is in the one-quarter to one-half million dollar level, and frequently higher. It will be less in cities of less population than 150,000, but average annual incomes of developers in cities of that size should be at least $100,000 annually.

Let's go over the goodies available to you once again:

1. A "nontaxable" piece of the action (15 to 25 percent interest) of the project.
2. Leasing and management fees.
3. Financing and refinancing fees.
4. Casualty insurance commissions.
5. Exclusive rights of resale at 5 percent of the **gross** sales price including mortgages given or taken back.

These benefits are available to you **right now!** All you need to do is develop or acquire income-producing properties following the guidelines and precepts contained in this book. Then you too can experience that booming economic success we all wish to attain.

your skills cannot be bought in the marketplace

During the 1960s and 1970s, quite a few (more than two dozen) large industrial companies sought to develop income-producing properties by organizing real estate subsidiaries for this purpose. Because experienced quality developers were already rich or had one-half million dollar annual incomes, their skills could not be bought in the marketplace. One strategy, and admittedly a more intelligent approach was to acquire development companies and give five- to seven-year annual employment contracts and bonus "earn-outs" to its principals. These development companies were usually acquired through "tax free" exchanges of stock. While the typical developer-entrepreneur is not the best place to find your typical corporate man, most of these subsidiaries contributed handsome yearly earnings to the parent company that acquired them.

Many of the developers left after their employment contracts expired mainly because large industrial corporate management endeavored to make real estate developments and their concomittant earnings to the developers in their subsidiaries operate in the same fashion as manufacturers. They sought to stabilize and **manage** earnings in the development arena, which is sporadic, volatile and long term. If the prior developer, now head of a corporate subsidiary could sell a property and earn a larger commission in the third quarter, he may have been instructed by corporate headquarters to delay the sale until the fourth quarter when other divisions or subsidiaries would show either losses or smaller profits. This attempt by large corporations to manage real estate development earnings added to the discomfort of the subsidiary heads. After all, they were former individual developers and thus didn't respond too well to direction from middle management. These middle management types frequently were paid less than heads of the subsidiaries and knew nothing about real estate developments. At any rate, the original developers acquired through tax-free exchanges are no longer working for the large industrial corporations. Many of them received their companies back through divestitures or left to start anew their own development companies after their employment agreements terminated.

Other major corporations had a different view of how to obtain profits from real estate developments. They hired young and intelligent graduates, usually with master's degrees from top universities (Harvard, The Wharton School at the University of Pennsylvania, Stanford) with their training in business administration. The results of following this strategy were worse than those of the major corporations that acquired companies owned by active developers who already had a history of fine earnings. I cannot recall a single major company that made any serious money by setting up subsidiaries with inexperienced but academically trained executives. Perhaps this is so because real estate academicians are rarely rich or enjoy one-half million dollar annual incomes earned from the exquisite suffering caused by earlier errors or failures. **I believe it is rather obvious that smart, educated, middle income persons cannot demonstrate how to become rich through developing income-producing properties.** They may be familiar with the development process but that familiarity hardly qualifies them to teach postgraduate students or practitioners how to make important money while making a serious contribution to our nation's inventory of apartment, office building, and shopping center projects. They have not had their money at risk. This is what separates them from the practitioner.

I hope we don't teach surgeons the way we are educating future developers. Perhaps the best method would be to mix academic learning with pragmatic know how by **requiring** students to assist local developers during their summer vacations. That would be better and hopefully more effective than any other method now employed by the academician.

What I **really** think should be done is to hire rich, experienced developers **who can also teach** regardless of their individual academic background. Of course **that** would take a Harvard or a Wharton or a Stanford University who need not worry about their professional academic standings, so excellent are their reputations. Most of the developers I know well rarely have more than a bachelor's degree if indeed, they have even graduated from college.

As far as I can project into the future, and my crystal ball is no better than yours, if you become a qualified developer your market skills are priceless. You will automatically become rich. Share your knowledge with those who need your help, and if they can't afford to pay you because they are young and just getting started, help them without a charge or fee of any kind. Someday they hopefully will help others, who are also young and just getting started. But if they need your help and are with a large corporation, are a rich individual, or with a well-heeled institution, be certain to charge a fair fee for your services and opinions. Your skills and know-how will develop quickly, but you will necessarily make a few errors no matter how hard you strive for perfection.

your future is secure

Because there is no investment alternative to investing in income-producing properties, your future as a developer or acquisition specialist is secure. You will be known in your community as a specialist in income-producing properties. As you develop or acquire income-producing properties, your reputation will grow. Investors will seek you out either for investment guidance (for which you will charge a fee) or will seek to join with you as an investor in your next venture.

Recently I was asked what I thought was the most important trait to have if one were to be a successful real estate developer. I replied, "Stupidity." The stupidity to go forward with a project when there is no clear evidence it will rent up; the stupidity to make a multi-million dollar investment decision without enough knowledge or concrete facts. This kind of stupidity is sometime called courage. Be of good courage.

office space plus a shopping mall. the mall is enclosed and contained on the first two floors. an architect's rendering of the esplanade, washington, d.c., 1978—cost $26,000,000.

glossary

AAA Tenant: a most credit-worthy tenant, so rated by Moody's Investor Services. Good examples are General Motors and Exxon.

Amortization: the constant payment of principal on a real estate loan, accompanied by interest and usually paid on a monthly basis. Also the annual deduction against income for federal tax purposes of any capitalized item.

Amortized: the process of liquidating debt by periodic payments. The process of deducting income for federal tax purposes of any capitalized item.

Annual constant: the percentage of the original loan amount that is to be repaid annually and includes both interest and principal.

Appraiser: a person who, for a fee, determines market value of real estate, i.e. the highest price in terms of money a property may bring on the open market, allowing a reasonable time for exposure for sale, with both buyer and seller having full knowledge of all uses to which the property may be put with neither buyer nor seller acting under duress. The techniques used by the appraiser cover three general areas: the cost to produce or reproduce the project (less actual and ordinary wear and tear); the economics, i.e. income less expenses; and market comparisons, i.e. actual consummated sales of similar properties in similar locations.

Assets: those things of value owned, such as real property, cash, stocks, bonds, jewelry, paintings.

Bankruptcy: the financial condition of a person or corporation wherein liabilities exceed assets. Technically, a person or corporation who on the petition of his own or his creditors has been judicially declared to have his estate administered under the bankruptcy laws for the benefit of his creditors.

Blind pool limited partnership: a limited partnership having many investors organized for the purpose of forming a large pool of cash with which to acquire or develop unknown income-producing properties, as distinct from a syndicated limited partnership wherein the purpose is to acquire or develop a specific project. Because of the larger number of individual investors, blind pool limited partnerships are necessarily public offerings and are usually registered with the S.E.C. as well as in the states where the limited partnerships units are being offered.

Blue sky laws: state securities laws designed to prevent promoters from selling citizens the "blue skies." Usually these laws require registration and full disclosure from any offeror. Extremely tough states with stringent registration requirements are Texas, California, New York, although most states are toughening up their securities laws.

Bonds: written promises to pay stated interest and ultimately the principal. They are issued by corporations, public and private as well as municipalities, counties, states and the federal government. Economists call bonds monetary assets characterized by a money claim, stated interest, and a due date.

Book value: cost of a project less depreciation and other amortizable expenses.

Borrow out: borrowing all the funds necessary to fully develop and rent up a property. It means there were no equity dollars invested.

Break-even point: a point in time of a rental project where the income and expenses are virtually the same. There is no cash flow at this point, either positive or negative.

Broker: in real estate a person who endeavors to bring together buyer and seller in order to effect a sale of the property from the owner (seller) to the buyer. Generally, the commission received for bringing together the buyer and seller is paid by the seller, although in some instances the buyer, by pre-arrangement pays the sales commission. It is unlawful in virtually every state to obtain a commission from **both** parties unless they are both aware of this commission arrangement. Most states require a **written** authorization from a potential seller before a property may be offered for sale or lease.

Broker, mortgage: a person who seeks long-term financing for a project, existing or to be developed, for a pre-arranged fee. Usually the mortgage broker represents the borrower.

Buy-out: an agreement by and between the partnership and a management and leasing company which provides for a predetermined payment to the management and leasing company by the partnership for the cancellation of management and leasing rights.

Capital: net worth, the excess of assets over liabilities.

Capital accounts: an individual's account of assets and liabilities in a given project. Assuming distributions of all cash flow, the account is increased pro rata by loan amortization and decreased pro rata by construction write-offs, investment credits, depreciation and other amortizable expenditures.

Capital gains: the profit realized by a long-term investor when the property owned is sold for a profit. Congress is always tinkering with the capital gains rate but it is traditionally a less costly tax than earned or ordinary income.

Capital interest: the interest of an investor in the capital or equity portion of an investment.

Capitalist: one who has capital, i.e. net worth—the excess of assets over liabilities; one who has capital for investment.

Cash distributions: in the context of a real estate limited partnership cash distributions represent ratable distributions of available cash to the partners, both general and limited. These distributions become available because of cash flow and other cash generated by refinancing proceeds, and proceeds of sale.

Cash flow: the remaining funds after all cash expenses and debt curtailment have been paid out of income received from the operation of any income-producing property. Usually expressed as a yearly figure.

Cash-on-cash return: the annual cash flow received for the cash down payment, expressed as a percentage. If the cash flow is $100 and the cash invested is $1,000 we express this as a 10 percent cash-on-cash return.

Casualty insurance: an insurance policy issued by an insurance company which may insure the owners and lenders against a multitude of perils such as fire, explosion, loss of rent, liability for negligence, acts of God and other risks.

Certificate of deposit: an instrument in writing issued by a bank, savings bank or savings and loan association which specifies the amount deposited, the interest rate, and the due date. As all the advertisements say, "there is a substantial penalty for early withdrawal." If you decide to redeem your certificate earlier than stated, the bank president gives you 20 lashes while the tellers look on. This is in addition to a substantial interest penalty.

Certificate of Limited Partnership: a written instrument which forms the partnership. It must be recorded with the clerk of the court generally where the real property is located, although sometimes it is recorded where the partners reside. The recording of the instrument gives notice to the world of the existence of the partnership and the intent of the partnership to limit the liability of the limited partners to the contribution requirements as set forth in the certificate.

Certified Property Manager: a person so designated by the Institute of Real Estate Management (IREM). Certain educational courses and a number of years experience as a property manager are the two main requirements.

Change order: a change from the original and agreed upon written plans and specifications, causing labor and material costs that exceed the original contract price.

Commercial lending specialist: see mortgage broker and mortgage banker.

Commercial loan paper: corporate promises to pay (I.O.U.s), usually for as short as one month up to three months, sold by dealers representing corporations of the very highest credit. The interest rate is usually a point or point and one-half below the prime borrowing rate as charged by the largest banks.

Conflict of interest: acting in a manner for gain which would tend to be at the expense of others. As an example, as general partner and as a selling broker to condition a sale to a third party upon retention of management rights.

Consumer Price Index: an index of items consumers buy or lease which include food, autos, rents and insurance. Many other items are included such as the cost of dry cleaning, shoe repairing and other services. The CPI is computed monthly by the Bureau of Labor Statistics of the Department of Commerce. It is used as a standard measurement to assess the increases in the cost of selected goods and services, hence it is a measurement to compute inflation. In 1967 the index was 100. In mid-1975 the index was approximately 161.

Contractor, building: a person or company that agrees to construct or re-model real estate for either an agreed upon negotiated fee or cost plus a certain amount (generally 5 percent) or any other financial agreement between the owner and contractor.

Corporation: a group of persons, under authority of law, having continuity of life, powers, and liabilities distinct from those of its members; a legal entity treated under law as a person.

Debentures: any one of several debt instruments issued by corporations. In usage, bonds and debentures are interchangeable although debentures are sometimes secured by an asset other than a general promise to pay.

Deed of Trust: instrument in writing which is a lien against the real estate. In actual practice, mortgages which are also liens against the real estate are used by practitioners interchangeably. The reason for two different kinds of liens are attributed to different laws among the states.

Depreciated: the process of entering an annual bookkeeping charge for actual wearing out of a real estate improvement (the building). The cost of the building (not the land) is depreciated annually using any one of several methods allowed by law. The amount depreciated annually may be charged as an expense and thus a deduction against income for federal income tax purposes.

Developer: a person or company supervising the total development process from ground acquisition, design, financing, construction, leasing, management and ultimate sale. Inasmuch as developers are not yet universally viewed as professionals, some persons maintain the word "developer" is a euphemism for promoter.

Divestiture: the act of divesting, to rid or be free from. Divestiture occurs when a company rids itself of a wholly owned subsidiary either through an exchange of stock or for cash or a combination of the two.

Draws: a monthly request to the construction lender for a progress payment to cover construction work in place. The request is usually made by the general contractor to the developer. The developer's architect is usually required to certify that the progress payment requested represents work in place. The developer then makes a request from his construction lender.

Gap loans: a loan or a commitment to make a loan that covers the difference between the "floor loan" (the guaranteed minimum loan committed by a major lender) and the "ceiling loan" (the maximum loan committed by a major lender, usually tied to a certain gross rental amount).

Entrepreneur: a person who organizes and manages any business enterprise wherein the essential motive is profit. The real estate practitioner uses this word interchangeably with promoter, syndicator and developer.

Equity: the remainder of value less debt.

Equity ownership: the ownership of all or a portion of all of the remainder of value less debt.

Escrow: funds kept by a third party (in our case, this is usually a bank) which will be released to someone else upon fulfillment of some condition. For example, our management company places 1/12th of our annual taxes monthly in an escrow account which monies are released for payment on a semi-annual basis to the city as our tax bills become due.

Fiduciary: a person to whom property or power is transferred for the benefit of another party.

First out: the cash investor(s) receive a predetermined percentage of the cash flow, based on the cash investment, prior to any distribution to the developer.

Fixed income securities: any general obligation to pay interest as distinguished from dividends.

Floating: this is an agreed upon rate that moves up or down depending on the prime rate charged to the most credit-worthy borrowers. The total rate charged therefore is floating, usually one to four points above the prime rate charged by Chase Manhattan, Bank of America, and Citibank.

Full disclosure doctrine: any written method of disclosure, such as a prospectus or a private placement memorandum which clearly reveals all facets of risk to a prospective investor as well as all of the rewards to the promoter, syndicator or developer.

Inexpensive money: loans made by institutional lenders at various times when the long-term interest rates are relatively low.

Installment sale: a sale for a specified sum wherein all of the cash is not paid at the time of sale. For federal income tax purposes an installment sale is one in which not more than 30 percent of the cash down payment is paid at the closing of the sale, the principal balance remaining is then payable in installments nearly always commencing in the calendar year next following the closing of the sale. Additional payments during the sales year are acceptable providing the total down payment plus additional principal payments do not exceed 30 percent. Because installment sales are a frequent occurrence in large realty transactions, many properties are offered at 29 percent down payment.

Joint Venture: a form of syndicate of persons wherein all the venturors share the risks, rewards and venture decisions.

L.E.E.P.: an acronym which identifies the four main facets of a qualified syndicate investor, L stands for living at a profit; E, education; E, previous investment experience of a certain kind; P, profession.

Leverage: the act of borrowing money at a rate of interest and repayment **less** than the cash flow. Leveraging intensifies the investment result in terms of a percentage cash-on-cash return.

Lien: a legal right to hold property or to have a right at sale for payment of a claim. In the case of a claim it is considered a "cloud" on the title until the lien is paid or otherwise released from the public record.

Liquidity: the ability to rapidly convert an asset to cash without loss of principal.

Mortgage broker: a person who attempts to place a loan for a borrower; a person who locates qualified lenders for a developer or syndicator for a fee, usually paid by the borrower. There is an unusual amount of negotiating done by the broker as there is not a great deal of standardization among lenders either as to risks or rates, length of pay-offs, and other loan features.

Net cash proceeds: all cash available for distribution after expenses, such as refinancing proceeds and proceeds of sale.

Off the top: a promoters' jargon for receiving fees first upon receipt of a project's cash rentals.

Old-money investor: a person who became wealthy through inheritance or trusts set up for his or her benefit.

Partnership: an association of persons (or corporations) joined together for the purpose of doing business.

Pension fund: a legally organized fund which is required to pay retirees an agreed upon figure. If the fund is administered with great discretion and is conservatively oriented in terms of risk, the retirees are the beneficiaries. If a risky policy has been followed and results in losses the retirees or pensioners could be adversely affected. The federal government has now required such funds to be reviewed by the Internal Revenue Service when initially organized. Additionally, the Pension Benefit Guaranty Corporation, a quasi-governmental organization insures pension funds of subscribers against losses by fraud and gross mismanagement in order to protect current and future retirees from loss.

Permanent lender: the lending institution who gives the borrower a long-term amortizing first mortgage, usually a life insurance company, savings and loan institution, savings bank or pension fund.

Points: a point means one percent. If you borrow $100,000 and are charged a point by the lender as an inducement to make the loan, you will be charged $1,000.

Portfolio: insurance jargon for all policies in force at any given time. Real estate investors sometimes call their collective real estate investments "my portfolio." The term is also used by investors in stocks and bonds who use the word "portfolio" to mean all their holdings at a given point in time.

Preferred stock: an equity ownership of a corporation with a priority right to receive dividends.

Primary market: the traditional source from which to borrow monies pledging the real estate as security for the loans. Savings and loan associations, savings banks, insurance companies and pension funds are the conventional institutional lenders.

Prime: this is property at its peak—usually occurring early in the building's life, usually during the first ten or twelve years from its completion.

Prime rate: this is the lending rate in effect by the largest banks such as

Chase Manhattan, Bank of America and Citibank for their most credit-worthy customers.

Priority right: a percentage right to the first monies of cash flow received by the partnership. Used interchangeably with a first out.

Private placement memorandum: a voluminous document prepared by a securities attorney as a substitute for a registered prospectus. If registration is not required by virtue of Rule 146 or by engaging in only intrastate transactions, a private placement memorandum is the "offering" made to a prospective investor. It must contain all of the possible risks and rewards involved in the investment as well as full disclosure of all benefits, however small, that will accrue to you as developer or syndicator. It should contain the partnership agreement, all accounting data and fully disclose in exquisite detail all of the risks inherent in the investment. It should also allow an investor or his offeree representative complete access to everything involved in the offering such as demographic studies, absorption market forecasts, development, leasing and management agreements, contracts with the general contractor, etc.

Pro forma statement: an annual forecast of cash income and cash expenses of a project to be built. All income is shown from which is deducted all cash expenses. Then a deduction is made from the remainder for annual mortgage payments including principal and interest. The bottom line or remainder is the cash flow.

Promoter: the person who initiates the organization that develops or acquires property.

Real estate investment trust: enacted into law in late 1960, a real estate investment trust was supposed to be the real estate industry's answer to the mutual fund industry. The owners of beneficial trust certificates pay taxes while properly organized real estate investment trusts in compliance with the law pay no taxes. There must be at least 100 shareholders and five or fewer individuals may not own more than 50 percent of all shares outstanding. There are other technical requirements requiring organizers of a real estate investment trust to deal with especially qualified tax attorneys.

Realtor®: realtor is a **service mark.** The National Association of Realtors® defines it as follows: "REALTOR® is a registered collective membership mark which may be used only by real estate professionals who are members of the National Association of Realtors® and subscribe to its strict code of ethics."

Recision: the act of putting every investor in the position they were in prior to entering a real estate venture as a partner. This effectively voids the transaction. Uusally recision requires a cash refund plus interest at 6 percent from the date of entry. Although the Securities and Exchange Commission may require a developer or syndicator to offer recision to all investing partners, because of various reasons, notably the tax effect, some of the partners may not accept recision and thus will continue to remain in the venture. Recision may also come about under order of your attorney if you have made a "false start", i.e.

made an offering prior to either state or federal registration or the preparation and distribution of a private placement memorandum.

Refinancing: going back to the original lender and negotiating a new and larger loan than the balance of the loan currently on the property.

R.E.I.T.: real estate investment trust which qualifies for special pass-through taxation under statutory laws and IRS regulations and results in taxes being paid only once. The owner of the beneficial trust certificates of the R.E.I.T. is taxed, not the R.E.I.T.

Rent control: a law imposed upon owners of residential rental real estate restricting free market rents. Rarely invoked by local or state authorities on any form of rents other than residential rents.

Rent-up: refers to the amount of time, generally in months, to fully lease and occupy a project.

Secondary market: a source of funds which will accept a risk higher than institutional first mortgage lenders. Consequently the rates of interest for borrowed funds in the secondary market are as much as 50 percent higher, or more, than conventional first mortgate sources.

Securities: generally stocks and bonds. The Securities and Exchange Commission (and the courts) has expanded this definition to include other forms of equities such as are found in real estate, gas and oil, cattle feeding programs, etc., especially if there is a public offering involved.

Securities industry: the entire group of persons known as stockbrokers who market stocks and bonds, usually for a fee or commission. It also includes professionals working on the various stock exchanges, money managers, investment counselors, and those specialists who make markets in various stocks. Those who do research in stocks and bonds also make up a part of this industry.

Short-term securities: a broad term used to describe numerous monetary assets such as: treasury bills, and bank certificates tied to the treasury bill rate; commercial loan paper; certificates of deposits—all of which are characterized by relatively short due dates and a good degree of liquidity.

Syndicate properties: properties owned by a partnership, joint venture, association or any group wherein the participants are investors introduced to the investment by an entrepreneur.

Syndicator: a person who forms a group of persons each of whom invests for the purpose of acquiring, developing, or otherwise seeking a profit in real estate. The investors collectively are capable of considerable financial strength as compared to each individual's financial strength. Since it is recognized that the larger properties are safer the pooling of investors' monies in one syndicate permits larger acquisitions and developments. It also is a good technique for investor financial diversification.

Take-out commitment: a commitment to make a permanent long-term loan issued by a major lender (insurance company, savings bank, savings and loan association or pension fund) with a specific interest rate, term, and sometimes mentioning a "floor" and "ceiling."

Tax incentives: special deductions for federal income tax purposes, either in the form of faster depreciation or tax credits. Such incentives may only be enacted by Congress. Business tax credits for hiring additional employees is an example of a tax incentive.

Tax loophole: any deductible item for federal income tax purposes allowed by statutes enacted by Congress. It has become a favored word by tax reformers and those tax experts that favor direct federal subsidies rather than either deductions or tax credits which are offsets in dollars which may be used to reduce taxes otherwise due.

Tax loss: during ownership of real estate, a loss for federal income tax purposes occurs when depreciation and other amortizable items exceed both the loan amortization and the cash flow. At sale a tax loss occurs whenever the net sales price is less than the book value. Book value is cost less the total of depreciation and other amortizable items.

Tax preference: any allowable deduction for federal income tax purposes that is over and above a "standard" deduction. For example, accelerated depreciation instead of straight-line depreciation creates a larger deduction. To the extent such deduction exceeds the amount which would be used in straight-line deduction, such excess is considered a tax preference.

Tax shelter: a situation wherein the deductible expenses of a project (depreciation and other amortizable expenses) exceed the principal repayment of the loan. In this event some, all, or more than all of the cash flow may be said to be tax sheltered.

Triple A corporate bonds: these are debt securities of the highest credit rated companies in the U.S. Assessments of credit-worthy companies are periodically made by independent analysts. Most banking institutions accept ratings as determined by Moody's Investor Services, a well-known credit rating company. AAA is the highest rating and many mortgages bear the same interest rate as the Moody AAA 25-year bond rate. Many, but not all of the Fortune '500' U.S. Corporations are rated AAA.

Underwritten: to assume liability by agreeing to insure a risk, e.g. from fire. Underwriters assess risks for insurance companies.

Windfall: borrowing **more** than all the funds necessary to fully develop and rent up a property.

Write off: any deduction allowable by the tax laws such as construction interest, real property taxes during construction and depreciation.

index